JS
113
.B35

D1103830

LARRY A. JACKSON LIBRARY
LANDER COLLEGE
GREENWOOD, SC 29646

FROM BIG GOVERNMENT TO LOCAL GOVERNMENT

The Road to Decentralisation

From Big Government To Local Government

The Road to Decentralisation

T. J. BARRINGTON

227459

INSTITUTE OF PUBLIC ADMINISTRATION
DUBLIN

LARRY A. JACKSON LIBRARY
LANDER COLLEGE
GREENWOOD, SC 29646

© Institute of Public Administration
57-61 Lansdowne Road
Dublin 4
Ireland

All rights reserved

ISBN 0 902173 67 7

Chapter 3 of this book, "The Geographical System of Government" (pp. 44-60), is reprinted from *Addendum to Report of the Public Services Organisation Review Group, 1966-1969* (*Devlin Report*), 1969, with the kind permission of the Controller, Stationery Office, Beggar's Bush, Dublin 4.

This book has been set in ten on twelve point Linotype Times New Roman and printed in Northern Ireland by W. & G. Baird Limited, Antrim.

CONTENTS

PREFACE

The papers reprinted in this book are the product of work for the Institute of Public Administration. They stretch over a period of twelve years, but they represent, so far as I am concerned, a time of much longer concern. With one exception the papers appear chronologically and the subjects as they arose were to some extent accidental. They were attempts to respond to the interests of different groups concerned with some aspect of what might be called the geographical or areal dimension of Irish government. At one time the problem might be that of the county, at another that of the region, at another the district. Hence the papers show some back-tracking and duplication. Nonetheless, I think it best to leave them as they were when they first appeared (barring an occasional change in phrasing): this at least illustrates how the focus of attention has shifted over more than a decade. To adopt this plan makes it necessary to relate together the common elements in the papers, and to put them in a general context: that is the purpose of the Postscript.

The basic argument of this book is that government is growing so big, absolutely and relatively, that it is in danger of losing its way in the mass of executive detail. Only central government can devise and decide on national policies; but there is no similar need to centralise detailed executive work. If the task of policy-making is impeded because so much decision on detail is sucked into the centre, then the whole country suffers. Government needs to adapt its methods to the consequences of size.

There is no self-correcting mechanism here. The forces of democracy, as we practise it in this country, make for the increasing centralisation of an increasing number of services. The natural tendency is for the problems flowing from centralisation to become more acute. The centralising forces of democracy tend to be self-defeating because government becomes progressively ineffective. The health of the democracy itself calls for a turning back of those forces.

A careful programme of decentralisation of executive work would enable central government to separate what only it can do from those things that can be done by other bodies under government's general supervision and control.

The report of the Public Services Organisation Review Group recommended ways by which the policy-making function of central government could be strengthened while the detailed executive work was decentralised to functional executive agencies similar to state-sponsored bodies.

There is another, complementary, way of effecting this decentralisation of executive work—by committing it to geographical executive agencies, regional, county, district, and other. This has advantages in evoking comprehensive development, in strengthening democratic institutions and, for appropriate services, in efficient, co-ordinated and flexible action.

These issues need more dispassionate discussion than they have hitherto received. In particular, we need to tease out the roles special to central government, to functional government and to geographical government if government overall is to give its best performance. The main purpose of this book is to identify the issues that define a useful role for local government—taking that term at its widest—in any such programme of decentralisation.

I believe that many of the points made in this book may also be true of countries other than Ireland. But the whole subject is at such an early stage of consideration that there is a danger of premature generalisation. As between that danger and that of seeming too local, too parochial, I have, in the present state of the art, chosen the latter danger as the lesser one.

Much of what is written here comes from discussion with colleagues, so that it is difficult to tell at times who was the parent of this thought or that idea. But the two most formative influences on my thinking have been my colleagues and dear friends Desmond Roche and the late Paddy Meghen. Perhaps they would disown nothing that is written in this book, but would have expressed it with such greater elegance.

Chapter 1

DECENTRALISATION AND DEVOLUTION*

I propose to argue that much of what we say in this country about the decentralisation and devolution of government services is misconceived; the real problem comes from the growth of the *quantity* of government. We are about to develop into a mainly socialised society. If we wish to maintain the values of a free, christian society in the conditions of the late twentieth century we should look to our institutional *structure* of government.

In a governmental structure designed for modern needs there is a big role for the local government system ; but only if it is modernised for 20th century problems and techniques. That is to say, local authorities must be permitted to become grass roots development corporations.

I. WHAT IS DECENTRALISATION ?

Decentralisation of government departments has been discussed in this country for many years. In public, decentralisation is accepted as a good thing: but with little obvious result. Substantial decentralisation raises practical problems ; but these have not been solved, because, I believe, the protagonists of change have not done their homework. An emotional attitude that wishes to see civil servants in Athlone or Castlebar is not sufficient to get them there. In any event, why only civil servants ? The onus is on those who wish to bring about change to produce good reasons for the changes proposed.

Hitherto the discussion has been about the dispersal of government departments: that is sending either parts of departments to different parts of the country, or whole departments to favoured provincial towns, on the model of the sending of most of the British Ministry of National Insurance to Newcastle on Tyne. Let us look at the

*A contribution to a seminar of the Institute of Public Administration on "Local Government Adaptation", October, 1964. Reprinted from ADMINISTRATION, Vol. 13 (1965) 1.

arguments relevant to Ireland for such dispersal. The unemotional ones reduce themselves to three:

(a) Dublin is too big,
(b) too much decision and initiative are concentrated there, and
(c) our provincial towns need new life

It is nonsense to say that Dublin is too big either absolutely or relatively. Compared with the size, and the rates of growth, of modern capital cities Dublin is no more than a sluggish village. The modern world is becoming highly urbanised. With the eight or nine million people in London or Tokyo we must also consider the enormous conurbations that begin to be the shape of modern living: for example the built up stretch from Boston to Washington in which about a fifth of the people of the United States now live, or the future shape of south east England. Calcutta, if present trends could continue, would have over 60 million inhabitants by the end of the century. Even in relation to Ireland's population, Dublin is not large, as a number of writers have already pointed out.[1] Indeed, Dublin is too small to support the intellectual and cultural apparatus of a capital city; it is still a provincial town taking in intellectual and cultural washing from overseas. Arguments for change, based on the bigness of Dublin, are likely to carry little weight amongst thinking people.

The argument that there is in Dublin too much concentration of decision and initiative carries, to my mind, more conviction. This is a feature of modern Ireland that strikes discerning foreign visitors. One has only to live for a short while outside Dublin to realise how centralised is our administrative system. This can be looked at in two ways. Either the overall volume of decision making is adequate, but too much of it is going on in Dublin, or the overall volume is inadequate and not enough of it is going on outside Dublin. I suspect that the latter alternative is the truth. But if the former is true, and the real problem is of an undue concentration of decision in one place, does the dispersal of concentrated groups alter the problem? Cannot concentration be just as intense in, say, Castlebar as in Dublin? So long as we think, in the sphere of government at least, of all effective decisions being taken at a single focus, then, in relation to any particular branch of activity, it is a matter of indifference whether that focus is Dublin or Skibbereen. Simply to disperse concentrated blocks of decision makers is not to decentralise decision.

No doubt, there is much to be said for giving a shot in the arm to

---

[1]Symposium: "Is Dublin too Big?" ADMINISTRATION, Vol. 2 (1954) 3.

provincial towns by dispersing civil servants to them, but this is to shift the argument from centralisation to the need to build up, say, our county towns. There is not much difficulty in showing that simply to disperse civil servants, without really tackling the problem of centralisation, is not the only, or the best, way to strengthen these towns.

Perhaps we could take a topical illustration of this failure to think the issue through ? Recent discussion has centered on a proposal that the Collection Branch of the Department of Lands be transferred to Castlebar. The Collection Branch is concerned with the centralised collection of land annuities from virtually every farmer in the country. As things stand, this collection will be just as *centralised* if it is directed from a single provincial town as it is in Dublin. But there is another approach. For many years there has been a desultory discussion as to how the system of land annuity collection, of rate collection, of the distribution of agricultural grant could be simplified into one operation. There is a long standing but remote relationship between land annuities, agricultural grant, and rates ; but this has never been given operational significance. Decentralisation of the Collection Branch, as opposed to dispersal of it, would involve taking the problem of taxing land and the reliefs for these taxes as part of one simplified operation, conducted by each county council from its own county capital. The farmer would get one simplified demand and would pay into one simplified collection system. By this means there could be both economy and simplicity combined with a decentralised operation. This is a very small, if topical example, of what adequate *administrative* decentralisation and devolution would mean. If, in addition, real local power to determine levels of taxation on land and of reliefs appropriate to the local circumstances were also to be given to local bodies, then we should be coming close to the heart of the matter.

Perhaps at this stage it would be useful to set out a few international definitions.[2] In simple terms, *decentralisation* means transfer of governmental functions from the centre. This can be by way of either *deconcentration* or *devolution*. *Deconcentration* involves transfer of the central government functions to field or regional units of government departments. One can see it exemplified in the regional

---

[2]United Nations: Decentralisation for National and Local Development, 1962. An excellent discussion of this whole issue is James W. Fesler: *Area and Adminis-tration,* University of Alabama, 1949. A discussion in relation to a particular country is J. L. Roberts (ed): *Decentralisation in New Zealand Government Administration,* Oxford, 1961.

units of British government departments, established during World War II, often headed by officers of under-secretary rank, and largely disbanded after 1945.[3] We do not in Ireland practise deconcentration to any significant extent and I do not propose to discuss it further. *Devolution* is the transfer of central government functions to local authorities.

In this country the discussion of problems of decentralisation is never in these terms. What we talk about is *dispersal,* either local or functional. Local dispersal is the dispersal of complete government departments to provincial towns, or the dispersal of parts of them to different places. We tend to forget that this dispersal is already considerable. For example, over 60 per cent of British civil servants serve *outside* London.[4] In this country the proportion is rather less. This is natural for a small country. But it suggests that if, in Britain, there are good grounds for complaining of too much centralisation, the situation here is rather worse. *Functional dispersal* (which does not come under the heading of decentralisation) is commonly practised in Ireland when state-sponsored (functional) bodies are set up to carry out functions hitherto performed by government departments.

So knotty a problem as decentralisation requires clear thinking about where our society is going. It is unprofitable to consider the structure of government without being clear how that structure fits into the kind of society that we want. This takes us away from the fascinating problem of whether the Department of Local Government is best sited in Athlone, or the Department of Defence in Clonmel.

II. THE SOCIALIZATION OF MODERN SOCIETIES

There are, in the context we have been considering, two leading problems of modern government: first, the growth, absolutely and relatively, in the volume of public business, and secondly, the problem of how to engage popular participation in government. These are separate problems, but, as I hope to show, they are related.

One of the striking features of the modern world has been the growth of governmental activity in the past few generations. This rate of growth has tended to be stimulated by the two great wars; it has also received powerful impetus from economic and social crises. Only simple minded people now believe that a modern economic community

---

[3]J. W .Grove: "How Central is Central Administration?" in D. Lofts (ed): *Local Government Today . . . and Tomorrow,* p. 117. London Municipal Journal, 1962.
  [4]Grove, *loc. cit.*

can grow and keep stable purely by the activity of businessmen. The 'invisible hand' of Adam Smith is now palpably the hand of the politician and the public servant. Increasing, and more sophisticated, intervention by government contributes as much to economic growth as the self-interest of economic man. Secondly, economic growth has involved extensive social changes, and has raised great social problems. It has also, of course, provided the means for alleviating these problems. These increased resources do not, however, automatically make themselves available for tackling social problems. Here government must act substantially outside the economic system if great social evils are to be remedied. Indeed, a big part of modern government is now, and has for a long time past been, concerned with social problems. Thirdly, the cataclysms of the great wars, and the desperate insecurity of modern peace-keeping machinery, have led governments into enormous expenditures on defence.

Thus, while modern societies have been growing at fairly rapid rates, there has been a more than corresponding growth in government. We have seen in the past, and in the present also, societies in pursuit of development moving from a traditional, orderly equilibrium into the dynamic, monetary economy. We are now witnessing, particularly in the free societies, the transition from the monetary economy into a situation where the business of government occupies, quantitatively as well as qualitatively, the principal place. Indeed, the relative size of government in the economy as a whole tends to be an index of the degree of development of a modern free society. This has not gone unnoticed. There were the warnings of Colin Clark and others that where government handled more than 25 per cent of the current resources of the community, there would be inflation and break down. Yet the public sector in the United States and the United Kingdom now engulfs something like 40 per cent of the resources of the community, and there is no sign that this relative growth is coming to an end.[5] Our own society follows steadily in the same direction: in 1962 about 36 per cent of the gross national product was public expenditure.

[5]Sir Richard Clarke in *The Management of the Public Sector of the National Economy,* University of London, 1964, pp. 6-7, points out that the public sector in Britain accounts for 40 per cent of national expenditure, 45 per cent of yearly fixed investment and employs nearly 25 per cent of the nation's manpower and probably 60 per cent of those with full-time higher education. He goes on to say: "The size and structure of important private industries, such as agriculture and aircraft production, are in effect determined by the decisions of Government; and the purchases of the public sector provide a large part and in some cases a dominant part of the demand for the products of other industries, notably construction, pharmaceuticals, electronics, electrical engineering, telecommunications equipment, and so on."

There is, as yet, no clear sign that this relative growth will end. As long ago as 1958 in West Germany the proportion was 44 per cent. Indeed, as the wealth of societies grows, and as the possibility of helping the weaker members of society becomes greater, it is likely that more and more of the resources of the community will be diverted to social ends, and this, almost certainly, will involve their being handled by government. Even more mystical than 25 per cent is the figure of 50 per cent. (In Britain, at the peak of total mobilisation in World War II, the figure was 52 per cent). A few years should see the mid-point passed in the advanced societies. When that happens the socialised part of society will be quantitatively greater than the unsocialised one. We are witnessing the rapid and progressive socialisation of society. The money economy in the western world, after a reign of some three centuries, will shortly lose its pre-eminence and will be succeeded by a predominantly socialised economy. We may not care for this development, and we may wonder where it is going to stop: but anyone who wishes to live in the modern world must come to terms with these facts. For a largely Catholic community like ours, this is one of the many contributions of the late Pope John, in *Mater et Magistra,* in coming to terms with the concept of 'socialisation' in a free society. But while we have to recognise this relative and absolute growth of the public sector of society, we must also recognise that this growth poses problems for us that will become steadily more acute.

The absolute and relative growth of the amount of government is likely to have, administratively, three main effects: the clogging of the centres of decision, atrophy at the periphery, and bureaucracy.

First, the clogging of the centres of decision. More and more business is likely to come on the tables of those who are the crucial decision makers in the community. A century ago John Stuart Mill was warning Britain: "It is but a small portion of the public business of a country which can be well done, or safely attempted, by the Central Authorities; and even in our own government, the least centralised in Europe, the legislative portion at least of the governing body busies itself far too much with local affairs, employing the supreme power of the State in cutting small knots which there ought to be other and better means of untying."[6] With the growth of public business this clogging of the system has spread from the legislative to the administrative side of central government. Professor Fogarty in a recent book[7] argues that Whitehall now handles so much detailed business that there is no

---

[6]*Representative Government*: ch. XV. Everyman edition, p. 346.
[7]M. P. Fogarty: *Under-Governed and Over-Governed*, Chapman, 1962.

time to consider the really important decisions. This, he says, explains much of the failures of modern British government. In this country Mr Whitaker has hinted at a similar danger: "I am not sure now if the biggest problem after all will not be one of organisation—how Secretaries and other senior officers can organise their time and work so as to get away from their desks and the harassing experiences of everyday sufficiently to read, consider and consult with others in order to be able to give sound and comprehensive advice on future develop- ment policy."[8] The clogging of the centres of decision occurs at a time when the increasing pace of modern living calls for ever more speedy adaptation and growth, and therefore for speedier and more frequent decisions on big issues.

The second likely effect is increasing atrophy at the periphery of our society. As has been said, 'apoplexy of the brain leads to paralysis of the limbs'. If the decision making in Dublin gets clogged, and there is no system by which decision making can occur in the various other parts of our society, then we are likely to move into the mastodon phase, which eventually leads to collapse.

The third likely effect is that more and more of our lives will be governed by decisions taken by gentlemen in public offices, whether in Dublin or in Castlebar. Even if we establish an adequate system of administrative law, as the French and many other people have done, as well as some sort of ombudsman system (as the Scandinavians and certain other people have done) the fact that most of the decisions of the community will be taken by public officials poses a major political preoccupation.

The growth in the absolute and the relative size of government in our society poses, therefore, three important problems—the clogging of the centres of decision, the atrophy of the periphery, and the bureaucratisation of decision making in society. One sees no evidence that any real attempt is being made to adapt our political and adminis- trative systems to cope with these problems. The growth leads to organisational changes, of course; but so long as these are simply *ah hoc* responses to immediate problems they make the situation worse because more complicated.

A recent study of the problems of tourist development in Killarney showed that some dozen official bodies were directly involved, not to mention the many voluntary bodies. This complexity baffles the citizen or the group and it makes it extremely difficult to initiate development as the remarkable failures with Killarney, potentially

[8]T. K. Whitaker: "The Civil Service and Development", ADMINISTRATION, Vol. 9 (1961) 2, p. 87.

our great tourist growth point, show too clearly. The remoteness of the centres of decision and the division of responsibility between so many bodies make for unresponsive administration and for frustrated citizens. The present tendency to remove more and more of such decision-making from bodies accountable to public representatives to unaccountable bodies aggravates the problem.

Whatever its other disadvantages, the price system does leave a good deal of decisions about his life to the ordinary individual. He can decide to buy this or that, or not to buy, or to save, to earn more or less. Within broad limits, he can make his own life. That is to say decisions are widely decentralised. Moreover, there is a rapid and effective way by which the cumulative effects of those decisions can be reflected in effective demand. But in a society where a large part, perhaps a majority, of the decisions governing his life will be concentrated, and will be taken by gentlemen in public offices who may not be amenable to rapid pressures, there is the danger that such freedom as the individual possessed under the old economic system will be lost to him and the system itself, for all its faults, made less responsive and adaptable.

This raises an important issue of what is the end or purpose of government.

III. THE SOCIAL TIE

This is a big issue that cannot be discussed here, except summarily. Basically, perhaps we could accept the end or purpose of government as being to serve the common good, or in the pregnant phrase of Bertrand de Jouvenel, to strengthen "the social tie itself."[9] These are concepts not without a great deal of difficulty, but one can perhaps give them some operational significance by saying that to strengthen the social tie is to create a closer sense of community. It is to bring about a situation where the physical, human and spiritual resources of the community are fully used; where the products of using these resources are fairly divided and the weak, sick and handicapped are truly cared for; and where each human personality has the opportunity for reaching its full level of development.

This has been set out with his usual lucidity by the Taoiseach, Mr Sean Lemass:

> We believe in a democracy which is deeply rooted amongst the people, which unites them in mutual understanding of national

[9]See Bertrand de Jouvenel: *Sovereignty,* Cambridge, 1957, ch. 7.

purposes achieved in full and free discussion of all matters of public concern, and in which the economic and social welfare of all is the constant concern of each. We believe in a form of society in which individual citizens and intermediate groups willingly accept the obligation to contribute to the common welfare, keeping their own interests in harmony with the needs of the community; a society in which all men are free to develop in a human way, free to act responsibly and entitled to the assumption that their acts are responsible, and free to cooperate with each other for their mutual advantage.[10]

In this context the greater degree of socialisation of the community's affairs is both an opportunity and a challenge. It is an opportunity because the more the affairs of the community come under rational choice and control and cease to be governed by blind impersonal forces, such as disease, poverty, the market, the more the community as a whole will rise to a higher level of explicit self-awareness and action so that the social tie, the sense of community, is strengthened. The increasing socialisation of the community is also a challenge, because this development could lead to the tyranny of big brother, or to the contrary evil, where the apathetic ordinary citizen feels no need to be responsible, or to worry, because the men in government will know, and do, best. Either of these results is the antithesis of what one would expect as the result of a free, responsible society. Either way, the social tie is weakened.

With the increased socialisation of society come a number of important developments that have the effect in themselves of increasing the independence, responsibility, and interest of the ordinary citizen. Both a condition and a consequence of increasing affluence is the spread of education at all levels, and the opportunity this gives for increasing self realisation. Communication within the society and as between societies has been increasing very rapidly, and the people, being better educated, have a greater understanding of what is going on both at home and abroad than they had in previous times. This process is likely to continue. With the increase in education and in knowledge there is also likely to be an increase in leisure, so that the ordinary citizen will no longer be crushed under the weight of merely earning a living. We may perhaps expect to see growing, gradually but steadily, the kind of situation that occurred amongst the citizens of the Greek states—the citizen will have the education, the knowledge, and the leisure, to play a significant part in public affairs.

[10]Speech to Dublin Lions Club, 3 September, 1964.

B

Thus the very growth of the circumstances that poses the problems of the place of the citizen in the new society also puts forward the remedy—that the citizen will be able and willing to participate more fully in the process of government. In this way the ordinary man can help consciously to guide the political and administrative forces that operate on him. Gunnar Myrdal foresees the development of society "beyond the Welfare State" when the state will restrict itself to two main things, maintaining a basic structure of society, and the rules relevant to life within the structure, leaving the rest for local self-government and for co-operation and bargaining between the organizations in the infra-structure. He goes on to say: "I have intentionally meant to depict a utopia. The reality in all our Western countries is far from realising it. I would nevertheless insist on the relevance of the utopian, decentralised and democratic state where, within the bounds of ever more effective overall policies laid down for the whole national community, the citizens themselves carry more and more of the responsibility for organising their work and life by means of local and sectional cooperation and bargaining with only the necessary minimum of direct state interference. This utopia is, in my belief, a real goal. It is inherent in those ideals of liberty, equality and brotherhood that are the ultimate driving forces behind the development of the modern Welfare State. If we made the ideology of the Welfare State more explicit, i.e. if we clarified our direction and aims, this utopia would stand out as our practical goal."[11]

This development can itself contribute to development both in politics and administration by increasing public understanding of the ends and means of political and administrative activity, thus leading to greater participation and more responsible responses to governmental action, and also to a greater public willingness to adapt and change to achieve such things as speedier rates of economic development.[12]

Mr Henry Maddick, putting forward a scheme[13] of decentralisation and of deconcentration, with the problems of developing countries chiefly in mind, claims: "the objectives of the system are, through decentralisation, to aid:

[11]Gunnar Myrdal: *Beyond the Welfare State,* Duckworth, 1960, pp. 67-70.

[12]That this popular participation may be an essential ingredient in well devised government institutions emerges from Mr John P. Mackintosh's devastating examination of whether a non-representative regional administrative organisation has made any special contribution to Scotland. See *Public Administration,* Autumn, 1964.

[13]Henry Maddick: *Democracy, Decentralisation and Development,* Asia Publishing House, New York, 1963, p. 230.

(a) the growth of popular control,
(b) economic and social development, and
(c) the growth of popular participation and support."

Of course, most of what has been said here about strengthening the social tie is concerned with values, and these tend to transcend normal discussions of administrative ways and means. But in our free, christian, democratic society it is likely that a great majority of people share the kind of values that we have been discussing. If these values are to be realised in the Ireland of the future, they will have to be given operational and institutional significance. This is a task for forward thinking administrators, amongst others.

IV. WHY DECENTRALISE ?

Administration is the study of organisations and their behaviour. Organisations can be considered at three levels: the individual organisations, the systems formed by individual organisations, and the structures of organisational systems. Each of these is at a higher level of abstraction. An individual organisation is the Department of Agriculture or the Wicklow County Council, or the Electricity Supply Board. A system is the civil service, of which government departments are a part; or local government, which comprises county councils and others; or (except that it does not yet exist) the state-sponsored bodies, of which the Electricity Supply Board is one. By a governmental structure we mean not only the individual government departments or local authorities or state-sponsored bodies, or even the systems of the civil service, or local government, or the state-sponsored bodies, but the fitting of all these into an integrated structure, where each individual body, and each system, has its role clearly defined and integrated. A great deal more thought needs to be devoted to the roles not only of individual public bodies, but of the systems and of the governmental structure itself. Above all, thought needs urgently to be directed to consider how best the overall business of government can be systematically allocated within the structure and as between the systems.

For this purpose it is necessary to diverge a little to discuss a philosophic issue, namely, the significance of hierarchy in systems and structures. If we look at the structure of the human body we see that it consists of a very large number of levels, each being at a higher level of abstraction than the last. Thus a human structure depends ultimately on sub-atomic particles, on atoms, molecules, cells, systems (nervous muscular, circulatory, etc.) until eventually the whole structure is created. At each level there is a grouping of similars to form a larger unity. At each level these similars work autonomously and do not invoke the higher level until a need for higher activity intervenes. Thus, the lungs work, the blood circulates, digestion takes place each within its own level; but when sudden danger comes, the nervous system, the muscular system, the release of adrenalin, the concentration of the brain—all these things join together to mobilise the resources and the actions that will obviate the danger. The point about the success of the working of the human structure is that at each level appropriate actions are carried on without invoking a higher level. It is only when something out of the ordinary is required that a message is sent up higher. Similarly in thinking. A great deal of our thinking is carried on at subconscious levels so that the brain can be kept clear for dealing with the new and the knotty. When we read, and the faster we read, we transcend individual letters, and words, and phrases—even sentences and paragraphs, when we read very fast. There is a hierarchy in these things, and each level has its own mode of operation that involves a high degree of local autonomy so that what requires to be done at any given level can be carried on within its own terms, and without outside interference; but if external interference becomes a part of the normal situation, the whole working of the hierarchical system becomes clogged and obstructed.

There is, of course, a danger in arguing by analogies, but analogy is still one of the great tools of thinking. It seems to me that the analogue of how a hierarchy works effectively is as applicable to systems and structures of human beings grouped in organisations as it is to the groupings within human systems and structures. This notion of the segregation of like activities, their grouping into levels, and the conditions for invoking higher or lower levels at any time, is one of the universal facts of human experience, and can be of great assistance to us in considering problems of organisations. One sees in it two broad factors: the differentiation of functions on the vertical plane (that is, the level of increasing abstraction), and the significance of the autonomy of each of the levels on its own plane. It is in this context that the principle of subsidiarity, referred to by Pope Pius XI in *Quadragesimo Anno*—that what can effectively be done at lower level should not be taken over by higher level—gets operational significance when one considers systems and structures of government.

Mr Lemass, in the speech already quoted from, puts the issue thus:

A true democracy is an educated democracy, because only people

who have been educated in its values, and understand its requirements, are able to maintain it. The promotion of this
education and understanding is not primarily a function of the
public authorities but of individual men, and groups, who understand that the work of the nation must be done, and know
that it can best be done, at the lowest level of authority at which
effectiveness is realisable, and that the higher up the pyramid of
power the function of taking decisions is moved, the greater the
danger to the kind of democracy we wish to preserve.

In the fiercely competitive world of today, there will always be
temptation to meet the pressure of current difficulties by resort
to control and regulation in the interest of greater national
efficiency. It is not the general experience of mankind that totali-
tarianism, or the excessive strengthening of central authority,
leads to greater national efficiency except for limited purposes
and for a limited time. The dispersal of responsibility throughout
the national community, the giving of effective power of decision
within their competence to vocational groups and intermediate
authorities provides a far more secure and, when fully understood and properly operated by an educated people, a far greater
assurance of the efficient performance of the nation's business.

In effect, one should centralise only what needs to be centralised,
and decentralise the rest. To repeat a slogan, we might centralise policy
and decentralise decision. This is to echo John Stuart Mill's maxim:
"The Authority which is most conversant with principles should be
supreme over principles, while that which is most competent in details
should have the details left to it. The principal business of the central
authority should be to give instruction, of the local authority to apply
it. Power may be localised, but knowledge, to be more useful, must
be centralised. . . ."[14]

Briefly, the argument to date has been that the real case for decentralisation comes from the growth in the quantity of government and the
growth poses in acute form the problem of popular participation in
government in a free society. This in turn leads one to look at the
structure and systems of government and one is not long doing this
before one comes up against the notion of subsidiarity. This in turn
leads one to the need to examine the role of local government in the
structure of government as a whole.

[14]*Representative Government*: ch. XV. Everyman edition, p. 357.

V. LOCAL GOVERNMENT AND DEVELOPMENT

If we look at the local government system as it operates in Ireland we see that it has three features—it is reasonably local, it is highly representative, and it is reasonably efficient. However, it would be unrealistic not to take into account the many criticisms that are made of the system. I propose to set down some of these, without necessarily agreeing with them.

The first criticism is that made of public representatives. They seem to represent only the consumers of public services, and one often gets the impression that they are actively concerned not with the public interest but with a series of special interests. For this reason, it is said, much of the best people in the community are shy of putting themselves forward for membership of local authorities, and a vicious circle sets in.

A second criticism is that, basically, the functions of local government are out of date. Local authorities in our system were set up in the 19th century to tackle problems that were new and vital problems in that century. In the 20th century they continued to discharge services that are basically 19th century responses to 19th century problems. The new, exciting 20th century problems have substantially by-passed the local government system. It seems to be unable to make itself really relevant to new and emerging problems.

A third criticism is that, basically, the functions of local government in our system are extraordinarily inflexible outside well-worn paths. One does not find in the local government system any really new initiative for development. Much of the blame, of course, for this inflexibility and out-of-dateness can be attributed to the heavy load of controls imposed on local authorities—the control of central government departments, the financial controls, and the pervasive control of the grossly over-elaborated doctrine of *ultra vires,* themselves the relics of out-dated thinking.

Each of these factors contributes to the vicious cycle and one sees what is basically a good system of local government becoming less and less relevant to the needs of the times. In such circumstances how could local authorities become "development corporations"? We lack any good intellectual foundation for the local government system, for dividing political (and administrative) power by area. How deficient is the theoretical basis either for more or less areal division of activity emerges vividly from an American symposium.[15]

[15]Arthur Maas (ed): *Area and Power, A Theory of Local Government,* Free Press, Glencoe, 1959.

Are these weaknesses of the Irish local government system inherent or are they remediable? I believe that they are remediable. They will not, however, be remedied unless urgent steps are taken to make the local government system relevant to the problems of the 20th century. This means loosening up the attitudes of those involved in the system and the kinds of controls that they exercise on one another. It involves widening the functions of local authorities. Above all it means giving them the power of initiative. As Mr Bryan Keith-Lucas points out in relation to England[16]: "The history of the 18th and 19th centuries shows how much the country owes to the experimental enterprise of individual local authorities in the social services. There are few if any parts of our welfare state which do not owe their origin to the experiments and initiative of local councils, long before the central government took up the ideas, and made them general." He goes on to say "So the frontiers of local municipal enterprise have almost ceased to expand and local government has lost the excitement and the opportunities that it once had. Joseph Chamberlain went into local government because he saw the challenge and the possibilities that it offered."

If local government could thus be modernised and made relevant it would most likely call for the best individuals in the community, those most anxious to contribute to the creation of a really virile democracy. We are witnessing at this time a great experiment in induced development, economic, social, cultural and institutional. This is a by-product of the basic experiments in planning for development that are taking place in this country. Because planning necessarily involves itself in taking an overall view of the community, it rapidly becomes aware that planning at the centre is not enough. It must be supplemented by regional and local planning. By this I mean not merely physical planning, but planning as a general technique over the whole field of administration, whether it is concerned with economic matters, social matters, cultural matters or institutional matters.

One of the striking developments of the past few years has been the piecemeal realisation that central planning, successful as it is in guiding decisions—whether by fiscal or other means—of decision makers in the private sector of the community, has been nothing like so successful in guiding decisions in the public sector, or in that vast hinterland where a marriage has to be arranged between public and private conceptions of the public interest. This has been one of the motivations behind the interest in stimulating community development in very underdeveloped communities. Unfortunately, comparable

[16]In Lofts, *loc. cit.*, pp. 30-31.

techniques of doing this in moderately advanced communities have not yet been adequately worked out. In the more advanced communities still—in France, in the Netherlands, and now in Britain—some progress has been, or is being, made.

A number of current problems of local development have been identified in Ireland in the past few years, and various *ad hoc* efforts have been made to cope with some of them. For example, the existence of local authorities has enabled real progress to be made in improving roads for tourism, but other local problems of tourism, such as accommodation, the development of antiquities,[17] and of amenities, problems of local supplies, have not been adequately tackled. The setting up of the local regional tourism organisations is an attempt to cope with these problems in isolation. Similarly, the county development teams represent another *ad hoc* approach to the problems of economic development in the small farm areas. A third kind of approach was the setting up of the special government department for the Gaeltacht areas. Perhaps one will soon see some form of integrated approach to the various disparate attempts now being made, and being planned, for educational development. Other local, developmental problems that have been identified but for which no real organisational solution has yet been devised, are the problems of development centres, of agricultural co-operation, and of the various forms of community development, such as those raised by local tourist and industrial development bodies, and by the pilot farm areas.

These are all substantially local problems and they are by-passing local government. Because they raise problems that are not really technological, the question of the adequacy of the size of existing local authorities does not really arise. Many of these problems may well be capable of being dealt with by bodies covering quite small areas. A striking example of a local authority covering a relatively small area —but a nominated not a democratic one—is the Shannon Free Airport Development Company (SFADCO). It is concerned with only a small part of the County Clare, but it represents a high concentration of ability and resources on this small area. In the recruiting of a large number of people with a high level of ability and in the investment of substantial capital resources, SFADCO presents a model of what local development requires. We need such bodies dotted around the country. But, if what has been said before about popular participation

[17]The recent strengthening of the Office of Public Works to improve the care of our extraordinary heritage of antiquities is to be welcomed. But the limits of the suggested programme of work over the next few years shows what a huge task remains to be tackled. Is this best *executed* by a central body?

as a value of our society is valid, they should logically be brought within an adequate democratic framework. Moreover, the scale of the problem of local development does not seem to have been widely grasped. The capital indebtedness of SFADCO (that is, the amount of public invest-ment in development other than that in the airport itself) in 1964 was £4.3 million, that of the Clare County Council, with development responsibilities over so much greater an area, was £1.7 million. This contrast shows what *real* development involves by way of public in-vestment and how the local government authority has, in effect, become largely irrelevant to the public development needs of the new times. However, it is not the *scale* of operations, but the insistence on *development* and the freedom to tackle new facets of development (such as the transition from building an industrial estate to tourist promotion) that is the remarkable *developmental* feature of SFADCO. This organisation is not, according to the values we have been trying to identify, the complete answer to problems of local development, but a number of the priorities have been got right in relation to it.

To summarise, the growth of the business of government and the importance of evoking popular participation in it, lead to the need for a better and more democratic structure of government in our society. In this structure there is an important part for local government to play if its role and scope for initiative are drastically recast so that it be-comes relevant to 20th century problems; if, in fact, local authorities can be turned into development corporations. If we are to have a society that is to be governmentally dynamic, two big problems arise. The first of these is how best to allocate the *existing* work of govern-ment throughout the structure of government, and the second is how best to get *new* development going.

In the task of allocating the work of government, it is important to tease out the appropriate roles of central, local and functional government. I have discussed this at some length on another occasion.[18] Here, may I say that the inescapable task of central government is to deal with those overall tasks—such as foreign affairs, defence, overall planning—that cannot by their nature be sub-divided. Leaving aside the special case of functional government (such as generating electricity), virtually all the detailed business of government could be devolved to local authorities. That is to say, we should have local *government*. This has the advantage of bringing the discharge of business nearer the people in respect of whom it is discharged. It much simplifies the business of government, which is now a nightmare of criss-crossing

[18]See "Machinery of Government", ADMINISTRATION, Vol. 11, (1963) 3, pp. 187-206, now the second paper in this book.

responsibilities, and it offers the opportunity of making the whole system of public administration democratic, by enabling it to be brought within the representative system. It is now forgotten how 60 years ago it was hailed as a great democratic revolution that the old nominated public bodies should have been swept away and elected representatives put in their places. Have we really lost our faith in the value of the representative system—that is in elected representatives, not nominated ones? (One can see the struggle to effect this transition from nomination to election as part of the freeing of African countries in recent times.) Anyone who had watched the growth of governmental bodies with nominated members over the past 38 years in this country would say that there was a strong and increasing drift away from democracy back to the old system of nominated representatives. Is it really true that successive native governments have less faith in the sense of the plain people of Ireland than the Tory Government of 1898? Is it utopian to look forward, like Myrdal,[19] to a system by which the central government reserves to itself only a small proportion of the functions of government, those that are genuinely indivisible; devolves on local representative bodies all the detailed business of government, including the raising and spending of taxation; extends the role of popularly elected representatives to moderate the detailed administration of these services by officials accountable to them; and gives, except for functions specifically reserved to the centre, clear responsibility and initiative to the local governments for development within the overall national development plan? There are certain other improvements one would like to see made—such as the setting up of local administrative courts for resolving local disputes between the citizen and the local administration. One would also like to see some provision for small local bodies (for example for the baronies) with some taxing and borrowing powers to carry out minor works of local development and amenity. It seems to me that, for example, an area with the dramatic potential of the Dingle Peninsula should be able to have for itself some sort of a body that, at least in the tourist, fishing and agricultural interests, could do for that Peninsula what the Shannon Free Airport Development Company has done for the much less promising part of East Clare with which it is concerned. Possibly there is also room for such small groups as the local development authority for a small town or village and its surrounding rural area with some statutory powers, including a limited power of taxation.

If some such scheme as this were adopted for general decentralisation

---

[19]Mr Roberts, *loc. cit.*, has a similar utopian vision for New Zealand.

of functions from the centre, and their devolution to responsible representative authorities, the central government would be free for that overall planning and review that are the essentials of modern government and for the setting of standards and targets by the subordinate bodies that is the essence of high-level government.

I think there is little likelihood of such drastic change, unless, as a first step, action is taken to establish an office with ideas and powers for dealing with problems of machinery of government.

Now that the Irish people are free, are becoming self-confident and more alert, having before them better opportunities of education and of the benefits of modern living, is it utopian to urge that we could devise and adapt a governmental structure that will evoke, free, and harness to the common and local good the boundless dynamism of the human personalities of our people? It is in such a context that, in my view, the terms "decentralisation" and "devolution" become meaningful.

Chapter 2

MACHINERY OF GOVERNMENT*

The expression "Machinery of Government" has been in use at least since the report of the Haldane committee on Machinery of Government in 1918. On the whole, the expression "machinery" is not inappropriate for describing the organisation available for carrying out the business of government. One thinks of the business of government as a substantially rational process carried out by a number of organisations that operate on substantially rational lines. One thinks of a clear allocation of functions between these organisations and within them. The analogy of a clearly articulated and coherent machine, carrying out certain set tasks, is a persuasive one. However, let us look more closely at a machine—such as an engine of a motor car. We see that it is composed of a number of clearly distinct parts linked together to form some sort of process. Thus, in a car engine, there is the ignition system, the fuel system, the conversion system, etc. Each of these systems has a clearly defined purpose. These purposes taken together serve an overall purpose. Within the systems themselves the same differentiation and overall unity can be seen to be at work. Thus, if a part were to fall out of a car engine, one could, with very little knowledge, know which part of the engine it came from.

If one considers the "Machinery of Government" one cannot speak with anything like the same assurance. A piece of business, left lying about, could belong to any part of the system of government. It is true that, nowadays, we consider the machinery of government as a more complex affair than in Haldane's time. He had in mind principally the operation of the civil service. We now would regard the machinery of government as comprising also local government, and functional government (i.e. that carried on by the state-sponsored bodies). To this might be added, as will be argued later, a fourth branch, which we might call appellate government. One has only to look at these forms of government to see that one cannot clearly distinguish them or their

*Reprinted from ADMINISTRATION, Vol. 11 (1963) 3.

component parts, as one can distinguish the ignition from the conversion part of the car engine, or the parts of the conversion from parts of the ignition. One finds, to press the analogy too far, bits of the fuel system in the conversion and bits of the ignition in the fuel system, and so on.

ASSUMPTIONS

If we are to follow the implications of this analogy certain assumptions are necessary. These are :

(i) Civil government is carried on by a single entity, the PUBLIC SERVICE ;

(ii) The mark of the tasks discharged by each branch of the public service and of their mutual relations is APPROPRIATENESS ;

(iii) Tasks are allocated to each branch of the public service according to PRINCIPLE.

Are these assumptions reasonable ? If they are, then a number of consequences follow that suggest substantial changes. It is thus important to scrutinise these assumptions very carefully. If they pass this scrutiny, then the analogy of "Machinery of Government" can be pressed a great deal farther. In this sense, too, the *method* of engineering design can be used to help in arriving at a possible design for machinery of government.

(i) *Public Service*

The assumption that there is such a thing as "the Public Service" is now coming to be accepted. The business of government, carried on for ultimately the same master—the plain people of Ireland—may be diverse in its activities, but it is capable of being comprehended as a single task, namely that of serving the common good in the overall task of national development. Whether one serves in central, local or functional government is immaterial, in this sense : all three services are but aspects of the public service. Of course, the public service is divided by a number or organisational barriers and loyalties, based on history, accident, career structure, superannuation etc. but, in principle, these barriers and loyalties are consequences, not antecedents.

(ii) *Appropriateness*

This is a much more difficult concept. It is one frequently used when a new state-sponsored body is set up; we say this is because its proposed functions are not "appropriate" to central or local government. But what precisely do we mean by "appropriate" in this sense ? To continue with the example of the state-sponsored body, we might consider a genuine trading body as appropriate to this form of functional government ; but in fact most state-sponsored bodies are not trading bodies. What is usually implied by "appropriate" is *not* the nature of the thing done, but the giving of a greater and more appropriate freedom of action in doing it. But this is to raise another issue altogether, distinct from the concept of "appropriateness" as commonly understood. This new concept is the one of whether the constraints on effective action imposed on central and local government are necessary and cannot be relaxed ; and that the only way of evading them is by setting up a different form of organisation. If we are to hold to the concept of "appropriateness" in the classification of work, we can only give it some sort of meaning by considering the special features of each service and matching it to the "appropriate" branch of government. This, in turn, leads us to consider the "appropriateness" of the role of each branch in a properly articulated system of government.

(iii) *Principle*

Principle is a guide to action by which like things are dealt with in a like way. Its mark is consistency, its aim coherence, and its result efficiency. If we find widespread, contradictory and long standing disparities, evidence of half measures, and complaints of friction and extreme complexity, we are unlikely to have a principled, that is an efficient, system. To remedy this, to bring order into the disorder, is basically a problem of design.

But here we have brought in a new term, namely, "efficiency". What do we mean by this? Basically, an efficient system is one that gives the highest possible return for a given quantum of resources, or, alternatively, gives a given quantum of return for the minimum use of resources. In the context of administration, efficiency is often used in the second sense. In a community like ours where there is a surplus of resources of men, capital and land, efficiency is more appropriately taken in the first sense. Here it will be taken in that sense, unless the contrary is stated. In general, efficiency is served by orderly rational process, hindered by the survival of ideas and practices that cannot demonstrate their rationality.

The argument to date is that the analogy of "machinery of government" assumes that the functions of government can be rationally allocated, each according to its nature. This, in turn, involves making assumptions on which to base this purportedly rational structure. These assumptions can be stated and analysed. If, after this, they are acceptable the possibility of re-designing on rational lines the machinery of government presents itself. The more rational this re-designed machinery can be made to be, the more efficient it, potentially, becomes.

A DESIGN PROBLEM

In engineering, in architecture, in industrial design, the solution to a design problem comes not from looking into one's heart, from subjective and emotional reactions, but from applying an identifiable design method. Is it possible to apply this method to the design of machinery of government? The marks of the method are an orderly concern for A. Purpose, B. the Situation, C. Formulation, and D. Feedback. These can be analysed further:

A. Purpose

1. Define OBJECTIVES.
2. Order PRIORITIES.
3. Define STANDARDS of performance.

B. Situation

4. In the light of the objectives, SURVEY the situation in order, not so much to find answers as "progressively to clarify the questions" by
    (i) discerning DISCREPANCIES,
    (ii) making FORECASTS of existing trends, and
    (iii) relating discrepancies, forecasts and standards so as to define what calls for ACTION.
5. In the light of the survey, define the PARAMETERS or limiting factors of the situation.
6. Divine the ORDER of the parameters.

C. Formulation

7. Relate objectives, priorities, standards, and parameters together by formulating a DESIGN.

8. In the design, define ROLES.
9. Devise a PLAN for achieving the design, or parts of it, over a given period.

D. *Feedback*

10. Insert a CONTROL to give feedback, to ensure that the design is related to the purpose at any time.

A. PURPOSE

1. OBJECTIVES

The main objectives of the machinery of government are to discharge the tasks of government:
a. Effectively
b. Acceptably
c. Comprehensibly.

a. *Effectively*

This objective does not call for discussion. Government is not an end in itself; it is simply a means of doing things in the national interest or common good.

b. *Acceptably*

But the common good is not served if government does things that are not acceptable to the people, or are done in a manner that is unacceptable to them. Sooner or later a government, even a tyrannical one, that loses the assent of the people will fall. One of the arguments for democracy is that it enables this question of acceptability to be tested every so often. The flexible nervous system that is given by public representatives holding office by public support provides a stream of information to governments showing how far they can go in mobilising unused resources, and where precisely are the sensitive areas that must, at least temporarily, be avoided. For example, this is one reason given to explain why it was possible for Britain to mobilise a greater proportion of her resources in World War II than Nazi Germany succeeded in doing.

But there is more to acceptability than this negative constraint on activity. A good part of the business of government can only be carried on with the understanding and sympathy of the governed. This is not simply a question of pleasing, or bribing, the electorate. The more complex government becomes, the more the public understanding of its objectives and methods becomes necessary. An extreme example of this was the system of food rationing in Britain during World War II. This was a difficult, potentially dangerous, task of government, depending on a high degree of public assent. In fact, the degree of assent available and the skill with which it was used enhanced both the standing and the scope of government. The more complex government becomes—this is one of the marks of modern government—the more important this objective of acceptability.

c. *Comprehensibility*

The third objective is that of comprehensibility. If public assent is to be maintained, it is essential that what is done must be comprehensible to the public. Thus, other things being equal, the simpler, the clearer, and the more orderly the procedures for carrying out the business of government, the better. The more incomprehensible, the more mysterious the system as ordinary reasonable men come in contact with it, the readier they will be to believe ill of the system as a whole.

2. PRIORITIES

These objectives clearly conflict to some extent. What is effective may not always be acceptable (and no government that is actively governing can always expect its measures to be wholly acceptable, especially in the short run). The complexities by which acceptance is gained lead to results that are not always comprehensible. Thus, there can be a clash between these objectives. Against this, these objectives can also assist each other. What is comprehensible is usually acceptable, and if it is acceptable it is usually effective.

Nonetheless, the possibility of clash is always there, so it is necessary to draw up an order of priority for these three objectives. Sometimes one of these objectives may in a given situation be more pressing than the others; but it is feasible to arrive at a normal order of priorities. Perhaps one can put this order of priorities as (i) effectiveness, (ii) acceptability and (iii) comprehensibility. In doing this, however, one must bear in mind that each objective is both a limiting and enhancing factor of the other, and that some situations may call for a different order. The main point is that, at each stage, we must know what is the order of priorities.

3. STANDARDS

It is not enough to know what is aimed at, and in what order, but also one must know *how much* of it is required in a given time, what standards of performance may be expected. What sort of standards can be applied to assessing the facts about the existing machinery of government? Can we arrive at any means by which we can judge what is a good system of organisation and what less good? It is unfortunate that very little work has been done in non-monetary terms on trying to devise standards of effective performance. One would expect, however, in general terms to be able to divine some intellectual standards that can be applied. These standards would seem to demand *principled, ordered,* and *effective* activity. In short, one would expect like to go with like and be differentiated from unlike, in a coherent, consistent scheme of organization, which facilitates and does not inhibit action. The special standards one would expect to see established here are generalised and congruous organisation leading to efficiency.

B. SITUATION

4. SURVEY

We survey, from the standpoint of the objectives, to identify the facts:
a. to discern the DISCREPANCIES between the standards and the situation;
b. to FORECAST the effects of existing trends (e.g. whether the discrepancies will widen or narrow);
c. and so to define what calls for ACTION.

The object of this exercise is, in effect, to distinguish the 'is' from the 'ought'.

a. *Discrepancies*

It is impossible here to point to more than a few salient facts. The striking fact is that of DISPARITY, internal and external. A full survey of the disparities of Irish government, considered from the viewpoint of organisation, would take a great deal of space. One can get a fair idea of the size and nature of the problem by taking, as it were, a few trial borings.

For this reason it is useful to consider, because of the central position of the civil service, its relations with the other arms of the public service, that is, its *external disparities*—e.g. of (i) central-local relations, (ii) trading and promotion, and (iii) quasi-judicial, or appellate, procedures.

(i) *Central-Local Relations*: Why, in alphabetical order, do the Departments of Agriculture, Education, Gaeltacht, Local Government and Social Welfare carry on activities almost identical with one another and with those of local authorities? To take the simple example of housing. A good part of house building in Ireland is conducted by the local authorities. However, the Department of Local Government and Department of the Gaeltacht give grants for building and reconstructing houses.

In some cases local authorities give grants for these purposes too, but only where the central authority has first done so. Some of the new house grant is offset by the stamp duty on the sale. A good part of the houses built for private occupation are, in addition, financed by loans from local authorities. House building is also a function of the Department of Lands, and a specially created state-sponsored body to build houses now exists, the National Building Agency. Local authorities also assist the building of new houses by giving substantial remission of rates. They are also responsible for controlling the standards of building and design of houses. They derive much of their own income from taxing houses.

One can consider the question of housing as a national problem. No doubt the final responsibility for the state of the nation's housing rests with the Department of Local Government; but considered from the viewpoint of any given area—a town or county—who is responsible for the state of housing, considered as a whole, in that area? The answer is "no one". No one is clearly and ultimately responsible. This lack of final responsibility somewhere is a mark of bad organisation of government and thus of bad government.

The Departments of Agriculture, Education, Health, Lands (Fisheries), Local Government, Social Welfare and Transport and Power all operate in some degree through local authorities specially orientated towards them. In each case the conception of the role of local authorities, the kind of organisation appropriate to the function being discharged, the relations with the Department, are different. The most striking example of this is, of course, that the idea of special committees as separate local authorities has been abandoned over the great part of Irish local government and been replaced by the management system; but this applies not at all to the local authorities that come under the Departments of Agriculture, Education, Lands, and (in part) Social Welfare. The concept of local government operated by these departments does not make the distinction—statutorily enshrined in relation to local government generally—between the *representative* and the *administrative*. The Department of Transport and Power occupies an intermediate position.

Again, the Department of Education conducts one broad branch of its educational services through local authorities; but this is only one of four. Each of the four is radically different.

Local bodies are strictly bound by the doctrine of *ultra vires*, apparently to ensure that they display no initiative that is not permitted by statute. On the other hand, those other organs of government, the state-sponsored bodies, are specially constituted so that they may display initiative.

(ii) *Trading and Promotion*: In 1957 Gaeltarra Eireann left the civil service and was constituted as a state-sponsored body. In engages in *trading* activities, but it also is clearly a social service body and receives a grant of £100,000 a year. Against that, a body more closely akin to a genuine trading body, namely, the Post Office, constitutes half the civil service.

If *promotional* work is not appropriate to the civil service, but is appropriate to state-sponsored bodies like the Industrial Development Authority or Bord Failte Eireann or Coras Trachtala, why is so much promotional work still inside the civil service? It is probably true to say that much the greatest part of civil service work still is promotional work.

If rigidities of *recruitment*—O shades of the great reform embodied in the notion of the Civil Service Commission—are reasons why state-sponsored bodies should recruit their own staffs, why are the staffs of the Industrial Development Authority and Foras Tionscail almost all (but not wholly) civil servants?[1]

If a state-sponsored body (Aer Rianta) should run Dublin Airport, why does the Department of Transport and Power run Shannon and Cork Airports?[1]

(iii) *Quasi-Judicial*: Why is there such a jumble of quasi-judicial bodies? A sizeable part of the work of a number of government departments is concerned with considering appeals by aggrieved parties against decisions taken by the Department. If it is a basic rule—as it is for example in relation to all appeals against the decisions of local authorities—that the decisions on these appeals must be given by Ministers, what about the position such an officer as the Commissioner of Valuation, who (subject to appeal to the Courts) adjudicates on decisions taken by his own officers, or the Revenue Commissioners in customs matters (but not for income tax ones)? If it is important that a judge participate in appeals about land acquisition, as is done in the Land Commission, why are similar decisions taken by the Ministers for Local Government and Health? If the Minister for Lands has nothing to do with these appeals in his Department, in what way should he differ from the Minister for Local Government? If there can be legal delegation in the Department of Social Welfare from the Minister to deciding officers and appeals officers—and indeed an elaborate appeal system and procedure provided there by legislation—why is this not possible in other departments?

---

[1]These discrepancies have since been removed—Foras Tionscal has been incorporated in the Industrial Development Authority and the whole set up as a normal state-sponsored body. Aer Rianta now manages all the civil airports.

These points are made, not to find fault, but to indicate the remarkable disparities that exist throughout the system of government. These are examples of *external disparities* of behaviour as between departments and other groups. Similar examples could be given from within public bodies themselves.

b. *Forecast*

It does not need much sophistication to see that this proliferation of *ad hoc* solutions to individual problems will, as the tasks of government grow, lead to more complexity and less public comprehension, thus making the system of government less acceptable and, thus, less effective. This might have to be faced if there were no solution to these problems; but that they are insoluble is unlikely.

(c) *Action*

It is natural that in developing bodies disparities of this kind should grow up; but it is not natural that their *continuance* should be accepted as natural. The generalising process, essential to good administration, has not been evoked. The existence of such widespread disparities shows the lack of periodical survey and generalisation. It is on this front that action is required.

If our standards call for principled, ordered and effective activity, what, as a result of our survey, calls for action? The basic assumption here is that once one has discovered a disparity one has some moral impulsion to do something about it. What calls for action here is, of course, the *gap* between *standards* and *facts*. The existence here of a gap (or, more accurately, a whole series of gaps) calls for re-thinking of the whole machinery of government, a necessity to grasp and make meaningful the concept of "appropriateness" and for an effective scheme of action.

5. PARAMETERS

The business of government is clearly limited by a number of factors, or, in engineering terms, parameters. These suggest limits to what can be done and to the way in which what can be done must be done. To define these limits is to arrive fairly clearly at the broad outline of the design that can be appropriately devised for this problem. The parameters here are:

    a. legislation
    b. representation
    c. subsidiarity
    d. efficiency of size

    e. sovereignty
    f. disputes
    g. control
    h. time

a. *Legislation*

The first parameter is that government must be based on *legislation*. This involves public discussion of the issues, the assent in some way of public representatives, the acceptance of the rule of law, and (the activity closest to the heart of administration) the careful formulation of legislative proposals. "Legislation" in this sense is *not* simply a function of central government. It is an aspect of every organisation—especially of public ones—in which rules have to be made.

b. *Representation*

In a free democratic society, legislation is enacted by representatives and the principle of *representation* involves election periodically, the participation of the representatives in the taking of the large decisions, the accountability of the administration to the representatives, the acceptance of the value of a sensitive nervous system between the administration and the administered which the representatives constitute, and the concept of fairness, that is, not only consideration for the administered but also the scrupulous dealing of like treatment in like cases. Here again, the representative principle has its part in every organisation. In business the directors are the shareholders' representatives, the shop stewards the workers'. It is a mark of democracy that representatives are *elected* by those they represent, of bureaucracy that they are *appointed* by some authority, no matter how well-intentioned.

c. *Subsidiarity*

The third factor is that of *subsidiarity*. That is to say, other things being equal, the smaller the better. Smallness may conflict with efficiency, and then it must give way; but in many areas increase of size does not add to efficiency. One cannot be dogmatic about this. The point about the principle of subsidiarity is that bigness has to *demonstrate* that it is best; one must not take this for granted. Again it follows that the lesser organisation should have as much autonomy as is necessary for it to discharge its functions and here again the onus of proof is on whoever impedes the free functioning of that autonomy.

d. *Size*

This brings us to a controversial topic, namely, the efficiency of *size*. Clearly there is no straightforward answer to this. The issues that arise are :

  (i) technology
 (ii) the operating unit
(iii) combining (or "tuning") units
 (iv) criteria of size—
        1. process, 2. viability, 3. career, 4. history, 5. generalisation,
        6. functional, 7. compendious, 8. balance.

(i) *Technological* considerations may demonstrate the efficiency of very great size indeed: it seems that there is, so far, no upper limit to the increase in efficiency that occurs when one makes extremely large electricity generating stations. But where such clearly technological factors do not operate, or when their advantages do not decisively outweigh their disadvantages, the question of the efficiency of size is a most vexed one.

(ii) It is probable that where there are not substantial technological factors, the individual *operating unit* is most effective when it is kept small. But once this is done, and its appropriate autonomy of action preserved, there seems, so far, no upper limit to the efficiencies that may be yielded by the *combination* of units into an organisation. The important point here is that the economies of scale in this kind of organisation must not be bought at the expense of the frustration of the autonomy of the operating units (this is the main argument against the unsophisticated use of such so-called aids as "common services" even where they can demonstrate—as they frequently cannot—this technical efficiency).

(iii) The best *combination* of units, so that the greatest overall efficiency can be achieved, does not mean that each of the units should be working at maximum efficiency; and conversely, it may be wise to forego some overall efficiencies in the interests of the more efficient working of the operating units. In the first instance, we have to guard against the danger of "sub-optimisation". In tuning an engine (to return to that analogy) it would make greatly for simplicity if all one had to do was to adjust each of the operating factors to its most effective level.[2] The trouble is that what is most effective for each of the units does not make for the most effective overall performance. This problem of "tuning" is not fully recognised in discussion about organisation. The same point has been demonstrated by workers in operational research. To achieve the best overall performance, we may have to put up with something less than the best performance by each of the participating units. In the same way, many large organisations have found that it is better to give each of the operating units, say, its own sales force, at the cost of considerable duplication, rather than to have a single sales force. What is

---

[2]'They all rowed well, but none so well as stroke'.

to be gained by the singleness of purpose of the sales force attached to a single operating unit, and the detailed knowledge of the product, is less than what is lost by the so obvious duplication of effort, travelling, etc. This may be the main (but by no means the only) argument for taking a hard look at the overall effect of common services insofar as they delay action.

Another aspect of "tuning" is balance. In the context of public administration, this is usually the problem of the right balance between the capital and the rest of the country. Dublin is not a big city, as they go; but relatively it is—a quarter of the population of the state lives in or about it. It is hardly big enough to support an adequate (e.g. cultural) superstructure; but is now beginning to show many diseconomies of scale. At the other end, our county towns—that is the principal town in each county—are mostly too small and some at least of them could, with advantage to the areas they serve, be built up. As wealth grows, the demand for cultural facilities will rise and this is a case for better and bigger county towns to support those activities. These in turn contribute to the process of national development. In administrative terms, this problem is often posed of transferring single Government departments to individual county towns; but there is another solution—to transfer the bulk of the detailed *business* of government from central to local government. That is, to have a wide devolution of functions. This would also facilitate the process of regional and county development by locating effective powers *within* the developing areas themselves.[3]

(iv) What are, then, the *criteria* that determine size?

    1. The first is that size is not an absolute but a stage in a *process*. We must have—at least until we know a great deal more about this subject—no *a priori* ideas about optimum size. What is important is that the process of evolution of the organisation should be permitted to realise itself to the stage or stages of development enabling it best to realise its potenitalities. This calls for the conscious recognition of growth, change, development as the healthy condition of organisation. If public bodies are to become 'development corporations' they must themselves have some freedom to develop. This means

---

[3]Foreign observers comment on the extreme centralisation of the Irish system of government. This is based mainly on the British model which, according to Professor Michael Fogarty (*Under-Governed and Over-Governed*, Chapman, 1962), is working badly because central government is so immersed in detail that it misses the main issue. A further consequence recalls the French 19th century saying 'Apoplexy of the brain leads to paralysis of the extremitites'.

considering size not only in terms of bigness but also in terms of subtlety and complexity, and of development in terms of levels of increasing sophistication.

2. The second point follows from this. The essential thing about any size is viability. The organisation must be big enough to enable it to achieve the purpose for which it exists. In some cases, for example, where no technological issues arise, where the potentialities of the purpose of the organisation are readily realised, this size can be very small indeed, and conversely if the organisation depends very substantially on technology, and there are substantial economies of scale in adopting for example, greater capital equipment, then the size is likely to be very large indeed.

3. Another determinant of size is one that will give a satisfying career to good men. Sometimes the operating unit may be large enough to permit this. If it is not, there must be some system of mobility of talent whereby the really good men can rise to the chances of realising their full potentialities. This implies either a single large organisation composed of a number of operating units, or a number of units with a common pool of talent—and an acceptable machinery for allocating it, such as the Local Appointments Commission. This factor will tend to make for organisations of increasing size. As men become more experienced and master greater parts of the job, they tend to seek wider fields for their talents and their energies. This is probably a major factor in creating growth in organisations.[4]

4. A further factor in determining size is history. Ancient nations may be very small in the context of the great nations of today, yet they may stubbornly resist technological and other forces making for larger nations. The same may be true in the business world and in public administration. For example, the historical boundaries of some counties in Ireland may be illogical, but they tend to persist because they happen to have existed for a very long time. The rationalisation of the structures of trade unions runs into the same sort of issue.

5. Another factor is the principle of generalisation. There seems to be something in the structure of human thinking that continually drives us to group things together and to try to derive from these groupings ever greater degrees of generalisation.

[4]See E. T. Penrose: *The Theory of the Growth of the Firm*, Blackwell, 1959.

Thus there is a tendency for ideas and organisations to abstract from more and more detail and thus arrive at higher, more abstract structures. Where this abstraction occurs, the *operating* units will be kept small. The degree of sophistication of the designers of the organisation is measured by the extent of the vertical differentiation they achieve. That is to say, they will achieve a structure in which the operational autonomy of the operating units will not be impeded, but high level activities such as long-term planning, major capital expenditure and senior appointments are dealt with at the high level their importance demands.

6. This leads us to two other factors that determine organisations. One is the *local* (or territorial). This has long been an operating unit where work tends to be thick on the ground. The other is the *functional*. Again, where the work is thick on the ground, there is a tendency for the functional to be caught up in some way in the territorial unit of organisation, because of the process of generalisation. At the beginning of a service the organisation tends to concentrate on a single function, and thus to be a functional one. Later a number of functional activities tend to be merged in a single organisation. Thus the local or territorial organisation becomes *compendious*. This represents the organisation at a fairly advanced state.

7. The grouping of functions in a compendious organisation enables that organisation to achieve a number of the advantages (as well as the disadvantages) of bigness and yet be related to a reasonably manageable local area. For example, the use of computers tends to give technological advantages to organisations, and those aspects or organisations that have hitherto been immune to the industrialised age. On a functional basis, the need to have an adequate computer may call for a very large organisation indeed. However, the versatility of computers is such that if a number of programmes are prepared, a single computer can just as readily be used over a variety of functions within a relatively small territorial area. Thus we can derive the advantages of bigness either by having single functions discharged over a relatively large area, or by having the maximum possible number of functions discharged over a relatively small area. What the size of that area should be will be determined by the possibility of "tuning", as we have seen, even at the price of obvious (but in the long run relatively minor) inefficiencies.

8. The alternative is to grow functionally, so that the organisation is a specialised one operating over a much larger area. Technology may dictate this (as in electricity generation) but unless it does, the costs of specialisation and remoteness have to be carefully balanced against the real (not assumed) advantages of large functional bodies.

Thus, as growth occurs, we have to choose between the complex and the remote.

e. *Sovereignty*

A problem seldom discussed is where, when all is said, residual sovereignty should rest? In the United States, for example, this rests with the individual States of the Union. Much the same is true of the French and German local authorities. The principle is, however circumscribed its use may be, in fact that the body exercising residual sovereignty can use initiative to engage in new activities where these are not already the responsibilities of the central authority. This is the sort of thinking that underlines the setting up of state-sponsored bodies in this country when they are granted "commercial freedom". Government departments occupy an intermediate position in this regard. Local authorities are bound so tightly that they may not do anything that statute does not specifically authorise them to do. This substantially follows English practice, where residual sovereignty rests in the State. This kind of thinking is all very well if we do not expect public bodies to exercise initiative. If we do, if we expect them to become "development corporations", then, quite obviously, the power of initiative must be given to them. Clearly the initiative must be contained, in some way, so that public bodies may be made rapidly accountable for their actions. This is, of course, one of the great arguments for the representative system.

f. *Remedy*

It is also a strong argument for having a simple, public, speedy and effective way to remedy the inevitable disputes between the administration and the administered. At the moment this is in a chaotic situation in our system of administration, and there are wide areas where no procedure exists for resolving disputes of this kind. Here again the representative system is a help, but it is not efficient where the disputes relate to technical issues. The lack of a good *system* of remedy is a major defect in administration. As we have seen, many *ad hoc* procedures exist; but even where they do exist they exhibit the failure of the generalising process. If there were a general means by which mistakes and injustices could be speedily and effectively remedied, the scope (and the acceptability) of administration could be greatly extended. This is all the more necessary if we expect public bodies to play their parts in a time of increasing pace of change. Change will be resisted unless there is a clear system of remedy. What is required is a procedure for resolving disputes (perhaps on the lines of the Continental *conseil d'etat*). In addition, for those residual cases that could not be covered by an adequate system of administrative procedures, some form of parliamentary commissioner or ombudsman would ensure that, so far as is humanly possible, administrative bodies would respect and cherish human rights, and thus receive a wider area of assent from those whom they administer.

g. *Control*

The parameter of remedy is often confused with that of *control*. Controls exists to ensure that what was aimed at for the organisation is being achieved, and to throw up the unexpected snags and details that impede real success. The control used in this way suggests ways and means of improving the effectiveness of the machine, in ever more accurately discriminating its various sub-purposes, so that the aim of achieving its overall purpose is served. This is to use control as a "feed-back". It is by this means that administration "progresses, not by finding the answers, but by progressively clarifying the questions".

h. *Time*

This leads us to the final parameter, that is the inevitable slowness of change. In an evolutionary, rather than a revolutionary, situation it simply is not possible to make radical changes rapidly. Therefore, a constraint on any design is that it should recognise that normally one can move from here to there only slowly by single steps, by "successive approximations". The design must, therefore, be open-ended. This leads to the need to have some unifying principle, even a slogan, by which to take decisions in the interim period. For example, if one were to give effect to the design that follows, perhaps the best slogan for reconciling the various objectives and parameters might be to "centralise policy, decentralise decisions". This suggests that the role of the centre should be to have a very clear idea of where the overall administrative effort is leading, while the role of other bodies might be to get on with their jobs in a spirit of initiative and freedom so that where their projects did not conflict with the overall public interest they would receive little or no interference from the central authority. Again, the kind of aid given by the central authority will be aimed not so much to give support from day to day, but to achieve self-sustaining activity. Hence the need to tackle such chronic problems as, say, the financial weakness of local authorities, and to do this less by recurrent subsidies than by radical reform of the scope and nature of local taxation.

6. ORDER

It is one of the marks of human action that matters must be taken in order. This is partly because resources are scarce, but it is also because events taken in process aid one another, but if dealt with out of this order will lead to frustration and inefficiency. A mechanic re-assembling a machine follows an order that permits him to do the job speedily and well. The same holds true in any situation. At any stage there is one parameter that, if eased next, will make a maximum contribution, another to follow that, and so on and on. To put the parameters in order and to deal with them in that order is to be most efficient in helping the best evolution of process.

C. FORMULATION

7. DESIGN

Principled and effective activity involves giving each of these parameters its maximum possible extension compatible with a properly "tuned" whole. The chart overleaf suggests an analysis of the elements and the powers of the machinery of government. This suggests the following leading features of the design:

a. Distinguish
   (i) FORMULATING from IMPLEMENTING
   (ii) In implementing, LOCAL from FUNCTIONAL
   (iii) In functional, TRADING from the REST
b. Allocate existing and new functions
   (i) according to the nature of the work;
   (ii) to the smallest viable unit;
   (iii) giving sovereignty according to function.
c. Provide
   (i) for the widest use of the representative principle
   (ii) a clear procedure for resolving disputes

8. ROLES

From this we can derive Roles:
a. The role of *Central Government* is concerned inescapably with:
   (i) Formulating, which calls for overall planning, preparing legislation and schemes, and with control and feed-back at the centre, and
   (ii) special cases, such as defence.
b. The role of *Local Government* is concerned with:

OUTLINE DIAGRAM OF THE PROCESS AND MACHINERY OF GOVERNMENT

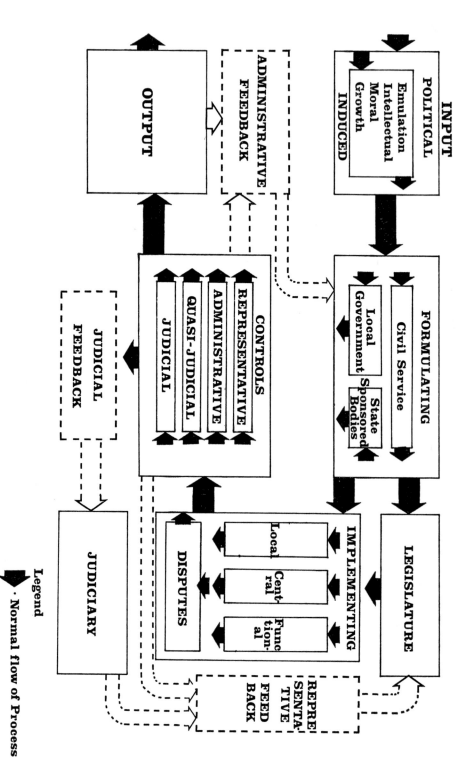

    (i) Implementing where the unit is horizontal and relatively small, and

    (ii) resolving disputes in parallel with the local administration.

c. The role of *Functional Government* (the state-sponsored bodies) is concerned with:

    (i) Implementing functionally commercial or industrial business through genuinely commercial or industrial bodies, and

    (ii) Implementing functionally where the business is promotional or social, cannot be combined with other functions, and the minimum unit of administration is the state as a whole.

d. The role of *Appellate Government* is concerned with:

    (i) speedy, cheap, public remedy of grievances in parallel with local administration, and

    (ii) remedy on a functional basis in highly specialised issues.

According to this scheme the really important business of government would stay with central government. This would be the policy work, the planning, the setting of overall objectives for the community as a whole, the residual watching over and fostering of the public interest.

According to this scheme the great bulk of the business of government would be devolved onto local bodies enjoying functional sovereignty and freedom of initiative so that they could become in a real sense "development corporations". This would envisage a very wide extension indeed of the functions, at least for the time being, of county and county borough councils. The transfer to them of massive blocks of implementing business from government departments (and from some state-sponsored bodies) would make them of substantial size, would bring a great part of the detailed administration of business under the proper scrutiny of public representatives, would meet the principle of subsidiarity, would enable bigness to be achieved of a horizontal kind, by virtue of making these bodies very compendious ones, would achieve a wide diffusion of residual sovereignty and would provide for adequate feed-back to the central government which, being freed of detailed implementation, would scrutinise the activity of local bodies where they were falling short of overall national objectives. Finally, this transfer of the detailed work of administration (the "decentralising of decision") could be done progressively so that the central bodies could gradually but steadily divest themselves of their functions.

In the same way, normal police work could, as applies in other countries, be decentralised to the local bodies. This would involve the establishment, in effect, of small local governments with a high degree of autonomy within carefully prescribed, but not narrow, limits.

The aim would be to have all government work of an implementing nature, that was not assigned to functional bodies, discharged by these local governments. The area of administration of these local bodies might remain, at least for the time being (until a stronger case has been established for enlarging the areas of administration) within the existing county and county borough boundaries. This is not to say that some re-arrangements of the existing very small counties may not be necessary, and some rethinking of the relationship of county boroughs to their surrounding county areas may not also be necessary. But in general the existing county is probably a convenient area of adminis-tration, provided it has enough to do. To maintain the generalising, the representative, and the legislative aspects of the machinery of government, all the business of an implementing nature transacted within the area of the county should be brought within the overall supervision of the elected body. So far as executive and administrative work are concerned, the existing administrative "pole of growth" which we have in city and county management might be developed along the lines that apply in European countries with their tendencies to vest in a single administrative official, the prefect or other, the executive responsibility for the oversight of the discharge of the work of govern-ment within a specified area. Three forces would be developed in this way. The first force would be the continuation of the process of vesting in the county council all the executive functions that have been so far given to local government. The second would be a massive transfer of implementing work from government departments, and some state-sponsored bodies, to local government. The third would be the develop-ment of the idea of county and city management to ensure that all the work of government within a specified area was under a single executive head. He would, of course, be in turn responsible to the elected local body.

The other "pole of growth" at present based on the county would be the remarkable institution of the district court. If all the work relating to appeals in disputes betwen the local administration (as so extensively widened) and those being administered could be dealt with in these courts, which are in continuous session, which dispense speedy and cheap justice, and which perform their duties in public, there would be achieved overnight a major revolution in our approach to the dealing with disputes. Of course, for certain specialised disputes technical assessors would be necessary to assist the justice. Provision would also have to be made for appeals on technical points to highly specialised functional appellate bodies at the centre (for example, to the special commissioners of income-tax or to the national appointed arbitrators for compensation for land). Apart from this, some fresh thinking would be needed as to the recruitment and career structures of district justices if their roles were to be so substantially geared into the day-to-day life of the community as is here proposed. If, in addition, provision was made for an ombudsman to cope with the grievances that slipped through the net of the appellate arm of government, the citizen could feel that his interests would not be lost sight of.

This leaves the problem of *Functional Government*. This is simple enough where there are genuine trading, commercial or industrial bodies. Such bodies as Aer Lingus or Irish Steel or the Industrial Credit Company clearly come within this classification. No doubt, the main activities of Coras Iompair Eireann also come within it; but there are clearly other activities which may or may not be integral with the rail and road transport system as a whole for which the justification is local and social. The generation of electricity is quite clearly a task for functional government; but in many other countries the selling and promotional work—the distribution of electricity to consumers—is the responsibility of other bodies. Is this task of distribution significantly different from, say, the distribution of water which is at present discharged by local bodies? In France, for example, local bodies buy electricity from the central authority and distribute it in their areas. *Implementing* work which is not specifically or integrally part of the work of an indisputably functional trading body could be decentralised, in the same way as implementing work could be decentralised from government departments. This is to say that the fact that business of government is inescapably trading or commercial or industrial does not establish the case that it should be attached to functional government. On the whole, on the principles already laid out, the onus of proof that the work is inherently part of a functional body, should rest with the protagonists of functional government.

There remain a certain number of special promotional or social tasks where the minimum unit of administration is the state as a whole. These would, no doubt, establish their case to remain part of functional government. One has in mind such work as that of Coras Trachtala or the *external* promotional work of Bord Failte Eireann. But much of the internal promotional work of the latter body might not survive the tests that have been laid down. And does it follow that there should be several marketing bodies for our exports, industrial, agricultural and invisible ? Or that the role of the Department of External Affairs may not need considerable development in this direction ?

D

9. PLAN

If there is a willingness to act (i) to achieve objectives, (ii) to remedy the situation created, and (iii) to apply the remedies demonstrated by the design, some form of *plan* is necessary. This is a coherent system of actions to be carried out in a specified order over a defined period in order to achieve an announced result.

D. FEEDBACK

10. CONTROL

In any plan of action there must be a constant reference back of information on whether objectives are being received. This is also true of the craft of government. That is the function of controls. But if these themselves throw up too little, too much, or irrelevant information, they are in need of reform. In this sense a control is an information system as to whether all is or is not going to plan.

CONCLUSION

This is a broad outline of the machinery for carrying on the business of government. The picture is not a comforting one, but to get it to rights is a big part of achieving administrative efficiency.

The exercise may have some interest, also, in that it shows an application of an *administrative method,* normally implicit in administrative behaviour. A considerable advance in the understanding of this behaviour, and thus its level of performance, can come from the explicit recognition of this method and of the fact that it can be helpful if we apply it to tangled situations.

If the logical implications of the tests that have been laid down lead us to decisions that are unpalatable, either the tests have not been adequately expressed or formulated or identified, or there is a defect in the logic, or we are being guided, not by rational, but by non-rational, considerations. The point about drawing up a scheme of this kind is that it forces into the open a great deal of hitherto unexpressed or concealed premises. If the functions of every public body could be scrutinised and re-allocated according to its nature following some such method as this, and new functions allocated in the same way, a logical and coherent structure would have been evolved. If there are defects in the design then to remedy these defects would be to make a better structure still. The important thing is to get discussion going on an explicit and an accepted set of premises, and to draw the logical conclusions from these. This does not mean that drastic changes can be carried out very rapidly. What it does mean is that once the scheme has been agreed upon, a broad process of reform can be got under way so that the changes can be achieved as opportunity offers in accordance with a coherent plan.

The main premise is that so long as we think of machinery of government in some way as resembling a machine, it is essential for us to make sense out of the administrative system and to allocate the functions of each part according to some consistent and coherent design. In this way, over time, individual decisions and reforms can get a coherent sense of direction. The existence of a design drawn from ascertainable premises and based on objective appraisal, permits the discussion to be carried on in a progressive way. The details of the design suggested here are less important than that somehow a method be adopted that will show how disparities can be avoided, that will give a result that will be internally consistent, and that can be operated flexibly over a period.

The kind of radical changes envisaged here as logically inherent in the notion of "machinery of government" will not occur of themselves, even if there should be widespread acceptance of them. Indeed, it is unlikely that there would be any effective acceptance of them, or other changes to the same end, unless there were established in this country, as there has been in other countries, either a permanent office or *ad hoc* group with the duty of concerning itself with precisely this problem.

A logical implication of overhauling a piece of machinery is a mechanic.

Chapter 3

THE GEOGRAPHICAL SYSTEM OF GOVERNMENT*

1. Our report is much concerned with rationalising the executive system of government; but we do not give an overall design for the geographical part of that system. In my view it is not enough to recommend (13.4.3) a special inquiry into regional areas and (13.4.8) into their relationship with the local government structure. We are concerned, too, with administrative planning and public participation; but not enough, I think, with the contributions here of an effective geographical system.

2. The material thrown up by our inquiry permits, in my view, the formulation of the broad outlines of a policy for the geographical system so as to achieve a decentralisation of some of the functions and machinery of government and for relating this to the regional and local government issues. In order of increasing distance from the core of our terms of reference, the ingredients of such a policy are:

    A. Departmental Deconcentration,

    B. Regionalism,

    C. Local Government, and

    D. Public Participation.

3. A governmental machine is as complex in a small country as a large : what is significant here is not size but sovereignty. Given this complexity, the task is not to aim for a spurious simplicity but to have each part of the complex machine in a smoothly working system, and to have these systems contribute smoothly to the overall working of the machinery. I think our proposals largely meet this test, but lack an overall design for the problems of the geographical system.

Addendum to Report of Public Services Organisation Review Group, 1966–69 (Devlin Report), 1969.

44

A. DEPARTMENTAL DECONCENTRATION

4. One of the notable features of the civil service departments is how much of their work is carried out away from headquarters: many departments are large mainly because their field services are large. The departments find it necessary to carry out much of their work close to their clients. (This is, of course, of the nature of local—and, so far as they exist, regional—authorities). Most of the larger, state-sponsored bodies—notably CIE and ESB—are in the same case. Of the 18 departments and major offices, only two—the Departments of the Taoiseach and of External Affairs—have not some form of field services; so, also, have some of the smaller offices.

5. There are three main features of these services—they are in varied geographical groupings; they are staffed by officers drawn from the professional, technical and departmental grades, not the general service; and the groupings and the officers in them have limited formal executive discretion.

6. It is a universal mark of the field services that there are geographical groupings, usually a special grouping for each service or part of a service. Sometimes the officers concerned live in the groupings, sometimes they live in Dublin but have their duties segregated according to these groupings. (This latter applies also to much of the distribution of work of wholly headquarters staffs). Depending largely on the volume of clients and the needs of supervision there is a hierarchy of groupings. Not all departments require the full hierarchy for all services, but a number of them use a number of the levels for several services. If one uses the terms sufficiently loosely one can discern, as between all the departments for all services, groupings at provincial, regional, county, district, and locality levels. Thus, in the educational services, there are three provincial centres for universities, nine regions for technical colleges, 31 counties for vocational education committees, districts for secondary school transport, and localities for primary schools. The postal services have head post offices in 51 districts, and some 2,000 sub-post offices in localities, but nothing between the headquarters and the district. A large organisation such as Revenue has two different geographical groupings and levels for their field services, Lands has three, and Agriculture several. The point here is not that anyone's definition of "province", "region", "county", "district" or "locality" often coincides, but that, over the whole of the field services, these five levels have meaningful operational content as administrative units.

7. It is not to be procrustean, therefore, to recommend that these units be clarified and standardised. The departments can be left free to choose which of the standard levels will suit their services; sometimes they will choose one level, sometimes several; sometimes all five. As with a lift, they may stop at all or any of the floors, but ought not to stop between floors. Moreover, some services at any level may not be sufficiently thick on the ground to justify wholetime attention there. This need not, especially at the lower levels, preclude grouping of units at that level; but what will be grouped ought to be standard units. Thus a system of free choice between standard administrative units and levels should provide enough flexibility for varying departmental needs. It is essential, however, that the units be well devised, and this will provide a major task for the Public Service Department and the organisation staffs of the various departments. Unless the geographical administrative units are standardised in this way it will be impossible to effect real deconcentration, much less decentralisation.

8. The field services are, as a rule, staffed by professional, technical and departmental officers. With some exceptions—notably inspectors of taxes—they illustrate the lack of, or limited, executive discretion given to such officers. Notwithstanding the existence of so many, often relatively highly paid, officers in the field, executive discretion is in large measure reserved to headquarters. Our recommendation for giving executive discretion to professional, etc. officers is likely, if adopted, to have its most dramatic effect here. The effects are clear in relation to the front-line officers, and their immediate supervisors; but the effects at the higher levels of geographical units and on the more senior officers depend on the degree of deconcentration achieved.

9. So far as the front-line officers are concerned the dominating influence is necessarily that of the client. But the departments, in their natural concern for specialisation and efficiency, have tended to lose sight of him as a whole person, perhaps bewildered, not very knowledgeable, with needs that do not coincide with departmental lines of demarcation, and these needs perhaps symptoms of more complex problems. No matter how well a function is clarified, and a service built around it, there will be some clients whose needs cut across the organisational lines. Each of the services may see only an isolated symptom, if that, and not the underlying malady. Thus, a department with a complex of services—agriculture, welfare and health are examples —may not be able to serve the real needs of its client; in agriculture, the first cross-over point between two similar field services may be high

in the headquarters of the department. This contrasts with the many-sided role of, say, the sub-postmaster whose *degree* of discretion may not be great but who can exercise it over a wide *range*. For these reasons our report recommends (13.4.7) that the key field officer of a department in direct contact with the client should be a general practitioner of all the departmental services, that is with a significant *degree,* and full departmental *range,* of discretion.

10.   The general practitioner concept will work only if the general practitioner is, as we recommend (13.4.7) backed by a group of specialists. These would be at district, county or regional level, depending on the intensity of the service. Here another type of cross-over is necessary, between the specialisms. We also recommend that at regional level there be created a focus for effective departmental decision-making in the person of the departmental regional director. This is the second main level at which a major problem of discretion arises. This offers a standpoint for the review of departmental progress in the area as a whole, and an appropriate input into overall departmental planning. It is at this level, above all in the context of development, that there should be a capability to link with like—in the telephone analogy, a freely operating local exchange. Otherwise, the unusual and the developmental will have to be referred to the centre where it tends to get delayed or neglected. Where the problems arise not so much as between the services of a single department as between the services of two or more departments, or departments and other bodies, the absence of local exchanges of this kind forces the decisions to the centre where, again, the local needs and the local urgencies may be lost sight of, and where there is inadequate machinery for inter-departmental action at executive level. The case for a degree of discretion and flexibility at the higher levels of the geographical units is a not inconsiderable one.

11.   What emerges from this discussion is that where clients are numerous, there are two levels at least at which deconcentrated discretion should be exercised—at the local level in relation to the client himself, and at regional level in relation to the development needs of significant geographical areas. It is also clear that departments have worked out for themselves cross-over points at those levels even if they have not, in general, granted much executive discretion to those levels.

12.   If executive discretion is given at the appropriate level of a geographical unit to the officers staffing it, there will be a significant

emigration of detailed decision-making from Dublin to the unit. Following the decisions will go considerable numbers of office staffs now located in Dublin. The new developments in computer technology facilitate this deconcentration.

13. The ingredients of a programme of departmental deconcentration are thus:
> (a) definition of geographical administrative units and levels to be standard for all departments ;
> (b) selection of those appropriate to the departmental service or services;
> (c) committing of operational decisions to general practitioner field offices;
> (d) committing of managerial, planning, developmental and co-ordinating discretion to more senior officers at e.g. regional cross-over points, and
> (e) emigration of office staffs from Dublin to those points.

B. REGIONALISM

14. So far I have been considering the problems of the field services in relation to each department—deconcentration within each department. But this is not enough as part of a real policy of decentralisation. For this, the deconcentrated units must be linked at the regional and local levels.

15. To organise the functions of government, even from the narrow viewpoint of administrative effectiveness, is a task of great difficulty. Two conflicting principles must be reconciled. On the one hand it is essential to clarify and simplify functions and commit them to specialised administrative units so that they are clear about what they have to do. On the other hand, since life is one and yet multifarious, it is necessary to build in to the administrative system a number of generalising or cross-over points, of administrative sub-stations as it were, into which the units are plugged. We have seen that the departments themselves require departmental cross-over points. The kernel of the problem of regionalism, viewed from the angle of deconcentration, is to link, at regional levels, the various departmental regional cross-over points so that regional issues can be dealt with as a whole. Similarly, as functions tend to move up from the local government structure to regional bodies, the same sorts of problems arise. This is what makes it so crucial that there be uniformity in the regional units, whatever they are to be.

16. Even a small country has a wide spread between those parts of it that are economically and socially developed, and those that are less developed. As development progresses these gaps tend to grow greater. To moderate these disparities, many countries are evolving regional authorities to give each area the special attention it requires to realise its potentialities for development and so enhance the rate of development of the society as a whole. For example, economic development is, even in its simplest form, a complex of agricultural, industrial, environmental, communications, etc. development. In its more sophisticated forms, come factors of social and educational development. Not a great deal is known of the development process in all its complexity, but it is well known that it results from a balanced "mix" of these ingredients, and that the balance of this "mix" varies at different stages of development, that is, that the priorities are different at each stage. Development is accelerated by planning. It follows that the tasks of the planners vary from region to region. Our report points out (9.1.4) that while planning for the private sector is indicative, planning for the public sector is imperative. Whatever the planning region, therefore, the administrative units should be provided with a regional centre of concentration so as to participate in meaningful planning for that region and to implement there the plans eventually decided upon. Planning demands the participation of the people planned for, so that factors of potential growth in each area can be incorporated in the planning and acceptable priorities set. In our report we have laid great stress on the planning system; but our proposals are not explicit on how this crucial regional issue is to be incorporated into that planning system. Yet, regional input is an important ingredient of the whole planning process. We need cross-over points between the various services, an appreciable degree of discretion at the level of that input, and an administrative infrastructure capable of comprehending the needs of each region as a whole, of translating inputs into workable and coherent proposals, and co-ordinating the implementation of such proposals in the overall interests of the region.

17. In modern administration descretion is of two kinds: developmental and executive. For developmental discretion there must be clear and coherent definition of roles and responsibilities so that there is no ambiguity about who is responsible for indentifying, and for solving when resources are made available, significant regional problems. There must also, as has been indicated, be an administrative sub-station at this level where problems common to a number of bodies can be considered as a whole and with the participation of all the relevant adminis-

trative agencies. This will not occur unless appropriate institutional arrangements are made. So what is required is an authority that will comprise in itself the developmental (and executive) functions of all the administrative agencies operating in the region. Otherwise the sub-station will not be effective. Our proposals for the field services of the Department of Agriculture and Lands show how this would work at regional level for one major service; but it is clear that as well as agriculture, all the major services—physical planning, tourism, education, justice, revenue, health and welfare, communications, etc.—would need to be linked together in some similar way. It follows that a great deal of developmental discretion should be given by the relevant departments to their regional directors if any such scheme has a chance of working, and that the regional authority must be able to bind together the general activities—as distinct from the specialised ones—of the regional directors. Much the same is true of executive discretion ; but as this is a main theme of our report not much needs to be said here: the regional directors must, if there is to be any real deconcentration, be given real managerial discretion by the appropriate agencies so that there may be rapid and effective response to varying regional needs. Finally, the responsibility in the first instance for functions that seem to fall between individual agencies should be borne by the regional authority until an appropriate allocation of function is made by the central administration.

18.   What is inherent in this, therefore, is a regional authority concerned with the whole range of public administration—specified or emergent—so far as it is relevant to the region. It would have functions, to a greater or less extent, co-extensive with the functions of nearly all of the home departments. Obviously, the relationships of the regional administration with the central departments would vary with the function—police functions, for example, would have a different relationship with the centre from, say, educational ones.

19.   It is apparent from the history of local government at the county level and from the experience of the Shannon Free Airport Development Authority (SFADCO) that effective deconcentration of discretion is meaningless unless the authority to which the discretion is deconcentrated is given real authority and funds, that is, that it is a clearly executive authority, not a consultative or ornamental one. I envisage that the Departments of Agriculture and Lands, Education, Health and Welfare, Justice, Regional Development, Transport and Communications and Labour, as well as the Revenue Commissioners and the Industrial

Development Authority will each be represented at regional level by a Director charged with the sort of discretion, in relation to his own area, that will be enjoyed by the Director of a centralised agency. Clearly, there will be a problem of the triangle of authority between the region, the agency and the assistant secretary of the appropriate aireacht. Nevertheless, long experience with local authorities shows that these types of difficulties can be readily overcome.

20. If planning for regional development is to be meaningful, a co-ordinating regional director, an officer of the Department of Regional Development, should be charged with the co-ordination of regional plans and execution, so that the directors work as a team with sufficient discretion to discharge their overall development and executive responsibilities, to make compromises, and to subordinate some departmental aims to the general welfare. The relationship of the regional co-ordinating director with the other regional directors should be one of planning, co-ordination and review, and he should have no executive control over them. (Below, reference is made to another unifying concept through public participation.) The co-ordinating director, as *primus inter pares,* would be the Government's main, and residual, representative in the region, and should be equipped at the least with a finance staff and a planning staff disposing of skills in addition to those of environmental planning.

21. The first requirements of a regional structure are thus:
    (*a*) the assignment, with full range of departmental discretion,
        (i) at local level of departmental general practitioners, with a fair degree of executive discretion;
        (ii) at (mainly) county level of supporting departmental specialists, and authority;
        (iii) at regional level, of departmental regional directors with considerable executive and developmental discretion;
    (*b*) the establishment at regional level of a co-ordinating and planning authority concerned with the whole range of public administration in the region;
    (*c*) the assignment to this authority of a co-ordinating regional director as leader of the team of regional directors.

C. LOCAL GOVERNMENT

22. Even when great care is taken to divide functions between public bodies there will be some functions that cut across the lines of division,

sometimes several of these lines. So, when a problem arises, each of the bodies may see only an isolated symptom, not the underlying malady. This is of special importance in relation to personal, family and community needs, that is, those problems that most directly affect the citizen. So that, against the advantages of a highly centralised system, such as we have in Ireland, must be put the disadvantages to the client the various bodies exist to serve. For example, a child in trouble may be dealt with as a delinquent (Justice), abandoned and/or handicapped (health authority, Health), in need of educational care (Education), etc. etc. The total solution of the child's trouble may call for a comprehensive response from the various bodies that they are not geared to give. Behind the child in trouble, as is now coming to be more clearly realised, is usually a family in trouble, even though no clear-cut symptom, other than the child's, may come to official cognisance. Again, we have no system for a complete response. Moreover, behind the individual symptom, as in the incidence of mental breakdown amongst older people, may be a community in trouble. Still less are we equipped to deal with such problems. These are examples from the mainly social area of administration, but other instances could be given from the economic and environmental areas.

23.   This is the case, therefore, for an administrative sub-station near the point of service where the field services of all agencies directiy concerned with the needs of individual, family, community, or group of communities can be linked together so that complex problems can be dealt with readily and in an integrated way. This, and the participation of the "client" in some at least of the relevant decision-making and priority-setting (so calling for some range of local discretion and initiative), are key arguments for a system of local administration concerned with the direct provision of services.

24.   Thus three important needs combine to require that the issue of local administration be clarified. These are the management needs of the central bodies themselves, the needs of their "clients", and the needs of integrated development. All three call for cross-over points at the local level, for public participation, and for the delegation of discretion.

25.   If these needs are to be met, three problems have to be tackled —that of the geographical administrative units—counties and/or districts ; that of the integration of public services at those levels ; and that of the appropriate administrative underpinning.

26. There is little agreement on the size, or degree of discretion, of the appropriate unit for the personal and environmental services. At the county and district levels there are conflicting principles. Where the service to be provided has a high technological content or where the clients are few, the minimum administrative unit may have to be very large. On the other hand, where the clients are numerous and the technology not considerable, the unit can be relatively small. A real problem arises where the two factors operate on two branches of a single service, and a compromise may have to be struck ; as between, for example, the needs of a modern hospital service and an effective personal health service. The county, our oldest administrative unit, is, in practice, too large as a primary unit for certain personal services—e.g. general medical care, police, agricultural instruction, first and second level education, postal services, etc.; for those the primary unit is, in practice, the locality, or at most, the district. The county is regarded as too small for other purposes—e.g. tourism, third level education, some physical planning, etc.—which are based on the region of three or four counties. The size of counties varies. Nonetheless the county is our standard local government unit and it is essential to settle, one way or the other, whether, if necessary, suitably remodelled, it is to continue in this role. Hence the crucial importance of the inquiry we recommend into this unit. Once a suitable local government unit has been decided upon, the lesser units can be settled striking the best possible balance between the special local needs of the various services—districts and localities for the personal services administered by "general practitioners" and the counties (either existing or remodelled) for the cross-over points for the local services. We are given to understand that some at least of these units are under review in the Department of Local Government. It is, however, inherent in the general points I have been making that these issues should also be reviewed in the context of the field services as a whole, and will thus concern the Public Service Department and the other Departments with these services.

27. In the context of a genuine deconcentration and decentralisation it is not enough to consider the county (and the district) only in relation to the existing local government services. They should also be seen in relation to the field services of all administrative bodies because the existing distribution of services is largely a result of the accidents of history. Those governmental services, therefore, that are sufficiently thick on the ground, as it were, to permit of having their cross-over points at county or district level should be integrated into the new county and district areas. It does not follow that they need become

local government services in advance of public acceptance of such a development ; but the new county and district units (if there are to be changes in the existing areas) should be devised in relation to the total range of public services.

28.   At this stage what is required is an integrated administrative under-pinning for all the public services provided at county and district level. At the county level, an administrative structure already exists, but requires to be pulled together in relation to the general range of public services discharged at the county and district level. One can envisage the county manager being used as the co-ordinating focus. He would act in three capacities—as co-ordinating executant and planner for all those functions that are regarded as local functions discharged under the system of county bodies with popular representation whatever they may be ; as co-ordinating local agent for the "regional directors"; and as agent, and co-ordinator with local activities, of other central activities in relation to his area. In these roles he would report, overall, to the Department of Regional Development. The practice of having a single officer serve both a local and a central authority, or authorities, can be discerned in the role of county manager as chairman of the county development team, and is a commonplace in other democracies. He is well placed to co-ordinate the local government service with the other public services discharged within the county. But if this is not acceptable the issue should not go by default. As a second best I re-commend the appointment in each county, as assistant to the Regional Co-ordinating Director, of an officer of the Department of Regional Development who would act as the county co-ordinating officer.

29.   The needs of the local government structure in this context are thus :

     (*a*) cross-over points at both county and district levels are needed for the integration of personal and community services;

     (*b*) for this purpose accept, or remodel, the county unit, and re-establish a district unit, in the light of the whole range of governmental services at those levels;

     (*c*) give the unit administrative underpinning by using the county manager as local administrator

         (i) for all local services with popular participation;

         (ii) for co-ordinating local responsibilities of the co-ordina-ting regional director; and

(iii) as agent for, and co-ordinator with other public services at county level of, all other public services in relation to his county.

D. PUBLIC PARTICIPATION

30. The fourth ingredient of an effective decentralisation policy is public participation. In practice this takes three main forms—direct election, as for county councils; a mixture of election and local nomination, as for committees of agriculture and vocational education committees; and central nomination, as for the boards of most state-sponsored bodies. It is clear that the nineteenth century, democratic concept of direct election has not met the needs for the association of specialised skills and interests in the representative area of public administration. It is no part of the task of a member of our Group to express views on the merits of any of these methods of popular participation in the administrative process as a whole. I merely note that the need for a considerable degree of public participation in the administration of regional and local services seems to be generally accepted, and that it has a significant part to play in the administrative process as a whole. Moreover, each department, as its local and regional services come to be deconcentrated on the lines I propose, will have its own ideas about how the public may appropriately participate in its administration at these levels. Whatever methods are chosen, I recommend that the Public Service Department keep them under review so as to gain deeper insight into the problems of public participation, problems that are likely to become acute.

31. Where central services are managed on a county basis the problem of participation is basically that of representing the consumers of the various services supplied. As we have seen, a major problem here is relating the services to each other. It is thus of great importance that they be co-ordinated with each other and with the local government services, and it has been recommended above that the county manager, or an officer of the Department of Regional Development, become the co-ordinating officer. The former proposal would suggest that the possibility of some link between the elected county council and the other representative bodies may be necessary. The Public Service Department should also examine this question.

32. At the regional level, the problem of participation is different. Here it is not really one of representing consumers of public services—

that can be done at county level. There are two issues here. The first is the need to create advisory bodies to each of the departmental regional directors. Whether these are elected, nominated, or representative of major interests, or a combination of these, will depend on the nature of the services: each department ought to be free to make its own arrangements.

33. The body concerned with the regional problems as a whole is the second and crucial issue. Here the problem is that of obtaining inputs to the planning process and of acceptable priorities (if there is to be a development centre in this region, and subsidiary centres, where ought they to be?); of ensuring that the problems of the region are seen in the round across departmental barriers; and of obtaining for the region enough discretion to discharge its responsibilities.

34. To take the last question first. It is not necessary to stress, after our study of the departments with local and field services, how strong are the centralising forces and how reluctant the departments are to yield discretion to local or regional organisations. Yet it is of the essence of the deconcentration envisaged that the regional directors be permitted a degree of discretion within their areas comparable to that exercised by the agency directors at the centre. The best way of ensuring this is to have a formal Regional Authority, free of the constraints that bind officials, to act as a counter-force to the centralising tendencies of the departments. Whether this authority should have elective, or nominated, members or, for example, draw them from representatives of the bodies at county level, or a mixture of all these, is not as important as that they be persons of sufficient standing and independence in the region to ensure genuine regional discretion.

35. The major task of the regional authority will be to ensure that the regional needs and the regional administrative operations are seen in the context of the region as a whole, and that there is comprehensive and integrated development planning for the region. It is inevitable that each regional director will be mainly pre-occupied with the needs of his own services and that overall regional needs will tend to take second place. It is essential that the regional authority ensure that this does not occur. That the lead role will be played by the co-ordinating regional director will not be enough, because he will not, of necessity, have executive authority over the other regional directors. To re-inforce his position, without weakening theirs in any essential, I recommend that he be the chairman of the regional authority. To ensure that the

other regional directors are fully seized of regional problems I recommend that they also be members of this authority. The number of non-official members should not be less than the number of official ones.

36. The third task of the regional authority will be to act as an input, both from the side of the public and the various interests in the region, as well as from the official bodies operating at regional level, in the process of drawing up, and reviewing, comprehensive plans for the region as a whole. The filter here would be, mainly, the advisory bodies attached to the departmental regional directorates ; but it is clear that the non-official members of the regional authority at least will require to be skilled in evoking a public input and in helping to translate planning proposals into measures acceptable in the region generally.

37. The needs of public participation are thus :
   (a) the establishment at county and district levels of bodies representative of consumers of deconcentrated services, and their linking with elected county bodies;
   (b) the linking at regional level of advisory bodies to departmental regional directors;
   (c) the establishment in each region of an Authority with, at executive level, co-ordinating powers, and at developmental level, full responsibilities for overall regional planning;
   (d) this authority to be composed, under the chairmanship of the co-ordinating regional director, of the departmental regional directors with at least as many non-official members.

DECENTRALISATION

38. In the context of deconcentration, regionalism, local government and public participation it becomes possible to make meaningful proposals about decentralisation.

39. Section II (10.5.3) of our Report points out that decentralisation can be considered from the viewpoints of dispersal, deconcentration and devolution.

40. It is clear from the concepts of aireacht and executive unit, that the former by its nature requires to be close to the minister at the seat of government in the capital. It is also clear that the devolution of executive authority to an executive agency permits it to be dispersed to a place away from the capital city. This is dispersal, not decentra-

E

lisation, because decision-making in relation to that activity remains just as centralised as before. Where the unit has no significant field services, its dispersal raises no major administrative issues. Where it has significant field services, then important issues do arise.

41. A genuine deconcentration, on the lines indicated in the preceding paragraphs, does permit and require decentralisation of decision-making to the regional and county centres where the deconcentrated units operate. Moreover, if the regional and county units are given executive discretion over a range of functions they become geographical executive organisations to which some general planning, co-ordinating and review functions can be devolved.

42. The argument for decentralisation is often to moderate the physical growth of the capital. But the basic argument is to help the development of the country as a whole by permitting the development process to be adapted to the varying needs of different geographical areas. It makes for public services better adapted to human and community needs. It makes for more meaningful public participation. Dispersal meets none of these conditions for effective decentralisation, and aggravates the problems. What is required is the integrated decentralisation of developmental and executive decision. The great mass of public servants are employed in the executive area. Jobs follow decisions. The decentralisation of decision, therefore, involves the decentralisation of jobs. In this way the growth of the capital can be moderated in a way consonant with the overall purpose of decentralisation.

43. For development to be facilitated it is not enough for the decision-making to be decentralised. This must be done in such a way that the bulk of the executive decisions about a particular area can be related together in that area, and there be some degree of priority-setting in that area. This involves the deconcentration of the appropriate executive units, their linking together in homogeneous geographical areas, and the devolution to the linked organisations of responsibility for co-ordination of decision, for overall plans and for review of the deconcentrated functions. This calls for skilled and sophisticated administration at the centre to reconcile local discretion with national needs and resources. It is the price of a genuine decentralisation for regional and local development, and underlines once more the crucial importance of the quality of those who staff the aireachts.

44. I accordingly recommend that the principle of the deconcentration

of appropriate executive activities to regional, county and, perhaps, district areas be accepted, and the deconcentrated activities be linked with the appropriate local government. As a first step toward giving effect to this acceptance of the practical application of the principle of subsidiarity, the Public Service Department should be charged with the task of instituting an inquiry into the geographical administrative areas appropriate for the various executive activities of government. The individual executive activities should be deconcentrated to the appropriate areas, and associated with an appropriate method of public participation. At each regional level there should be established a co-ordinating, planning and review body, with a degree of public participation and sufficient discretion to attend to the special needs of the region. At the county level there should be some similar means of integrating the various administrative functions.

45. There would thus emerge a positive programme of administrative decentralisation in the interests of regional and local development. This would rationalise the geographical system of the machinery of government.

46. In implementing any such programme there is a chicken and egg problem. Until the appropriate geographical units are defined no effective deconcentration can take place ; and these units cannot be adequately studied until it is known what they have to do. From our study of the departments it is clear that the following departments have extensive field and local services—Agriculture and Lands, Transport and Communications, Education, Health and Welfare, Justice, Regional Development and Labour, as well as Revenue. These are the prime candidates for deconcentration ; but there are others. A number of the departments are at present struggling with the regional issue, and decisions are being taken about it in isolation.

47. The most urgent step, therefore, is to get the Public Service Department to get going a series of studies on geographical units, and to give first priority to the study of regional areas for all likely administrative purposes. If this regional study threatens to be prolonged, provisional regions could be established, subject to review, and the various departmental field and local services assigned to them. The next step would be the establishment of the (provisional) regional authorities, and the appointment of the regional directors. It is essential that these steps be taken before the organisational structures we have recommended for the new agencies harden into (an otherwise highly centralised) shape.

48. Once these steps had been taken the study of county and, if necessary, district units could be allowed to proceed at a more normal pace.

49. A programme of decentralisation geared to well-adapted development thus requires:
   (*a*) a geographical executive and developmental system composed of well-devised units at regional, county and, perhaps, district levels;
   (*b*) extensive deconcentration of departmental field and associated executive activities to these units;
   (*c*) devolution of executive and developmental discretion to these units;
   (*d*) integration of public services at both county and regional levels by means of
       (i) effective administrative underpinning; and
       (ii) public participation.

50. I am under no illusion as to the degree of administrative re-thinking a programme of this kind will require. Nonetheless it is in my view necessary and urgent to make sense of our administrative system as viewed by the citizen outside Dublin, and to gear it into the varying developmental needs of the country.

Chapter 4

SOME PROBLEMS OF INSTITUTIONAL DEVELOPMENT*

It is clear from the nature of the discussions over the past few days that we have been considering a subject of great complexity. Moreover, the changes and the developments that are occurring seem likely to make the situation more complex, not less. The purpose of a discussion like this is to enable us to stand back a bit from the details of the various kinds of structural changes that are being mooted and to attempt to see them as a whole. Behind these changes there is an underlying structure of sorts. After the changes have been made another kind of structure will have emerged. How clear-cut and coherent will it be ? It seems to me that the future overall structure is likely to be a more effective one if we have somewhere in our minds a desirable framework to which individual decisions about parts of the structure can be oriented. There are a number of matters on which it is necessary to clear our minds before such a desirable state of affairs can come about.

If we are to have a Public Service Department as Devlin has recommended, then we ought to put on its agenda, first the institutional problems we have uncovered, secondly, the special problems of geographical or areal government, and, thirdly, the relevance of these to the whole issue of institutional development.

I. SOME INSTITUTIONAL PROBLEMS

1. *Hierarchy*

The first problem we have uncovered is that of levels of administrative organisations in a hierarchy. One may think of a unitary type of all-purpose local authority. That was the aim in this country in the 1920's when there were virtually no services performed in a county other than those provided by a county authority. But the growth of government in

*Text of a lecture delivered at Local Authorities Seminar held in Tramore, 13th-15th November, 1969. Reprinted from ADMINISTRATION, Vol. 18 (1970) 3.

the meantime has shown that it is not possible to be thinking in terms of one level of authority. For example, the Redcliffe-Maud report in England conceived of the main local government functions as being discharged by a unitary authority, the number of these being roughly equivalent to the present number of English county councils. But beneath these is contemplated some kind of community service body, and above them the provincial councils for the larger functions. So here we have three tiers being recognised even at the time when great effort is being made to concentrate powers in a so-called "unitary" authority*. One can see something similar emerging in this country even in the single field of the health services. The main authority here is to be a regional one comprising several counties, but it emerges that there will be county bodies to which the regional authority will delegate some functions. Above the regional authorities there will be, at least for the voluntary hospitals, three provincial authorities operating between them and the single national authority, the Department of Health. At the other end of the scale one can see emerging the problem of some kind of authority such as a local community service type organisation as is envisaged in the ideas that Dr. Ivor Browne has been propagating to cope with community and personal health services.

In what is left of local government proper, one can see, in the latest enthusiasm for regional planning bodies, the emergence of reasonably distinctive roles as between these regional bodies and the county bodies. The regional bodies will be concerned with planning, and the county bodies (or whatever is to succeed them following the decisions on the announced White Paper on local government) will be the executive bodies. It is quite clear that beneath these bodies again there is a growing need, at least in urban areas, for residents' associations to be assimilated into the system.

We can see this phenomenon of tiers, or of a hierarchy, manifesting itself in a number of other functions. The problem is to recognise this hierarchical issue of community, county, region and perhaps province, for what it is and to try to work out some sort of roles for the various levels.

2. Decentralisation

These considerations are also relevant to adequate discussion of the decentralisation of government services. It is quite clear to anybody who looks at the present state of Irish public administration that the great

---

*And in some areas the model of London, with a two-tier authority, is recommended.

range of administration that is carried on now in local areas is carried on not by local government authorities but by the field services of the central departments. If anything is to be done about decentralisation this issue must be tackled. Here there is something to learn from what is being done in other countries.

The second feature that is relevant to decentralisation is, of course, the degree of central control exercised by the headquarters of the various departments in Dublin. We know about the extent of this control over local government and local health bodies. It is perhaps tighter still over the field services of the central departments themselves. So long as this control remains so tight it will be almost impossible to bring about within a geographical area an adaptation of the various kinds of services to the emerging needs of that area and to the effects of its continued development.

The third feature relevant to decentralisation is that of coherence. It is natural and right that central services be divided clearly according to function: but this causes problems at regional, county and community levels, because the individual 'client' cannot be divided according to function—another system of administrative classification is needed so that his problems will be coherently dealt with. Even as between central government services themselves there is no effective coherence, either locally or, in smaller matters, at the centre. Similarly, there is no significant coherence between many central services discharged locally and many local services. This issue of local coherence is crucial to tackling the problems of decentralisation.

3. *Complexity*

Here may I interject that the problem in considering a national system of public administration is not mainly one of size of the nation but the nation's sovereignty. A small country needs just as complex an organisation of government as a very large one—except that some of the large ones are federations which interpose a further level of government at state level. But the Irish Army, for example, has, I am assured, precisely the same organisational structure as the United States Army, even though the scale of operation of the two armies is so different. The same is true in civil matters. Of course, great scale adds to complexity so that the problems of governing Ireland are not as great as those of governing the United States, but the problems are not proportionate to the differences in size. In principle, it is possible to think of a small country like Ireland as having only a single level of authority, that of the central government. But, in practice, wherever we look we see various kinds of

local organisations, at the district level, at the county level, at the regional level, at the provincial level. Even at the headquarters of the
centralised departments, one usually sees the headquarters' work also
divided up under a hierarchy of geographical headings. So, while it is
natural for work to be divided according to function in the field of public administration, it is just as natural for it to be divided according to
area. As soon as one tackles this area problem one sees emerging a
hierarchy of different levels for different purposes. Just as in human
evolution there has been a development from the simple to the complex
structures, and the complex structures themselves have constructed themselves according to a hierarchy, so also in the field of institutions and
government.

We need also to clear our minds about the nature of community services—education, health, welfare, agriculture, environmental, law and
order, industrial, taxation, etc. The more the technological arguments
require large units of operation and the clear division of functions at
those levels, the more important it is that somewhere near the point of
service, near where the ordinary human person, and family, lives there
be a service capable of dealing with these people as whole people and
whole families, not as separate and unrelated symptoms. This is because
in the human condition individuals, families and communities have complex problems which do not often fit neatly within the tidy functional
divisions of administrative agencies. This is why it is so important that
there be some kind of 'general practitioner' service within some authority—it may not need very extensive powers—to pull together in broader
groupings the various kinds of functions that play on individuals. This
is a major problem if public services are to be made both more humane
and more efficient.

The basic point here is that there are no simple solutions to issues of
such complexity.

4. Areas

The next big problem is that of areas. Here the crucial question is
what is to become of the county? For over forty years it has been the
basic unit of Irish local government. Its role has been that of an executive authority. Because, with present day methods of communication, it
is now held that the county is too small a unit for executive activities
which make heavy demands on technology, the county is tending to lose
a number of its functions. Other governmental functions which, in former times, might have been given to the county executive authorities
are being dealt with in other ways. It is perhaps not too much to say that

the county is likely, if present trends continue, to become obsolete as an executive authority. Am I too perverse in saying that a number of the decisions that have led towards this obsolescence have not been based on any very deep study of what is an optimum area of administration for various kinds of services? Is it not time, before the present drift makes our local government system increasingly irrelevant to the times, to engage in some such studies?

For example, one can accept the technological arguments for a large catchment area for a modern acute hospital. But less than a quarter of beds in this country are in acute hospitals, and it may be that some of these are being used for non-acute cases. The other three-quarters relate to the long stay type of patient, in mental hospitals, county homes, etc., where the technological arguments are not so compelling and seem to lead towards smaller, not larger, units. Moreover, so far as the personal medical services are concerned, the technological arguments do not make a great deal of sense. On the other hand, a number of the environmental services do pose technological problems—for example, adequate water catchment areas—which may well call for a transcending of county boundaries. Yet the evolution we see is the regionalisation of personal services and the maintenance at county level of a number of these environmental services!

It would be surprising if the county boundaries first drawn by King John in the 13th century should prove to be the most appropriate for present day conditions. Is not the first point to be examined, therefore, the detailed arguments for and against the enlarging of the functional area of the basic executive-administrative unit? While the bulk of the existing counties are reasonably uniform in size and population, there are wide variations between the smallest counties and the greatest. Does not this nettle need to be grasped?

The great argument for a geographical areal authority is that it provides opportunity for co-ordinating related services. Experience in other countries shows that this kind of co-ordination will only be achieved when an adequate role has been worked out for the co-ordinating authority. There is plenty of evidence to show that the attempt to co-ordinate other people's plans after they have been drawn up is a way of provoking strife and confusion, not of co-ordination. Co-ordination is a function of planning—using the term in its broad sense—and if we want a geographical area to bring about effective co-ordination then it must have a clear cut role as a planning body. Moreover, in relation to the activity it engages in, it must be in a position of some power. That is to say, some form of limited sovereignty, or range of discretion, is inherent in its position and should be recognised.

5. *Representation*

The final issue that cropped up in the discussions is the very important one of the relationship of democracy to these administrative structures. One of the great arguments for local government, when the term meant what it still says, namely, government as it operates in a local area, was the association of public representatives with the decision-making. As democracy advanced we came to accept that these representatives should be freely elected. It is quite clear that we are in full retreat from this position now. It may be that it is just as democratic to have public representatives nominated by ministers, or by vocational groups, or whatever; but this is an issue that at least should be discussed in the overall context, and its place in the overall framework clearly seen as being adequate to our aspirations.

II.   GEOGRAPHICAL GOVERNMENT

1. *Integrated Administrative Areas*

One of the arguments for an areal or geographical type of organisation is that it permits the working together of different bodies engaged in mainly the same sort of activity but having different historical, social and economic backgrounds. One can see, for example in the FitzGerald report,[1] the attempt to create a single hospital system incorporating both the voluntary and the public hospitals. Something of the same sort can be seen in the problems that are arising in integrating various kinds of schooling at the secondary levels. We all know the different origins of the primary schools, the private secondary schools, the vocational schools. However, if we try to look at the problem of educating children in the 12 to 18 year age groups as a single one—though perhaps pursued by different means—then the problem arises of relating together these three types of educational institution. Indeed it has arisen. A geographical authority where the various interested parties, including, of course, the parents, can participate in the decision-making looks as though it may be able to contribute at least part of the answer to this problem. Here again the issue of hierarchy arises. We have at one level the relatively numerous primary schools, at second level the junior secondary cycle, at a further level the senior secondary cycle, beyond these the regional technical colleges, and at a higher level still the three

---

[1]*Outline of the Future Hospital System*: Report of the Consultative Council on the General Hospital Services (FitzGerald Report), 1969.

university centres in each of the three main provinces. At each of these levels there are certain minimum, and perhaps, optimum, sizes of operation and it is a relatively easy thing to work out, given the need to provide a reasonable range of choices for children attending senior cycle secondary schools, and allowing for the fall-out from the education process at the junior cycle, to arrive at appropriate catchment areas for the various kinds of schools at each level. From this some conception of the appropriate administrative area for educational purposes can be arrived at.

It is quite clear that we need a large number of these studies to be made. What is the minimum area, given the sparse population conditions of this country, that will enable a reasonable general practitioner service to be provided in health, agriculture, welfare, and justice? Above this what is the kind of area that is required to support an effective executive authority equipped with a decent management structure? What services, precisely, have a technological content that requires them to operate on, say, a regional level? What other services can only be provided on, say, a provincial level or a national one? It seems to me, for example, that the discussion on the health services has failed to distinguish accurately between these different requirements. On the one hand the regions seem to be far too small for the really high-skill services—which of us who gets a skull or a kidney injury would not wish to be brought at once to the Richmond or to Jervis Street hospitals respectively? On the other hand, the kind of community services that are so badly needed for the psychiatric and geriatric services, and the growth of voluntary interest in these, are not necessarily well supplied by an organisation as large as a region. Something similar may be true also of the general practitioner and other personal medical services. At an intermediate level are those relatively minor surgical skills that may require relatively simple hospital care for their exercise.

The point that emerges is that it makes for both democratic and administrative efficiency for the steps of this government hierarchy to be recognised in relation to all the services and to have appropriate services pulled together at each of the steps. We need, therefore, a careful study of each of the services to find out what are the natural hierarchical groupings within the services and what is, at least, the minimum area required for effective participation and administration at each of these steps. If this work were done we could view with much greater confidence than we can at present the various changes that are being made in our administrative structures.

In general terms there are three crucial levels—those of community services, those of executive agencies, and those of planning bodies.

2. *Community Services*

About community services it is not possible to say very much because so little thought has been devoted to them in our system.

3. *Executive Agencies*

About executive agencies more can be said. As I have pointed out, for some forty odd years the executive agency has been the county authority. A good deal of thought and work was put into making these authorities into effective administrative units but at the same time they have been losing their credibility for two main reasons. The first of these is that new functions of government have not, as a general rule, been attached to them. The second is that some of their existing functions are being progressively taken away from them. All of this has been happening in an unplanned, *ad hoc* way. It is essential to stand back and clear our minds about what area an executive unit ought to operate over, and to assign it a coherent, if not a comprehensive, set of executive activities of government in respect of that area. For this I think that three lines of approach are necessary. The first is, as I have been indicating above, to determine the minimum area, at least, required by the needs of each of the main services. The second is to think through the implications of the increasing need for public participation in decision-making about those services. The third is to determine how much it is worth sacrificing under the first two headings to gain the advantages of a coherent integration of related services at the executive level, with effective overall management.

4. *Planning Regions*

At the third level there is the problem of planning. Planning is partly a process of getting an input from executive agencies and partly one of working out, more or less with their agreement, the framework within which their activities will operate for a period of time. In so far as executive agencies are concerned with the discharge of programmes, the task of planning is the integration and co-ordination of these programmes. The effective discharge of this planning function requires a good deal of discretion in the planning agency, and some degree of power in relation to the executive agencies. A so called planning body allowed merely to be a channel of communication between the centre and the executive bodies is a contradiction in terms. Administrative credibility goes along with genuine power and decision-making. If planning bodies, whether physical, economic, social or other are to be based on regions, then the powers that are inherent in the planning and co-ordinating process ought also to be given to such regional planning bodies. This is the first main problem of the region.

The second main problem of the regions is that of definition. In a somewhat disconcerting way, each government department has been defining its own regions. There are a very large number of these special arrangements. Fortunately, there seems to be a drift towards settling for seven, eight or nine regions in the country as a whole. There is a chicken and egg situation here. It is hard to determine what area the region should cover until it is known what it ought to do. It is hard to know what it ought to do until some idea of its potential size has been arrived at. However, here we have something to learn from the administrative genius of the Anglo-Normans. First, they were pretty clear headed about what they wanted their counties to do, and secondly they were quite clear as to their definition of a county. It was inconceivable under their system that the sort of thing that has arisen in relation to the county of Roscommon and regionalism could have occurred. Roscommon is in three different regions for the purpose of tourism, health, and planning and is divided between two regions for the purposes of the technical colleges. What sort of planning is feasible in such circumstances ? Admittedly, this is the extreme case, but there are several divergences between the regions that are now being constructed. It is really urgent that somebody get around to the task of defining regional boundaries for all purposes.

The problems here arise from the failure—natural from a departmental viewpoint—to take account of the need for *coherence* in overall government activity within any given area. Is it possible to think of 'government' as basically a single activity through a number of forms basically addressed to the same people in a single area? If so, then the internal consistency and flexibility of that activity become important. They become essential if what one aims at is the co-ordination and planning of governmental activity in the interests of more effective development. For planning to succeed one must have effective co-ordination. This co-ordination applies at five stages : input, formulation, assent, decision and implementation. At the input stage there must be common data. To be related together these must be for a common area. At the stage of formulation of plans based on the data, all those concerned must play a part sufficient to involve them in assent to, and commitment to implement, the subsequent decisions. This type of decision-making involves a degree of decentralisation of authority as regards central government, and a degree of concentration of authority as regards local administration. But if the area in which authority is to be used is not the same for all the purposes involved it will be impossible to obtain full commitment, and thus co-ordination. Agreement on areas is crucial to coherent and effective administration.

Some thought also needs to be given to the kind of organisation and structure of regional bodies. This depends partly on what their role is to be. Some of them are envisaged as purely consultative bodies for canalising mainly voluntary action. Some are considered as a means of bringing badly needed professionalism into the administration of a service (e.g., health). But, if there is to be development planning in the true sense, the body concerned with that planning must, as has been indicated above, be granted the powers necessary to give a realistic basis for the planning. These powers must derive from law, they must be administered by highly qualified people, and they must be backed by a good deal of money. Anything less postulates a degree of amateurism which is quite out of place in administrative structures.

III. INSTITUTIONAL DEVELOPMENT

These perplexities arise from the evolution of our administrative structures. Our institutions are adapting and growing to meet changing and more comprehensive needs of government. This kind of growth tends to be much less effective and efficient if it is simply adaptive and unplanned. Just as economic development calls for a positive fostering of the developmental process according to some generally accepted principles, so also does effective institutional development. The fact that, intellectually, the whole concept of institutional development is not well accepted by those who practise administration, and has as yet worked out very few guidelines, makes it all the more important that, if economic, social, political, environmental or cultural development is aimed at, we bring the degree of sophistication with which institutions are developed up to a comparable level. So we ought to be thinking about the aims that we wish the development of our institutions to serve. We ought to have some sort of structure in our minds to which these institutions can be adapted. It has emerged from the discussion that significant changes in administrative institutions occur perhaps once every twenty years, that is two or three times in the working life of any public official. For that reason not a great deal of experience of the process of institutional development has been accumulated even by officials of otherwise great experience. Moreover, many institutional changes are controversial and evoke a good deal of resistance from those whose interests may be adversely affected, or who are simply opposed to institutional change of any kind. So, what is desirable in relation to institutions may not always be feasible, and a good deal of compromise may be necessary. Nonetheless, compromise in the process of achieving a desired end is a different thing entirely from compromise when there is no clear cut aim at all. In the first instance important aims may be preserved in the process, but in the second they may be lost because their significance has not been realised.

If there is to be national development at an accelerating rate—and we have been going through a very rapid rate of development under various headings in our society—a very large number of decisions is necessary about the shape of our institutions. These decisions will be taken one way or another. It is highly desirable that they should be related to some acceptable aims to be achieved over a period of time. Moreover if these aims have been specified the decisions are less likely to be contradictory and conflicting and the whole process of institutional development and adaptation to changing needs is likely to be speeded up.

It has to be borne in mind that institutional development is in some ways very different from other kinds of development in that there is no natural built-in adaptive factor in institutions. Changes in them have to be consciously willed and brought about, sometimes after long negotiation, legislation and so on. Yet, we who have been living through a period of exceptional change in our society, intellectually, economically and so on, will have to face the implications of these changes on our institutions. In a changing world they alone cannot remain unchanged—when everyone is required to change and adapt in his economic, social and cultural life, they alone cannot drag their feet and limit response and change to the minimum. On the contrary, many of the public institutions are crucial to the whole process of economic, social and other change and development, and it is essential that they share in the whole development process, including the development of their own structures. For bureaucrats, above all, it is time to say: *tempora mutantur et nos mutamur in illis.* This might well be the motto of that crucial Devlin recommendation, the Public Service Department.

It was substantially because there was a belief that in a rapidy developing society the public institutions were not developing at a suitable pace that the Devlin group was set up, and its report is aimed to facilitate this process of change and development at the centre of our administration. It is clear from the discussions that the same sort of problem arises at the other end of the spectrum, as it were. There is need, as a preliminary to the First Programme of Institutional Development, for a comparable study of our geographical institutions, of our institutions as viewed, in effect, from the grass roots.

Chapter 5

THE DEVLIN CONCEPT OF THE PUBLIC SERVICE AND THE PROPOSALS FOR A PUBLIC SERVICE DEPARTMENT*

My theme is the concept of "the Public Service", a central issue in the Devlin Report. The implications of this concept are of some importance.

This paper falls into three parts. The first part relates to the basic assumptions on which the concept of "the Public Service" itself rests. These basic assumptions are : that one can meaningfully conceive of a single system of government for the community as a whole ; secondly, that, within that system of government, it is possible to devise meaningful roles and areas of discretion ; and thirdly, that system requires, if it is to work effectively, an instrument of long-term management.

That is the first issue. The second issue is—what is comprised in the concept of "the Public Service"? The third issue is—how might this concept of "the Public Service" work out in practice ?

I. BASIC ASSUMPTIONS

First, therefore, the three basic assumptions on which the concept of "the Public Service" rests.

1. *A single system of Government*

The first of these assumptions is that one can meaningfully comprehend and discuss the government of a country as a single system of interrelated parts.

The terms of reference of the Devlin Group asked us, because of the growing responsibilities of Government, to look at the appropriate distribution of functions as between departments, and as between departments and other bodies. One can think of three meanings for the word "Government". In the first place, of course, it means the

*Address delivered to members of the Institute of Public Administration on 13th January, 1970. Reprinted from ADMINISTRATION, Vol 17 (1969) 4.

F

body of ministers to whom the government of the country is entrusted. In the second place, it can have a very wide meaning comprising all the institutions of government — legislative, executive, judicial. In the third place, it can have the relatively narrow meaning of the administrative institutions that are available to the Government for carrying out its responsibilities. It is in this third, narrow sense that the Devlin report takes the expression "Government". What the Report is concerned with, therefore, is the process of government so far as administrative institutions engage in it. The Report took this process in a restrictive sense, in that it did not address itself to the problems of large institutions of government comprised by the Garda Siochana, the administrative underpinning of the Courts, or the huge area of the public service comprised by the various bodies of teachers, while the Army was touched upon only in a special way. When the Report considered distribution of functions, therefore, it considered them within the traditional administrative areas of the civil service, local government, and the state-sponsored bodies. However, perhaps to be a bit perverse, we took a fairly broad definition of what came under the heading of state-sponsored bodies. The crucial problem here is whether those bodies that we did take — 16 government departments, more than a hundred local authorities, and eighty or so state-sponsored bodies—together comprise a meaningful *system* of government? Are there criteria that would enable us to determine what might be held to be within that system, if it exists? If so, what are the special features and problems of that system?

It is inherent in this whole discussion that the volume of business to be carried out by the Government—what the terms of reference call "the increasing responsibilities of Government"—is now so great that it is not possible for the members of the Government to carry out all of these functions themselves. They need administrative institutions of one kind and another to help them to discharge their responsibilities. So, the first common thread running through all the bodies that could be held to be comprised within a system of Government is that they are engaged in serving the Government and in facilitating the Government in discharging its responsibilities to the plain people of Ireland.

The volume of this business is very large ; it also is extremely complex. That means that there are not only lines of communication up to ministers but a tremendous number of criss-crossing lines of communication between the various public bodies themselves. There are, in these inter-relationships, a number of special features. Again, government impinges on nearly every individual and organisation in the community, but on the public sector one can see a different degree of impingement from that on the private sector.

Let us try to list a few of these differences:

First, in the private sector the initiative for the establishment of the body and its objectives are clearly primarily matters of private interest, even though they may also serve the public interest ; but in the public sector nearly all the bodies are the creations of positive law, or of some other form of government initiative.

Secondly, although public money, and power, support many organisations in the private sector, nonetheless private sector organisations are basically self-sustaining ; this is very unusual in the public sector ; that is to say, they depend for their survival or development, or both, on public money.

Thirdly, certain standards of public accountability are expected of the public sector that are not applied in the same way in the private sector.

Not to make too fine a point of it, once can say that private individuals and organisations very properly serve their own interest, but public bodies must serve the public interest. In operational terms this expression "the public interest" means the better government of the community. This in turn means the service of the plain people of Ireland. As Bishop Philbin put it a number of years ago, for public servants their profession is patriotism. This is not to suggest that those in the private sector are no less patriotic. It is simply to say that the primary aim, the professional task, of those who work in the public sector is patriotism, and that they discharge this task by effectively contributing to the process of the government of their country. Thus, there is a large group of public bodies of one kind and another—of diverse origins, with diverse forms of organisation—all engaged in basically the same task, which is the process of government. It follows that it ought to be possible to understand the complexities of this process and to apprehend the system that comprises it. I think that no one who has tried to grasp the complexities of this system will underestimate the difficulties of doing so. He will sympathise with the reasonable perplexities of those who work in an isolated part of the system when they are asked to grasp the system as a whole. Nonetheless, wherever we work—whether in the civil service, in local government, or in the various types of state-sponsored bodies—we are part of that system. At least, that is the basic assumption of the terms of reference of the Devlin Group, and the basic assumption on which its Report rests.

CHART 15.1: THE NEW PUBLIC SERVICE. Structures and Systems

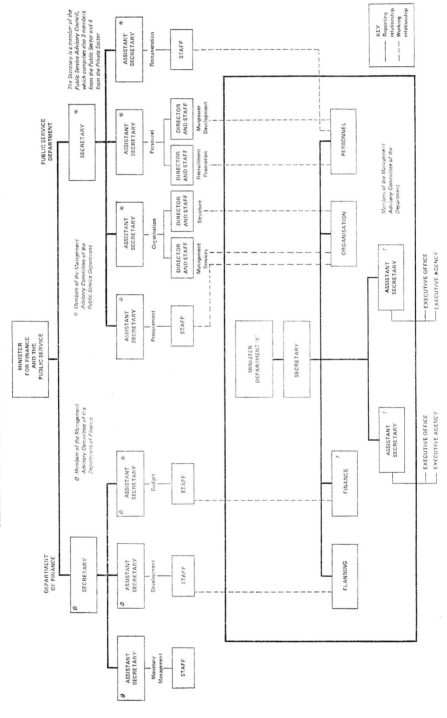

If you look at chart 15.1 from the Report (opposite) you will see in a nutshell what we mean by the system of government under the Devlin proposals. Here perhaps I might issue a warning. The presentation in this chart has had to be drastically simplified. The purpose of this system is to serve the Government and the plain people of Ireland— one might get the impression from the chart that the system exists for contemplating its own navel. This is not so. All of the bodies shown in the chart have many purposes, and thus relationships with many bodies. To make any graphical sense of the system we have had to show them throughout as if each had only a single major purpose and only a few relationships. The trouble about a chart is that it can show relationships in only two dimensions. The chart does not mean that we are not aware of the limitations. Yet, when all is said against it, the chart is an extremely elegant picture of what we mean by the system of government.

2. Role and Discretion

Assuming, therefore, that there is a system and that there are various types of bodies operating within it, how does one determine the roles and the degrees of discretion appropriate to each type of body ? We are all familiar with the statement that when a new state-sponsored body is being established it is because its functions are not "appropriate" to the civil service. What is "appropriate" to civil service work? What is "appropriate" to the work of state-sponsored bodies of various kinds? What is "appropriate" to the work of local government? These are three strikingly different forms of organisation. One might think, as form is supposed to follow from function, that the different forms suggest different functions. However, even a cursory examination of our system of government shows that this is not so in practice.

It is clear, therefore, that one of the problems of Irish government is to point out what are the roles to be played by the various types of public organisations. The Devlin Report finds, very broadly, three kinds of roles. The first of these relates to policy formulation and review. The second relates to the carrying out, or the execution, of policy. The third relates to the redress of grievances.

At the level of execution of settled policy the distinct roles of local authorities and of the various kinds of state-sponsored bodies are relatively clear, though they are becoming confused. But it is when one comes to look at the civil service departments that the real problems of roles emerge. There is very considerable overlapping of roles between departments, on the one hand, and the executive bodies on the other.

This comes from the fact that the departments are discharging all three roles of policy formulation, execution, and redress. This question of roles is discussed further by Mr. Devlin.[1] I mention the problem here simply to bring out the point that within this system of government that we have been postulating it became necessary to segregate roles—to ensure that each kind of job—policy, execution of various forms, and redress—had its own appropriate type of organisation.

One is here faced with a paradox. As soon as one grasps the essential unity of the system of government, one is immediately forced into the task of dividing it into distinct and separate areas.

Much the same sort of problem arises with the question of discretion. One can think of the problem of discretion in two ways. The first is the discretion that may be exercised by various types of organisations themselves. The second is the degree of discretion that may be exercised by individuals within those organisations. This issue of discretion, and its related issue of accountability, are crucial ones in modern large-scale organisations. Once roles have been defined, once objectives over a specified period have been set, once resources have been allocated, the modern tendency is to let people get on with the job for a period. Then, at the end of the period, they are held severely accountable for the results achieved with the resources allocated. In the business world, this is true both of executive bodies within a large complex and of managers within those bodies themselves. It is quite clear that if one looks at the problems of centralisation as they have manifested themselves in government departments under the concept of the minister as corporation sole, or if one looks at the degree of central controls exercised over local authorities, one sees big differences — but not mutually consistent ones — between the practice of our governmental system and that of large organisational systems abroad.

But even within our system itself there are large differences. The concept of the state-sponsored body — initially in the commercial and industrial sphere, but now also in the promotional, regulatory, research, training, marketing etc. spheres—was to give a wider degree of discretion to the organisation to get on with a fixed task. It is clear that the whole drift of Irish public administration is now towards that type of solution. When there is a problem of getting ahead with a new task, as well as with existing tasks, the general practice now is to set up a new state-sponsored body and to give it a degree of discretion quite unknown to government departments or local authorities. Events have forced a series of *ad hoc* decisions that have given substantial

[1]Liam St. J. Devlin: "The Concept of the Aireacht, the Four Staff Units, and the Executive Area," ADMINISTRATION, Vol. 17 (1969) 4.

degrees of discretion to new forms of public bodies. So long as we act in this pragmatic way but still cling to techniques of centralisation that are no longer appropriate to the scale of modern government, we are, as the Report points out, continuing to fail to think through the problem of discretion in relation to departments and local authorities. The point is that in the laudable aim to ensure that administrative organisations are *subordinated* to Government we have continued to rely on *techniques* of centralisation that are inappropriate to large scale modern government, and when these have broken down we have been content to devise *ad hoc* solutions without taking a hard look at the root causes of the breakdowns. So, while we arrive at the unifying concept of a system, we find in practice that it forces us into two careful processes of *segregation*—the segregation of role from role, and the segregation of areas of discretion.

3. *Unification*

The problem of reconciling these needs of segregation within a single system raises the third major assumption of the report. That is, to arrange this system of government so that roles and areas of discretion are segregated, and yet that the system be unified over all.

There are, of course, a number of built-in unifying factors. The first of these is the authority of Government itself. This is basic; but like many basic weapons it can in practice be used only as a last resort. It has been clear, for example, from the complaints in the NIEC report on Economic Planning,[2] that day to day operations even within the civil service itself call for some unifying machinery. Secondly, there are the four co-ordinating and communicating sub-systems discussed by Mr. Devlin.[3] Thirdly, the concept of the Public Service is a major force for unification in itself. This can be looked at from two standpoints. The first is from the aspect of a piece of machinery—the Public Service Department. The second is from the aspect of "the Public Service" as a great dynamic resource.

First, the machinery. It is clear that if the system of government is to be kept in tidy working order, adaptive to the changes that the future will amost certainly bring upon it, and effective in a real sense, it will require a great deal of overall management. Part of this is a question of raising the level of management within the various public bodies themselves. But part of it is also a question of the management of those overall and long-term issues that relate to the structural

[2] National Industrial Economic Council: Report No. 8, 1965.
[3] Loc. cit., pp 376–378.

problems of the machinery of government as a whole. We came across what seemed to us to be a very large number of these structural problems which continued to exist because there was no adequate machinery for diagnosing the nature of the problems and for working out solutions for them.

These structural problems were, substantially, of two kinds, which I might describe as external and internal. The external problems were those I have touched on already—the roles, responsibilities, relationships, and accountability of the various types of public bodies, and the degrees of discretion that, consonant with the public interest, could be allowed to them. The internal structural problems are perhaps even more fascinating. To some people it has seemed to be a surprising feature of our Report that it seems to give so much weight to structural questions, and much less weight to questions of personnel. This is because over the years a great number of barriers, fences, and areas of no-man's land have grown up between organisations in the public service, so cutting one off from the other. Even within the same organisation artificial barriers have separated people into almost impermeable vertical and horizontal classes — general service, professional and departmental. In one department, we were told, the staff were divided into the 'Blacks' and the 'Whites'. There has been a proliferation of grades. There have been various *ad hoc* arrangements for filling higher jobs and for meeting superannuation problems. All of these have had the effect of preventing the development of human dynamism and of keeping the human resources in the public service cribbed, cabined and confined. Every time I think of the hundred barriers to the free movement and development of human talent in the public service I am reminded, if I may be forgiven for repeating the quotation—and for the exaggeration—of Burke's description of the penal laws in Ireland—as "a machine of wise and elaborate contrivance and as well fitted for the oppression, impoverishment and degradation of a people and the debasement in them of human nature itself as ever proceeded from the perverted ingenuity of man." However, what we have here is, not so much a *contrivance* as, something that grew up at haphazard, in an absent-minded sort of way. It has grown up in this way because there was not some central management agency concerned to ensure that this kind of thing did not occur and that its ill effects were remedied. The price we have had to pay for this has been the restriction of the personal development of very many people and, I am sure, much less effective performance by our organisations overall than their inherent human resources would have permitted them to have achieved. Now it is not enough to say with Voltaire "Ecrasez l'infame".

We must also devise a piece of machinery to ensure that nothing like this can occur again. This is the basic purpose of the Public Service Department.

Thus, we come to the aspect of the Public Service as a vast pool of human ability, energy and dedication available for the service of the plain people of Ireland. And let me stress how vast it is. Counting the civil service, the local service; the services of the state-sponsored bodies, as well as the Army, Garda and teachers, it amounts to nearly 200,000 persons. That is to say, almost one third of all *employed* persons in Ireland are employed in the public service. Thus, also, we arrive at our conception of the Public Service Department as the organisation that will ensure the development and deployment of so much ability, energy and dedication so as to give the best possible service to the plain people of Ireland.

These, then, are the three basic assumptions of the Devlin Report —that there *is* a system of government, that it is necessary to *divide* it into appropriate roles and areas of discretion, and that it is necessary to *unify* it by a number of concepts, of which a most significant one is that of the Public Service and its handmaiden, the Public Service Department.

II. WHAT IS THE PUBLIC SERVICE ?

The second main point of this paper can be developed more quickly. What is the Public Service, as we envisage it ?

The concept of the Public Service that emerges from the three basic assumptions is a two-fold one. It is the Public Service Department, and it is the people who are working in the various kinds of public service agencies. The structure of the Public Service Department is set out in chart number 21.1 overleaf. As one reads from left to right, one sees that the proposed Department has an assistant secretary for each of four main functions—procurement, organisation, personnel and remuneration.

The slightly ambiguous word "procurement" is intended to cover vestigial functions from the Office of Public Works, functions from the Stationery Office, Stores Branch functions from the Department of Posts and Telegraphs, and the Combined Purchasing functions of the Department of Local Government. I do not propose to say anything more about this except that it is hoped that the Central Procurement Office will give an advisory and consultancy service to the various types of public bodies in buying and supplying their own needs, and that it will not itself be primarily a supplying body.

CHART 21.1: PUBLIC SERVICE DEPARTMENT PROPOSED ORGANISATION

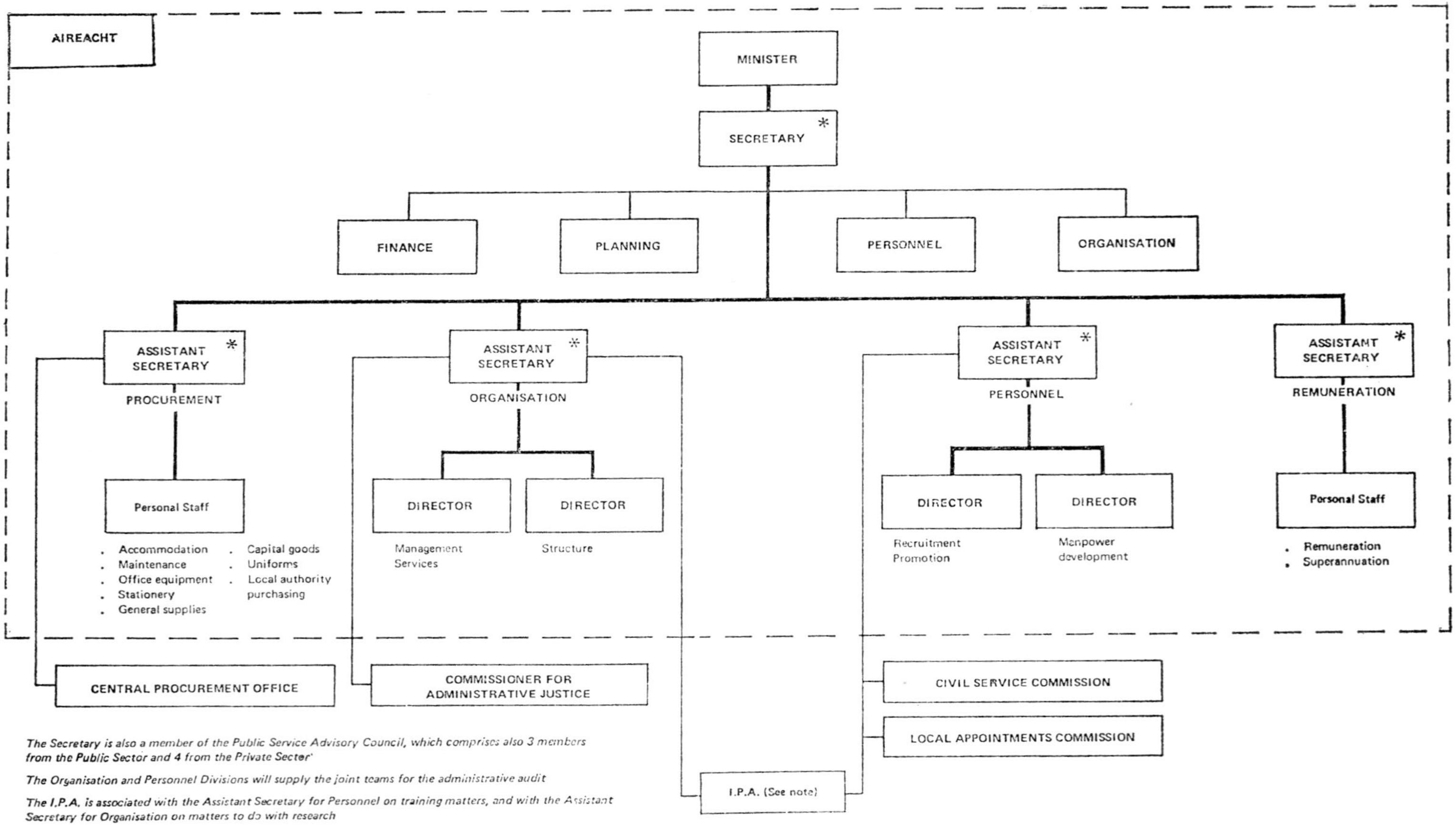

AIREACHT

MINISTER

SECRETARY *

FINANCE — PLANNING — PERSONNEL — ORGANISATION

ASSISTANT SECRETARY *
PROCUREMENT

- Accommodation
- Maintenance
- Office equipment
- Stationery
- General supplies
- Capital goods
- Uniforms
- Local authority purchasing

Personal Staff

ASSISTANT SECRETARY *
ORGANISATION

DIRECTOR
Management Services

DIRECTOR
Structure

ASSISTANT SECRETARY *
PERSONNEL

DIRECTOR
Recruitment Promotion

DIRECTOR
Manpower development

ASSISTANT SECRETARY *
REMUNERATION

Personal Staff

- Remuneration
- Superannuation

CENTRAL PROCUREMENT OFFICE

COMMISSIONER FOR ADMINISTRATIVE JUSTICE

I.P.A. (See note)

CIVIL SERVICE COMMISSION

LOCAL APPOINTMENTS COMMISSION

The Secretary is also a member of the Public Service Advisory Council, which comprises also 3 members from the Public Sector and 4 from the Private Sector

The Organisation and Personnel Divisions will supply the joint teams for the administrative audit

The I.P.A. is associated with the Assistant Secretary for Personnel on training matters, and with the Assistant Secretary for Organisation on matters to do with research

* *Management Advisory Committee. The Assistant Secretary (Budget) in the Department of Finance is also a member*

At the right hand of the chart one can see an assistant secretary for remuneration. Here again, I do not propose to say anything about this obvious activity except that its functions would extend outside the public service as we have been considering it hitherto and include also the remuneration problems of Army, Gardai, Teachers, etc.

The two crucial functions, for the purposes of the Report, are those of organisation and personnel. Sir Geoffrey Thompson deals with the personnel function including remuneration.[4] It is not necessary for me to say anything about this, except perhaps to stress the point already made, that a personnel function cannot operate effectively if the organisational structures are not adequate. These structures depend on adequate overall management for the public service as a whole. This is what makes the organisation function so crucial to the whole concept of a dynamic public service.

The assistant secretary for organisation will be concerned with two executive agencies—the office of the Commissioner for Administrative Justice and the Institute of Public Administration so far as administrative research is concerned. It is expected that the establishment and management of an effective system of administrative appeals throughout the public service will be a very considerable organisational task. Once the system has been established it will be an important communication system as to the effectiveness of public organisations in giving public satisfaction.

The assistant secretary for organisation will be assisted by a Director for Structure, and a Director for Management Services. We would envisage the management services organisation based on the Public Service Department as providing the public service with a really high-class management consultancy service and encouraging the early adoption of management techniques. That is clear enough.

The difficult job is that which will be discharged by the Director of Structure. His task will be threefold. He will be concerned, first, with the internal structures of organisations so that jobs, relationships and areas of discretion will be adequately defined. Primarily, of course, this will be the responsibility of the management of the executive agency, and, at one remove, of the appropriate aireacht. But there will be certain issues that can only be tackled from the centre, and these will constitute a good part of his job. Secondly, he will be concerned with the very complex problems of the types of administrative structures, of their roles and of their relationships, and the adaptation of these to future conditions. For example, one would expect him to

[4]Lt.-Gen. Sir Geoffrey Thompson: "The Devlin Report: The Personnel Problems," ADMINISTRATION, Vol. 17 (1969) 4.

be able to have an overall picture of what will emerge from the present experiments in relation to regional authorities and ideas of decentralisation.

Thirdly, he will be concerned with achieving the pre-condition of a dynamic personnel policy. This will require the removal of all unnecessary barriers to personal development and to the broadening of experience. These barriers of class and grade are internal to the organisations. There are also the barriers to promotion, to personal development and to mobility that are external to individual bodies but internal to the system as a whole. A major task here will be to have defined the organisational needs for manpower and skills of the various public bodies now and in the future so that the personnel side can provide and train the necessary people.

All of this, I should like to insist, is in the interests of making the best use of the very substantial human, financial and physical resources that will be comprised in the conception of the public service.

The Public Service Department would not discharge the old establishment function of detailed control of numbers, called in Britain, the "complementing function." That would remain with the Department of Finance to be delegated to the aireachts with other supply-type operations. Thus, the procedure for allocating resources for staffs would be similar to that for allocating any other type of resource and would, allowing for the other changes recommended by the Report, resemble the present procedure for allocating staff resources to existing non-commercial state sponsored bodies.

The Public Service

What do we mean by the Public Service itself? It would comprise what we call the *new* civil service, the local government service, and the services of the commercial state-sponsored bodies.

The new civil service would comprise three groups. First, it would include those working in what would be left of the old-style civil service, that is to say in the aireachts. Secondly, it would include those members of the old-style civil service who would be working in the new executive agencies. Thirdly, it would include those persons now working in the non-commercial state-sponsored bodies. In this way a 'Department' would consist of the aireacht and the associated executive agencies. The agencies, the commercial state-sponsored bodies and the local authorities would comprise the executive system of satellites revolving about their appropriate aireachts.

I need not say that the Report envisages that there will be a wide degree of executive discretion within the satellites. At the same time the persons working in those satellites would feel themselves to be part of a larger service with opportunities for making a career for themselves within this larger service. This will apply whether, if I may adapt a delightful metaphor first used by Mr Scannell, their bent is towards the cloistered monks of the aireacht, or, towards the mendicant friars of the executive system, or towards the curial complexities of the appellate bodies.

These two proposals—to have a single Public Service, and a Public Service Department—would they make any real difference? We believe they would. The existing agglomeration of various types of administrative agencies, however good they may be individually, leads, when they are considered collectively, to a great deal of confusion of purpose. This does not provide, overall, a good service to government, and it fills individuals working in these bodies with a great deal of quite unnecessary frustrations. We believe that to have a Public Service Department that would concern itself with problems of this kind, that is, basically structural and organisational problems, would greatly enhance the effectiveness of the new administrative set-up which we recommend. Secondly, the conception of a single Public Service, is, at its simplest, the conception of a single career service that will permit any able and ambitious young man or woman, no matter where he or she begins in the service, to have a fulfilling career, to get personal development and experience, and to get a sense of achievement consonant with his or her ability.

III. HOW CAN THE CONCEPT OF THE PUBLIC SERVICE BE GOT TO WORK ?

The short answer to the question of how the concept of the Public Service can be got to work is—by raising the level of administrative management both in relation to the agencies and in relation to the system as a whole. In a nutshell, this involves solving the twin problems of administrative discretion and of administrative accountability. It is perhaps to simplify too much to say that the Report is basically about the problem of administrative discretion in a democratic society; this is at least a major theme. But it is inherent in such a situation that if there is to be wider administrative discretion, as we propose, then there must be a more effective system of administrative accountability. In a modern, complex, developmental situation the nineteenth century systems of audit of appropriations and of general parliamentary accountability are no longer the full answer. We have accordingly proposed no less than five new administrative systems for assessing the level of administrative performance. These are, in effect, based on the new-style Department of Finance and on the Public Service Department.

First, very briefly the accountability systems under the Department of Finance.

It is no secret that much of the trouble we have experienced in this country in relation to planning for national development has been organisational. The Report recommends a machinery throughout the public service aimed to overcome these difficulties. An effective planning system that identifies objectives to be achieved in a given period is a powerful system of accountability. Failings and shortcomings in achieving objectives come to light, and pinpoint places where organisational and personnel improvements are needed.

In the strictly financial field programme budgeting brings to light failures to get adequate returns from expenditures on certain services, and the system of effectiveness audit makes obvious where resources as a whole are not being managed to full effect.

We have recommended that the Department of Finance delegate real financial discretion to the various public bodies. It is clear, therefore, that in return it should be at the heart of the systems of accountability in the planning and financial fields.

So far as the Public Service Department is concerned, it is proposed that public bodies will undergo—perhaps at five-yearly intervals—an administrative audit to assess their level of management, their organisational effectiveness, and their use of personnel. This will also bring into the open significant defects in these areas. The extensive appellate system under the Commissioner for Administrative Justice will provide continuous evidence of how far statutory services are giving satisfaction to their clients.

Apart from the striking of a proper balance between administrative discretion and administrative accountability, an essential feature of the system we recommend is the creation of what might be called a common market for talent throughout the public service by knocking down all the organisational impediments to movement within and between agencies so that every member of the Public Service will have the chance of achieving his own best level of operation.

This brings one back to the crucial importance of our proposal for a Public Service Department. As Mr Devlin[5] has pointed out we have

[5]Liam St. J. Devlin: "The Devlin Report—An Overview," ADMINISTRATION, Vol. 17 (1969) 4.

recommended a separate department for this purpose in order to ensure that organisational and personnel problems are not subordinated to finance problems. These organisational and personnel problems are themselves extremely difficult and complex. They require high level attention. Hitherto they have not been getting that attention. For the purpose of approaching structures and personnel in a dynamic way the Public Service Department would be a crucial instrument. It would ensure that the public service has built into it the necessary adaptive factors. These will enable it to adjust itself in an orderly and effective way to the changes that continually occur. The primary responsibility for the effective use of people — and for avoiding the creation of unnecessary barriers in their deployment and development — will rest with the executive agencies themselves ; in addition the organisational and personnel units in the aireachts will be concerned to see that, overall, the best use is made of the people and resources that come under the aegis of the aireacht. But in the last analysis there must be a place where we can pin the responsibility for ensuring that these tasks are in fact performed throughout the public service as a whole. There must be a place where those general problems that affect everybody but may be the responsibility of no one in particular are tackled in a positive way. That place is the Public Service Department.

What happens if the Public Service Department itself is not fully seized of its responsibilities? This is the purpose of the Public Service Advisory Council that we have recommended and which is referred to in the top right hand corner of Chart 15.1 on page 76. This is to be composed as to half from the private sector and as to half from the public sector. It will be required to submit a report each year to the Oireachtas. In addition each Department would be required to submit an annual report to the Oireachtas. With these and with the information thrown up by the programme budgeting system and the planning system a good deal of information about the administrative system and its operation would become available to members of the Oireachtas. One would hope that the Oireachtas, if necessary as a result of some organisational changes of its own in the direction of special committees, would take a special interest in the progress and maintenance of public service reform, adaptation and development. Moreover the publicity that would be associated with the publication of the reports on the Public Service would stimulate and inform public discussion on these broad issues of general institutional development.

CONCLUSION

What I have been trying to say, therefore, is this — that the concept of the Public Service is a basic one in the Devlin Report. It rests on three fundamental assumptions. First, that there is a *system* of government in which all the various kinds of public bodies interrelate to a greater or lesser extent. Secondly, within that system there is the problem of teasing out separate roles for different kinds of bodies and for giving them appropriate ranges of discretion. This parcelling out, as it were, seems at first sight to undermine the concept of the fundamental unity of the system and calls for some special means of ensuring that the system as a whole works in a unified way. Two new administrative concepts are needed for this. The first is the Public Service Department for the long term management of the system as a whole. This management includes the structures of the various bodies and their relations with one another. It includes their internal organisation. It includes also the effective use of the people who are employed in these various bodies. The second administrative unifying concept is the notion of a single Public Service to which all those employed in various kinds of public bodies, of no matter what description, would belong.

The second main point that I have tried to make is that the notion of the Public Services comprises these two things — first, an agency or piece of machinery, such as the Public Service Department, and secondly an idea, the idea being the essential unity of purpose of all those employed in the interests of the plain people of Ireland. This idea of the Public Service would comprise the new civil service as we see it, incorporating those working in the aireachts, those working in the agencies who were formerly working in government departments proper, and those working in the non-commercial state-sponsored bodies. The public service would also comprise those working in the local government—and no doubt the new regional—authorities. And it would comprise those working in the commercial state-sponsored bodies.

The third main point is how to be sure that we can get the concept of the Public Service actually to work. Here the problem is to reconcile administrative discretion with more effective means of administrative accountability. The new forms of accountability involve both the Department of Finance—so far as planning and financial accountability are concerned—and the Public Service Department in relation to the system of administrative audit and the appellate system proposed in the Report. These should mean that the organisation and personnel units in the agencies and in the aireachts are seized of the need to ensure that in the bodies with which they are concerned the structures and personnel practices are well adapted to the needs of the times. Secondly, they involve the Public Service Department in being concerned with those general problems in relation to structures and personnel that are not the specific problems of any of the individual agencies or aireachts. Thirdly, they involve that a reasonable review system of the progress of the Public Service Department, and the progress of the departments of the Public Service as a whole, exists for reporting to the Oireachtas and to the public so that the problems of institutional development can be seen to be important problems for the community as a whole.

G

Chapter 6

BIG GOVERNMENT AND LOCAL COMMUNITY*

What I have to say is this. Modern government is big government and is getting bigger. Big government is different from the kind of government we have been accustomed to. It requires, and results in, new techniques of public participation. Our existing public institutions are not well adapted to these techniques. I conclude by throwing out a few ideas on the lines on which this adaptation might take place, with particular reference to the place of the local community in the whole complex.

I. BIG GOVERNMENT

In Ireland, as in other western, free societies, government is big and is getting bigger. In Ireland it handles over two-fifths of the GNP and of those employed for salaries and wages nearly one-third are employed by government. More cash transfers, better health facilities, longer education, will increase the quantity of government.

In quality, government is also big. Government participates in about three-quarters of all the investment in our community. Government policy about tax systems, school syllabuses, foreign policy, are major influences on our decisions, values, and aspirations.

The drift towards bigger government has come from the approval of ordinary people. They want more of the services that only government provides. But the size and complexity of modern government and the new demands made on it have changed the nature of government: now it has to be not only responsive but positive. Government action can accelerate economic, social and cultural development. Positive government calls for clarifying national objectives and mobilising idle resources.

Positive government has led to planning. Planning needs greater collective effort and thus greater public understanding and acceptance. Planning requires foresight, over the budgetary year to come, over the length

*Paper read to the Christus Rex Congress at Nenagh, Easter, 1970.

of the current development programme of four or five years, over twelve
or fifteen years such as in the Report on Full Employment,[1] and over
the coming generation for important environmental decisions. It needs to
foresee how coming changes interact on one another—for example, the
apparent connexion between affluence and delinquency—and how to
obviate the unacceptable ones.

Positive government identifies the changes needed in society so as to
respond successfully to needs and aspirations. It involves major commitment to modernisation and growth and to the implications of technological advance both in the private and the public sectors. It involves
commitment to achieve defined aims—such as full employment by 1980.
It is certain to involve substantial adaptations when we become members
of the EEC. There are many other problems for positive government. The
greatest of the problems is to anticipate emerging problems, not simply
to respond to existing ones. This makes government much more difficult,
intellectually and morally.

Positive government calls for wider public education and consultation
with those affected by proposed decisions. But consultation is not
enough—there has been a great deal of consultation about incomes
policy! Some degree of consent to the emerging proposals has to be
achieved. This is not easy. A system of education, consultation and consent, if it is to be effective, leads to some degree of participation in the
decision-making of the community. This participation has to be sufficiently real to involve commitment to the ends and the means proposed
to achieve more national development.

The effects of successful national development are more affluence,
more education, more leisure. An affluent, educated and leisured community can play a bigger part in decision-making. It is likely to demand
this.

So we have, on the one hand, the need for more positive government
and, on the other, a people ready and demanding to take a larger part
in the decision-making. Each is a condition of the other.[2]

These developments pose two main problems. The first is of over-
loading the top with business. The second is how to make a reality of
participative government. If we are to continue with a system whereby
so great a part of every process of decision-making takes place at the top
of government departments in Dublin, then as the business of government grows, as the main decisions to be taken become more difficult,
and as the public demands more participation, the centralised system is

[1]National Industrial Economic Council: *Report on Full Employment, 1967.*
[2]I need not develop this further because it is well discussed in Charles
McCarthy: *The Distasteful Challenge, 1968.*

likely to break down at a faster rate even than it is breaking down at present. If we continue to refuse to face this issue, and continue to rely on *ad hoc* administrative expedients, we shall have a disorganised and unresponsive machine drifting towards a bureaucratic neo-feudalism where the elected government would not be in effective control of the process of government.

We have three choices. We can try to reverse the trend towards big government, at best a long haul. We can do nothing and so accept the present drift. Or we can try to grasp the complex interactions, and devise for them a system of overall democratic control that reconciles effective action with effective public accountability. This is the course now being chosen by many democratic governments, and the Devlin Report provides the most comprehensive advice given on this issue to any government. These proposals may be good, bad, or a mixture: but they are addressed to a serious problem. It is too easy to run about inflaming prejudices with emotional petrol bombs such as the 'Public Service sees itself a Fifth Estate, independent of Politicians'. This is not how public servants see themselves; but if they did, all they need, for the wish to become fact, is for the present drift to continue.

We are faced with a major problem of politics. The political system is, or ought to be, the channel through which all the really important decisions of the community are identified and decided. It is a major unifying force in the whole community, and channel of communication throughout. When it is working freely it ensures that the significant issues in the community are adequately identified, adequately discussed, and settled at the widest practicable level of consensus.

To play this role it is essential that the political system be in full communication with the various problems and groupings in the society. There is some evidence—as witness the Tuairim pamphlet. *Government and People: Creative Dialogue*[3]—to suggest that there is an increasing divorce between the participative groups in our society and the political system. This drift from politics to syndicalism bodes ill for the future health of our democracy.

We look to the political system to provide leadership and decision-making in the important matters to society. Below the political system we look to the various kinds of public institutions to underpin that role of leadership and decision-making. Politics keeps the complex governmental system under democratic control. It is essential that politics be highly relevant to what is going on within the whole system. It seems to me that this is in danger of not occurring in our society. Our insti-

[3]Xavier Carty: *Government and People—Creative Doalogue*: A Report of the 1969/70 Communications Conference, 1970.

tutions—political and administrative—have not adapted themselves to keep abreast of the changes that have been occurring as a result of big government. On the one hand, the community groups, the interest groups and the voluntary organisations are bypassing the political system. On the other hand, the administrative innovations—such as the programmes for economic and social expansion—are bypassing the political system also. One may have two minds about the efficacy of economic planning in Italy, but at least the plan there is discussed in Parliament and passed as a law. After 12 years of economic planning in this country we have not yet found a system for bringing parliament into the adequate discussion of our economic, much less social, programmes. This role has been played, so far as it has been played at all, by an appointive, not an elective body, the National Industrial Economic Council.

These twin drifts—to bureaucracy on the one hand and to syndicalism on the other—pose major problems for the future of our society. A good part of the remedy is to tackle the problems of undue centralisation and of public participation. There is an extraordinary degree of centralisation in our society. This means that a small number of politicians and administrators take nearly all the decisions that are relevant to the government of the community and the great mass of politicians, the great mass of public servants and, above all, the great mass of individual citizens can play little or no part in this activity. Where there is a high degree of centralisation of decision taking about matters that are not of the highest importance we find delays, rigidities and failure to relate together separate decisions about related subjects. Human and community needs spill over the tidy, bureaucratic lines of demarcation. It is hard to get a decision along the straight functional line; but where the decision cuts across several functional lines one is in real trouble. Moreover, problems that are not specifically the problems of any one of these bodies tend not to be attended to at all.

This kind of centralisation impedes the planning process which depends on an adequate input of information from various parts and sections of the community and of the degree of consent to unpleasant courses that, in a democracy, is best evoked by popular participation.

The time has come to restructure our institutions to take account of the changes that have occurred and are occurring because of big government. So far as central government is concerned, the Devlin Report spells out what needs to be done at the administrative level. But a major contribution can be made from the other end, by a drastically restructured system of community and local government.

II. SOME PRINCIPLES

It is here I think that one can get some help from some general and fairly familiar ideas. These are the ideas of hierarchy, of subsidiarity, of emergence, and of co-responsibility. These are ideas of great generality; but perhaps I may illustrate their relevance by a simple example.

1. *Hierarchy*

When one looks at the evolution of a successful organism, such as man, one sees a progression from the very small to the very complex, but it is a particular kind of progression. Thus, if I may simplify, atoms cohere into molecules, and molecules into cells, and cells into systems— circulatory, nervous, motor—and the systems into an overall organism. There is a clear hierarchy here but it is a hierarchy not of subordination, but of freely operating roles.

2. *Subsidiarity*

The second general idea is that of subsidiarity. All the parts of the overall organism play their allotted roles with a very high degree of autonomy. So the heart does not need permission from the brain every time it has to beat, much less the actions of cells and molecules throughout the various systems. They have their jobs to do and they continue to do them without constant reference to the centre for orders or guidance. It is precisely because of this autonomous working of the various systems that the brain is in control of the whole organism. It is in control because it is not being kept continually cluttered up with the need to take small decisions that are capable of being taken by the autonomous systems themselves.

3. *Emergence*

One of the striking things about a hierarchical grouping is the phenomenon of emergence at various levels of the hierarchy. When a number of molecules are organised into a cell one still has the molecules; but one has something else as well, namely a cell. In the same way the cells can be grouped into a system. Here one has not only the molecules and the cell but also a system. As this grouping goes on up the hierarchical levels other new concepts emerge. Moreover, they emerge without derogating from the position of the lesser components of the whole structure.

4. *Co-responsibility*

The autonomy inherent in the ideas of subsidiarity and emergence are conditioned by the overall need to serve the interests of the organism as a whole. While the parts are autonomous, they are bound together in a spirit of cohesion, of co-responsibility—co-responsibility of the higher parts to respect the legitimate autonomy of the lower ones, co-responsibility of the lower ones to submit their immediate needs to the good of the whole.

In the well-organised organism one has this principle of hierarchy, the principle of the autonomy of the subsidiary and emergent systems at each of the levels, the whole bound together by the principle of co-responsibility. That is to say at each level there is responsibility at that level for doing the things that are appropriate to it, and there is responsibility to ensure that what it does is in conformity with what has to be done at higher and lower levels too.

I think it is helpful to apply the principles illustrated by this example to so complex a system as the system of government. Nature shows us how, by using these principles, to organise a huge mass of detail into coherent, efficient systems. I think that if we wish to make an equally successful task of organising our governmental problems we could do worse than learn the lessons to be derived from the concepts of hierarchy, subsidiarity, emergence and co-responsibility. That is to say, it is inherent in the proper functioning of a hierarchical system that the subsidiary systems be permitted an appropriate degree of autonomy in their operations without constant reference to the centre so that they can act co-responsibly.

The problem is how to get going a system of hierarchy and of subsidiarity, how to get it underpinned by appropriate institutions, in such a way that the Government will be in effective control of the whole and that the democratic values of positive government with popular participation will be maintained.

III. LOCAL COMMUNITY

A restructuring of our institutions calls for hard thinking about the problems of government services at the local and community level. There are some seven major governmental services provided at these levels for the mass of the citizens: education; health and welfare; agricultural services; environmental services; law and order; taxation; and, now developing, industrial promotion services. These services raise fascinating problems of areas, of roles, of coherence, and of participation.

First, areas. Are there within the overall system any 'natural' catchment areas for these blocks of government work ? Take the example of education. There are three levels: primary to age 12, second level to age 17-18, and third level. The second level is divided into two cycles—the junior cycle to age 15 and the senior cycle. At the first and second levels we have three distinct overlapping and underlapping systems: the system of primary education to age 14 based on the parish ; the system of secondary education from about 10 or 11 based on the teaching orders and on haphazard geographical groupings ; the system of vocational education geographically coherent but haphazard in selecting its younger students. The problem is to incorporate these three distinct systems into a coherent structure.

The *minimum* sizes of the various types of schools related to the population patterns and the present pattern of school going gives us an idea of the structure of a reasonably comprehensive school system. This shows a district pattern of one senior cycle to four junior cycle to eight primary schools.

For an *executive* area there ought to be several of the senior cycle schools with their attendant junior cycle and primary schools linked together for such services as school transport.[4] With an administrative structure of this kind it would be economical to use it for a massive decentralisation of executive work—school groupings, building grants, teachers' recruitment and pay, cleaning grants, perhaps syllabuses etc. etc.

A typical county seems to be big enough to provide these executive services.

This would give the opportunity for participation at the district and the executive levels by parents, educational and church interests, employers, trade unions, etc.

We have above the counties the emerging regional structures for regional technical colleges covering several counties, and above them again the 3 (or 4) provincial centres for university level education.

Here we see the principle of hierarchy emerging—in Devlin terms, the central *aireacht* under the Minister, the four centralised executive agencies,[5] the provincial or third level groupings, the regional groupings, the county groupings, and the district grouping around the complex

---

[4]Appendix XII of the OECD report *Investment in Education*, Vol. II, 1966, suggests that there might be five or six of these units in an average country.

[5]*Report of Public Services Organisation Review Group*, 1966-69, p. 324. The proposed four executive agencies were: Office of Primary Education; Office of Secondary Education; Higher Education Authority; Teacher Training Authority.

of at least one senior cycle school, with its attendant junior cycle and primary schools.

Similarly, under the new Health Act there will be three provincial councils based on the university schools of medicine, a number of regional councils comprising several counties, and, it seems, health committees still remaining at the county level. Beneath them, however, there is a new concept of community health and welfare services based on a relatively small community. The service that is nearest the community in this way is basically a general practitioner type of service —not only in the medical sense, but also in the welfare sense—pulling together for the benefit of individuals and families the various specialised services.

So also with the agricultural services. The Devlin Report[6] shows how the agricultural services might be operated on the hierarchical principle —at the centre the aireacht and the specialised agencies, the regional groupings, the county groupings, and beneath them the "general practitioner" agricultural services.

With the environmental services—communications, other parts of the infrastructure, the local government services—the picture is more complicated. But in local government the same sort of pattern is emerging. Local government services can be seen to operate on a number of levels. At present there is an effective executive unit at county level. Beneath this is an increasing desire of many small communities to get ahead with making improvements on their own with the necessary technical or financial support from the counties. Above the county level one sees growing up a regional approach to environmental planning. So, apart from the central department, we have three levels —the community services level, the county executive level, and the regional planning level.

The other bulk services do not fall clearly into this pattern but could be fitted into it. Not every service needs to be fitted into this scheme: each one can pick between the levels to meet its own needs. The point is that there is a principle of hierarchy here that can help us to define administrative areas.

We can also use this hierarchical principle in devising special roles for the various levels of this hierarchy. As an alternative to a huge mass of undifferentiated material being sucked into the centre in Dublin we can envisage a number of different levels each with its defined role, each dealing with its own problems so far as it can and only pushing up to a higher level the problems that transcend its own

[6]pp. 160-162.

responsibilities. This principle of subsidiarity is, I believe, the underlying structural reality.

A third major issue is that of *coherence*—how does one bind together major services that impinge on one another? This is important at the three levels we have identified. At the district level it is important if the real needs of the "consumer", where they do not fall within tidy departmental boundaries, are to be diagnosed and treated. However effective the general practitioner concept might be, some degree of separation of services and skills must exist between the main specialisms. It is necessary at the executive—or county—level to have a means by which action can be taken across departmental lines. At the planning —or regional—level this knitting together of diverse services becomes crucial to the whole planning issue.

As things stand in our system, there is only one place where these diverse issues are drawn together, and that is at the level of the Government itself. Obviously, only the most important matters get full attention there, and the problems of co-ordination and coherence at lower levels can get much less attention. So we need at the planning, the executive and the district levels means of binding all these services together in the general interest of the local area.

This in turn calls for a clear definition of these local areas—region, county and district—and their roles. Coherence becomes impossible if the areas and roles are not standardised.

Implicit in this is a high degree of local discretion. This could be bad if local standards were not high: but defining and enforcing of standards is a job for the central administration. Local discretion could be good for two reasons. First, planned national development calls for a mixture of a number of different types of development—economic, social, cultural, environmental. Of necessity, the appropriate mixture varies from place to place. The overall rate of national development thus depends, in part, on the most appropriate mixtures for the various parts of the country. This requires local knowledge and local decisions.

Local discretion could also be a good thing because government depends on the assent of the governed. Decisions to which people, or their genuine representatives, have been a part are likely to be more acceptable than those that seem to be imposed from outside. Machinery for enlarging the area of popular assent is likely to contribute to, not detract from, positive government. At each of the levels of community services, of executive action, and of planning, there is the problem of representation—of the representation of ordinary people, of the representation of significant local interests, of the representation of specialised knowledge, skills and talents. This is an issue that calls for more thought than it has been getting.

If, by adopting the principle of hierarchy supplemented by the principle of subsidiarity, we can have a clothing, as it were, of public participation—for handling grievances, for consultation, for decision-making, for planning, for reviewing—then we have the beginnings of a newly structured political system. Elements of this system are to be found in different degrees in different services. But we have no coherent system for all the services which would marry the administrative structures to the underlying political needs. This, in effect, will be the major task of the new Public Service Department. But as of now we do not have the political system fully carrying out its tasks of local leadership and local decision-making.

If this kind of comprehensive structure were created, if local decision-making were linked to the local political system, one could see the political system acting as the nervous system of the whole. Voluntary and interest groups wanting things done in their particular areas would impinge on the local political systems. Politics would then get a new relevance to the day to day preoccupations of Irish people.

IV. CONCLUSION

Perhaps because I am an official, much of what I have had to say has been about the administrative side of government. The administrative part of government is, as it were, but its bone structure. Unless it is clothed in the flesh and life of politics it just remains a skeleton. Each is part of the other, and some light may be thrown on the politics of big government by looking at the underlying bone structure.

What I have been trying to say, therefore, is basically this. Government is big and is getting bigger. The bigger it gets the more important it is to get the hierarchical system of government working properly. This hierarchical system involves familiar terms—subsidiarity and co-responsibility—for so many as possible of the members of a more alert, better educated, and more leisured community in the future. This will involve some fairly drastic re-thinking, and a fair degree of restructuring, of our institutions. If this is done it is likely that the political system will be made more relevant to the problems of community, county and regional areas of society, and will thus become more effective.

I think that these are urgent issues. Our society faces a number of problems that cannot be wished away. First, it needs to be a success

—to hold our people, to preserve our values, to improve—or at least maintain—our position in the world. Secondly, we are about to leave the quiet backwater in which Ireland has lived for thousands of years, and launch out into the mainstream of western Europe ; can we navigate those waters, or will we be swept away ? Thirdly, here as elsewhere the young people are putting us on notice. Our society cannot be a success, we cannot preserve ourselves in the great world we are about to enter, unless we can coax all our people—young and old, sick and poor, urban and rural, clerical and lay—to stay, to contribute, to participate in the new society we shall be forced to create here.

We cannot do this—keep a balance between urban and rural, provide good social service, achieve economic (or any other kind of) development—unless we bend our minds to this problem of the kinds of institutions that are necessary to run a modern, free, christian society in the Ireland of tomorrow.

Chapter 7

POWER TO THE PEOPLE*

When I was first asked to speak on "Power to the people" I had a vision of unruly young people in Paris chanting this slogan. They had another slogan that I, as a bureaucrat, found in poor taste. They said they would hang the last politician with the entrails of the last bureaucrat. However, last week the balance was restored when President Nixon, talking of "the flow of power and resources from the states and communities to Washington", announced that his purpose was to reverse it. It is in this sense that I propose to talk about power to the people.

I.   A COMMUNITY CENTRED SOCIETY ?

Power—political and administrative power—is exercised through institutions and it is about institutions that I propose to talk. The creation and development of appropriate institutions is part of the development of any society. The development of public institutions in this society has been towards a quite exceptional degree of centralisation. This has been for three main reasons.

First, a post-revolutionary government had to ensure that it really was in control of the activities of government. Secondly, in a small, poor country it was held that the simpler the institutional structure the better. Thirdly, there was the belief that centralisation makes for efficiency. These three reasons need to be looked at afresh in the light of what has happened in the past 50 years.

It is not to be disputed that the Government of a sovereign state ought to be in control of the business of government; but the *techniques* of government control appropriate to the 1920's have not been adjusted to the needs of the 1970's. This is a major point brought out by the Devlin Report. The problem is not to reduce the ultimate control of government, but to ensure that the systems of control match its present scale.

*A paper presented at a Tuairim discussion in February, 1971.

Secondly, smallness of itself does not make for simplicity: what is crucial is sovereignty: a small, sovereign country needs very nearly as complex a system of government as a big one.

Thirdly, we have come to understand better what we mean by "efficiency" in public institutions. Efficiency is a term that derives from technology. The technology appropriate to government institutions is of two kinds. On the one hand there is the technology that requires real bigness and intense specialisation, for example, the economy of big power stations, or the expertness of specialist brain surgery. It can plausibly be argued that the whole country is too small a unit to support real efficiency in these senses. On the other hand, efficiency can also be seen as humane response to human needs, and this is quantitatively the main area of present day government. We are coming to learn that small units of operation, perhaps backed up by specialist services, are likely to give a better return here. So we find ourselves obliged to distinguish between those things that must be handled by the largest unit we have, namely the state itself, and those things that can be more efficiently handled by relatively small units. What sort of units?

There has also been a change in the kind of people we are. The growth in government means that we bump against it at every turn and the growth in communication, in education, and in leisure, means that we know more about what is going on, and have time to consider what we ought to do about it. So one has an increasing sense of the need for a more participatory democracy than would have been considered necessary in past times.

These issues of the problem of control, the problem of efficiency and the problem of participation pose for us the question of the kind of society we want to create here. In effect, can we develop our institutions so as to achieve a more harmonious and community centred society ?

I will not hide my own preferences. They are that central government ought to concentrate on the great affairs of State and ought to shed the load of detailed administration. The load so shed should be given to various kinds of subordinate authorities in which the representatives of the plain people of Ireland should have a significant voice.

Times are relevant for thinking in these terms. We are, very shortly, to have a White Paper on new proposals for our local government system. We are, very shortly, to have legislation setting up a new Public Service Department that will be concerned with the overall structure of the institutions of government. There has been much public discussion about decentralising the functions of government. We see emerging a new and complex system of regional administration.

Any adequate discussion of the issue "Power to the people" must, I think, centre on three issues: that of regionalism, that of local government (which in our system is basically county government), and that of community or district government.

I propose this evening to deal only with regionalism. There is no point in discussing county government until the promised White Paper appears. District or community government raises issues that are not sufficiently ripe for action at this stage. So, if we want to talk in practical terms about "Power to the people" in the here and now we should concentrate on the issue of regionalism.

This involves two things. The first is to look at the decisions now being taken to set up regional structures. The second is to link these structures with adequate public representation.

II. REGIONAL SHAPES

As things stand we have set up, with a greater or lesser degree of formality, regional structures for health, for tourism, for physical planning, and for the colleges of technology. Regional structures have also been established by the Industrial Development Authority and by the Department of Labour placement and guidance service. There are various regional groupings of the field staffs of the Departments of Agriculture and of Lands, and of the Revenue Commissioners, the Gardai and the Courts, the ESB, CIE, etc. etc. Broadly, "region" in our system is a grouping of *counties* to perform a function common to them—e.g. tourist development, health services etc.

Two problems arise in relation to the shape of regions. First, should the regional boundaries coincide with county boundaries? Secondly, should a regional area be standard for all purposes?

For the regional technical colleges a number of counties are divided; and the Buchanan[1] Report also suggests the breaching of some county boundaries.

There is a wide variety in the size of informal regions; but the formal ones are settling down at eight, or nine or ten in number. For example, there are eight tourism regions and eight regional health boards. There are nine physical planning regions; these are identical with the regions for the Industrial Development Authority. These all rest on the existing county boundaries. There are ten regions for the

[1]*Regional Studies—Ireland* (Buchanan Report) 1968.

purposes of the regional technical colleges, and these, as we have seen, breach the county boundaries.

Of all these regions only two are identical—for the purposes of physical planning and for the IDA; but those for tourism, health, and civil defence are, overall, not significantly different from these, although there are significant differences in detail. The rest vary widely.

As to detail, the extreme case is the county of Roscommon which for all practical purposes is in three different regions for the purposes of physical planning, tourism and health, and is divided between two regions for the purposes of the regional technical colleges. Buchanan would also divide up Roscommon between regions.

The first question then is that of the county boundaries. Are they to be taken as fixed or not? We will know what the government's proposals on this are in the near future when the White Paper on local government is published. Clearly this issue should be settled one way or another. If we are to stick to the county, then let us be consistent in the subsequent decisions. If the county is to be significantly altered then let us be clear cut in what is done. Either way, let the region be made up of whole counties, whether existing or altered ones. This is the only way by which the region can be related to the local government (and, later, the community) structure. To fail to make this relation would be disastrous for all three.

If there is to be effective regionalism let there be a single region for every purpose. Why should this be? There is no doubt but that different regions for different purposes would best suit individual services. But it does not follow that what best suits individual services makes the best overall arrangement. The reason for this becomes clear if we consider what purpose a coherent system of regionalism can best serve.

A main argument for regionalism is that it can make a useful contribution to planning for national development as a whole. At the level of central government it is possible to deal only in aggregates. The needs and the resources of each region differ one from another. By identifying those needs and mobilising those resources one may get greater overall initiative and effort than would be possible if development were to depend solely on the information and direction available at the centre. This kind of regional mobilisation is also important in order to help to redress the imbalance between various regions and to prevent it becoming worse.

It is not generally realised how complex is our system of government viewed from any given geographical area. Apart from small and specialised bodies there must be something like 30 major government organisations operating in any given place. The problem of development in any regional area is, basically, to get all these diverse organisations to work in some sort of interrelated way in accordance with the special needs of the region.

We think therefore of regionalism as basically a means of serving the needs of a particular area and of mobilising the resources in that area that are available, or that can be made available, to tackle those needs.

If we are to think in regional terms and also in terms of getting going within the region the interplay of all the complex central organisations that operate there, then three conditions must be satisfied.

A. Regional Planning

First, there must be an adequate system of planning to ensure that local needs and the administrative equipment that is available for meeting those needs are effectively married. There must be agreement on common demographic features, agreement on objectives and agreement on the dove-tailing of programmes. This means not only a local-planning organisation but also a local focus where effective decision-making can take place as between the various administrative agencies that exist. If numbers of these are working to different administrative areas these conditions cannot be satisfied. So, if we look to regionalism as a means of achieving overall development within the region the boundaries must be clearly and uniformly defined for all services. Without that it would never be possible to transfer any effective decision-making power to the regions and thus to the people.

B. Regional Representation

The second condition for effective regionalism is a representative system. It is not easy to meet this condition and all I can do is throw out a few suggestions. There are two main interests to be represented. There is first, of course, the people themselves in whatever way this can be best achieved. I shall come back to this.

Secondly, there is the need to represent the various administrative agencies that are operating within the region. Here there is something to be learned from the representative side of the Regional Development Organisations now being established. It is clear that unless the various administrative agencies can be pulled together by some sort of representative system there is virtually no chance of their overcoming the centralising forces and of achieving an adequate degree of discretion from their central headquarters in Dublin. Should these forces not be overcome there would be little chance of getting the agencies to work smoothly together in the interests of the region

H

Representation for these agencies is relatively simple. If each of them were to have, as the Devlin Report recommends,[2] a regional director operating within the region with a considerable power of local decision then he would make an effective representative on a regional body. Not all of thirty or more of these administrative organisations operating within the region could be directly represented on the main regional body. So it will be necessary to think of a number of subsidiary bodies for broad areas of activity in the region—agriculture, industry, environmental services, educational services, health services, etc.—on which the appropriate official bodies would be represented by their regional directors.

Clearly, in each of these areas there are a number of interest groups, and provision should be made to have them represented, too. Clearly, too, the people at large should have some degree of representation on these subsidiary bodies, whether by direct election, nomination, or co-option. Finally, the chairman and one other person—that is, a public representative and an official—might represent that subsidiary body on the main regional board. The main regional board would thus consist of the nominees of the subsidiary boards. It should also contain popularly elected members if it is to be a genuinely democratic body.

How to achieve adequate and democratic public representation is a more difficult problem. It was formerly believed that popular election was the democratic way of getting public representation in the administration of services. It is clear that that does not now really commend itself to people in this country; hence there has been only limited recourse to popular election and most "representatives" are in practice nominated or co-opted. This is an issue that needs to be thrashed out. My own view is that in the short run the formula worked out for the Regional Development Organisations might, to begin with, make a suitable mix. This provides for nominees of the popularly elected bodies in the region, of administrative organisations, and of other interests. However, if there is to be genuine representation some element of direct, popular election is an essential ingredient of any real form of regionalism. If there is to be a board for the region as a whole, and if it is to have popularly elected members, then, once again, the area they represent must be clear-cut and the same for all purposes.

C. Regional Executives

The third requirement of the regional body is an effective executive. Its functions will relate to planning over the whole range of govern-

[2]*Report of Public Services Organisation Review Group, 1966–69*, p. 160–162.

mental responsibilities—social, economic, environmental and cultural—in the region; but it will not attempt to take on the jobs of the existing agencies. Nonetheless it must have power to insist that planning is done, that programmes are dove-tailed and that obligations are discharged.

This calls for two conditions to be fulfilled. These are, first, a strong chief executive, such as we are accustomed to in the state-sponsored bodies. In my view he should be not only chief executive but chairman of the regional body and be flanked with a small, but high-powered, staff equipped with the most modern administrative skills. Secondly, he must be supported by a genuine system of popular representation. Again, it is clear that these call for jurisdiction exercised over a clearly defined area.

If all of this is to be made work a further condition must be filled. Both the representative and administrative sides of regionalism will survive only if there is brought about a strong sense of community within the region itself. This in turn requires that there be a single region for all regional purposes with which individuals and groups can identify themselves.

If we want to get real power closer to the people these are the sorts of conditions that must be fulfilled. If there were to be a credible and effective general administrative organ in each region it would be feasible to think of decentralising large blocks of work from central government to the regions. This would provide a practicable programme for reversing the flow of power to Dublin.

III. POWER TO THE REGIONS?

So, if you want to see power to the people look closely, at least as a first step, at what is happening in the regions. Are they given uniform boundaries? Are they being given adequate public representation? Are they being given adequate administrative underpinning? Are they based on areas that can grow into real communities? Are there plans to transfer real powers to them?

Chapter 8

IS THERE A FUTURE FOR THE DISTRICT?*

I suppose the real question is: Is there a future for local government? I accept the premise of the White Paper[1] (2.1.1.) that "a system of local self government is one of the essential elements of democracy". If operational meaning is to be given to the expression, we must have a view of the place of "a system of local self government" in our society. This is not the place to attempt a philosophy of local government; but it is fair to say that we do not have in Ireland "a system of local self government": we have the unsystematic local administration of a dwindling number of services. It is not a system, it is not local, and it is not self government. The argument of this paper is that, if one wishes to have a *system* of self government that is genuinely *local* then one must grasp the crucial significance of the district.

1. THE CONTEXT OF REFORM

The argument for and against the district in a system of local government has to be seen, if it is to be properly understood, in a wider context than that of our existing local government. So two preliminary points must be made.

The first is that on which the comments[2] (3.1.) of the Institute of Public Administration on the White Paper rest. It is that the objective, in looking at the structure of local government, is to see it in the context of government as a whole. Is there a *system* of government in operation in any given place? This is to consider not merely the existing services of existing local government agencies, but all services of government. We normally consider government from the viewpoint of individual functions; this present approach leads us to consider all the functions of

*Based on an address delivered at a seminar on Local Government Reorganisation convened by the Institute of Public Administration at Galway, 25-26 November, 1971. Reprinted from ADMINISTRATION, Vol. 19 (1971) 4.
[1]*Local Government Reorganisation*, 1971, Prl. 1572.
[2]*More Local Government: A Programme for Development* (Chubb Report) 1971.

government within a given area. What are the operations of government in any given area? Would the discharge of governmental functions be improved or disimproved there if it were done in a related, systematic way? Would this involve taking some of the decisions within the area, and if so, what kinds of decisions?

Thus the enquiry starts off from the basis that if we could arrive at a suitable area for various kinds of functions it should be possible systematically to get sub-systems going, to relate them together and thus to decentralise some at least of the decision-making in relation to those functions to political and administrative centres within that area. In a nutshell, this approach derives from a value that leads one to choose as between function and area, *the area*; as between the special (and unsystematic) and the general (and systematic), the *general*; and as between centralisation and decentralisation of decision and discretion, *decentralisation*.

The second preliminary point is to give adequate weighting to three concepts crucial to considering the structure of government from the viewpoint of area, system and decentralisation. These are the concepts of (a) hierarchy, (b) roles, and (c) efficiency.

(a) *Hierarchy*

Of these, the basic one is that of hierarchy. It is often assumed that in a small country it is possible to have a "flat" system of administration and that a system of tiers of government seems too complex. However, when we examine the administrative structure of existing services we find not flat structures but hierarchical ones. Even more striking is that one can discern a pattern in the *number* of tiers of levels in each hierarchy. We are all familiar with the notion of a hierarchy of gradings within the headquarters of any organisations of size; but what has been demonstrated very clearly from the IPA study of the field services of the centralised organisations is that these field services of the centralised organisations are also organised on a hierarchical principle.[3] Considered as a whole, there is much confusion in the areas covered by each level of each hierarchy; but there is much uniformity in the *number* of levels. If we try to plot into a matrix what is happening we find a large number of hierarchical systems operating on five levels. Not every service uses the full five levels, and each tends to have its own definition of what should be covered by each level. Nonetheless, an overall picture emerges.

We see in operation a hierarchical system of five levels, stretching

[3]*More Local Government,* Appendix IV.

from (1) a *community* level, through (2) a *district* level, through (3) a *county* level, through (4) a *regional* level, to (5) the *centre*. One can conclude that whatever about the needs of any individual service, in practice there is need for five levels if all the needs of all the services are to be provided for.

This analysis cannot be applied to every national service. Some services are by their nature, so far as the nation is concerned, centralised (e.g. foreign affairs); but their number is less than most people have been prepared to recognise. Again, some services are so thin on the ground that they do not need—and it would be extravagant for them to have—a localised hierarchical structure. But these are special cases.

In general, if one approaches the mass of the business of government —that is the business carried out by the various kinds of agencies of state, central, local and functional—from the viewpoint of areas, systems and decentralisation, one sees the central importance of this notion of hierarchy. It is essential to work out the implications of this.

(b) *Roles*

The second concept, that of roles for each level of hierarchy, is a simple management one. If there are to be different hierarchical levels then it ought to be possible to work out a role appropriate to each level. That this is not being done or, where it is attempted, is being done in a confused way, makes it urgent to apply this basic management concept. If we could agree on broad outlines of roles for each level of the hierarchy we should make a significant advance. It is necessary to get the concepts clear, even if we must be flexible in applying them to individual services. It is inevitable that some services will never fit neatly into any comprehensive scheme. It is certain, at least in the middle run, that it will be a long haul to fit others in. But that is not to say that one cannot have clear ideas of what ought to be done, even though it may take a number of years for those objectives to be achieved in practice. This is what institutional development is about.

One can look at the problems of roles from two aspects, the administrative and the representative. These, of course, merge into one another but, as a first step, it is useful to keep them conceptually distinct. Let us begin with the administrative issue.

I would propose, as a basis for discussion, that the essential role of the central in administrative terms, is that of *leadership*—trying to tease out national objectives; to set national standards of achievement; to review progress; and, broadly, to allocate resources.

The role of the *region* I would see as that of identifying regional needs, planning for alleviating them, allocating resources available to the region amongst the various regional agencies in accordance with this regional plan, and reviewing results.

At the *county* level I would see the focusing of the technological services, mainly the engineering and architectural ones. It is clear that certain technological services—e.g. major general hospitals—will demand greater areas than the county and may have to be based on the region or perhaps something larger still.

On the *district* it is possible to base the personal services where technological issues are not significant or, in the context of "customer relations", predominant.

I do not see any significant administrative role at the *community* level.

In a sense it is easier to tackle the issue of representation. In principle, all that is required is that there be a level of public representatives for each of the administrative levels to take the major decisions appropriate to that level, and to represent the "consumers" of the services provided by it. Here it is possible to think in terms of five levels—the four administrative ones, with, in addition, representation at the community level. However, when we get down to devising representative schemes a number of problems arise.

First, it is clear that where we think of the provision of specialised services—education, agriculture, health—there is need to make provision for two kinds of representation: there are the consumers—such as parents and farmers—who need some special kind of representative system; and there are the specialised interests involved—churches, medical profession, teachers, and the like.

Secondly, as we move from the community level up to more specialised areas, especially the regional level, this problem of specialised representation becomes more important. Moreover, the range of the authority—which, if it were to cover all the functions of government at its level, would have to be very wide indeed—would call for very extensive and complex representative systems.

Thirdly, there is the problem of those services that hitherto have had no representational system at all.

Fourthly, the kinds of demands on public representatives, especially at a well-functioning regional level, are likely to be such as to call for new kinds of skills on their part, skills that may not be plentifully available.

To list these difficulties is not to suggest that the open democratic system of public representation is not a necessary and important part of any restructuring of our institutions of government. It is not to suggest, either, that the democratically elected public representative should not play the decisive role in relation to this complex representative system. But it is to recognise that some difficult problems will arise if we try to have a hierarchical administrative system married to a representative system of equal sophistication.

(c) *Efficiency*

The third concept is that of efficiency. This is dealt with in some detail later. Here it is enough to make a sharp distinction between "efficiency" as a technological concept—relevant at, say, the county level—and the kind of "efficiency" relevant to normal regional functions, and to district functions.

The essential role of the region, if what has been said about it is accepted, becomes planning and resource allocation. Efficiency here is thus related to quality of information and of decision-making. At the district level, which is our immediate concern here, efficiency relates to the quality of the services and the *manner* in which they are provided. District services are, as we have seen, personal services. At that level, therefore, efficiency, must be seen in these personal, human terms. At that level the *manner* in which a service is provided may be at least as important as its technological efficiency as when a distressed customer cannot have his problem remedied without a vast struggle in the bureaucratic toils. This issue may be all the more important where the customer is poor, ill, or miserable and where the service may not have much technological content—such as income maintenance. In such instances, the efficiency of the service is to be measured by its promptness, its imaginativeness, and its helpfulness.

So we have at each level of the hierarchy a different requirement of efficiency. At the centre it is effective leadership, at the region effective planning, at the county effective technology. But at the district it is, in the simplest possible terms, prompt and compassionate service. This, in turn, often calls for the relating together of two or more services at the individual or family level. One of the strongest arguments for providing decision centres at the district level is the possibility it opens up of relating together the personal services at that level, in the interest, to repeat, of prompt and compassionate service. Under our existing system this is almost impossible to achieve.

What begins to emerge from these considerations, therefore, is a conception of local government on a sophisticated level. First, the services are made as local as their inherent nature permits them to be. Secondly, this enables services of all sorts to be grouped together and systematised at each appropriate level so that there can be a comprehensive approach to the problems of individuals, families, communities, areas, etc. at each of these levels. Thirdly, it permits people and their representatives— directly elected, professional, interest and other—to participate in the decision-making which effects their lives at each of these appropriate levels. If local government is to mean anything in real terms these are the criteria by which it is to be judged.

II. THE DISTRICT IN PRACTICE

In this discussion *district* has two slightly different meanings. In rural areas, it is defined[4] as a sub-county unit with a relatively small population—three, four or five of them in a typical county with a population somewhere in the range of 10,000 to 20,000 or thereabouts. In a conurbation, such as around Dublin, the district must necessarily be a larger unit in terms of population. It would probably have a population somewhere in the 50,000 to 200,000 range[5], perhaps less, perhaps more, depending on geographical circumstances. Is it realistic to think of districts in these terms?

The district as a local government unit has, of course, a very long history. We think of the walled town of medieval times, and of the chartered borough of later times, each leading a life of some independence. During the 19th century many towns lost their borough status, but had added to them various other functions relating to public health, lighting, etc. So we have still, apart from the four county boroughs, 84 towns with their own form of local government, many of them very small places indeed. Nonetheless, these towns at the sub-county level, contain about half the total number of all the elected local representatives in the country.

The history of the district in the rural areas is more chequered. The oldest of these rural areas is the barony; and many baronies stretch back to at least the beginning of our history. In the last century the barony was gradually superseded by another concept, that of the union, a rural hinterland based on a town of some significance. Later in the century, for public health purposes, a rural district based on the "union" was created. When it contained an urban area a separate urban district was often created. As we know, unions and rural districts were swept away after Independence. But the rural districts continued to have some vestigial existence in that they are normally the basis for the electoral areas for county council elections.

[4]See *More Local Government,* para. 4.2.10.
[5]ibid, para. 4.5.8.

The purpose of this historical excursus is simply to show that a sub-county unit, whether urban, rural or mixed, has a long history in this country.

The district has however not only an historical existence but also some sort of continuing life. The most obvious is, of course, the continuance of the borough, the urban district and the town under town commissioners. Notwithstanding the great administrative weakness of the smallest among these, they seem to have some significant political will to survive, if the reactions of public representatives to the proposals in the local government White Paper are a reliable guide. In the rural areas also there has been some survival after death in that there has grown up on a wholly informal basis, under the existing county council system, a practice of committees of county councillors for an electoral area meeting together to discuss problems common to that area. Indeed, the White Paper proposes to recognise this to some degree and also to give it some formal existence.[6] At the administrative level, also, one can see from the information collected by the IPA study[7] that many of the existing county council services are in fact based on a system of district administration.

The same point can be seen in the existing field services of a number of the government departments—for example agriculture, lands, justice, posts and telegraphs, etc. This is not to argue that all the systems for these services are the same, but that in practice it has been found useful and convenient to base the basic direct services of these departments on towns and some form of district organisation. It is noted that when a special sort of problem, such as that of the Gaeltacht emerges, recourse must be had to some form of district organisation. Notwithstanding the great centralising forces operating in relation to education and to health, one can see within the centralised, or regional, structure attempts being made to systematise the personal services—schooling and community care services—on some sort of local, district structures. So that, even within existing systems of national, regional and county administration, some degree of life remains in the concept of the district.

It is perhaps not fully realised that in formally attempting to ignore the need for a sub-county unit of this kind, this country is exceptional.

We have recently seen decisions in England and Scotland to base the reform of local government substantially on the creation and strengthening of sub-county districts. Mention is often made of the attempts now being made in Scandinavia to reduce the number of local authorities; but when that process has been completed there will still remain a vast

[6]Para. 11.5.1.
[7]Para. 4.2.2.

array of authorities on what we might call a sub-county basis. The same is, of course, true of other European countries. For example, in France there are 38,000 communes. Even if we reduced that number to the relative Irish population, we could, on the French model, have almost 2,000 local authorities. We have something over 100, and the White Paper would reduce these to perhaps 50 or 60. The contrast is striking.

That the time has come to think afresh about these issues and perhaps to call a halt to the destruction of small local authorities, which has been a feature of our system since Independence, is suggested by the proposals in the White Paper itself. It certainly seems to be supported by the comments which have been made by very many bodies on the White Paper, discussed by Mr. Roche.[8] The Minister for Local Government in concluding a debate on the estimate for local government, specifically said[9] that there would be created in the Dublin area a number of local bodies catering for a population of the order of 100,000. The new Eastern Health Board, as part of its restructuring of its community care services, proposes to experiment with the idea of basing these community care services on something similar to the bodies the Minister for Local Government appears to have in mind.

So, when we talk about the district we are not talking about a chimera but of something with a long historical existence, with a remarkable capacity for surviving, under the surface as it were, to meet administrative needs, and with very considerable promise of getting formal recognition to meet significant political and administrative needs in the future.

III. COMING TO GRIPS WITH THE DISTRICT

Let us look a little more closely at the issues that seem to be emerging. One can understand the role of the district by considering the issues that arise from two crucial concepts—those of growth and of efficiency.

A. CONSIDERATIONS FROM GROWTH

(i) *Growth of Government*

The growth in the size, the pervasiveness, and the importance of government in the modern state, both absolutely and relatively, requires from us new thinking about the structure of government in our society. The growth of government from such activities as the stimulating of economic activity may, perhaps, be self-liquidating. But now a great,

[8]D. Roche: "Local Government Reorganisation: The Issues Involved," ADMINISTRATION, Vol. 19 (1971) 4.

[9]*Dáil Debates*, 27 October, 1971, Col. 408.

and steadily increasing, part of government comes from its redistributive function.

Economic growth of itself does not distribute its benefits to the members of the community in a manner that most people in modern society would consider adequate. So, it is necessary for the state to step in and build up a complex redistributive mechanism to ensure that the old, the poor, the handicapped, the widowed, etc., get an increasing proportion of whatever affluence is available in the community. Given our present state of political and administrative sophistication there does not seem to be any likelihood of a change that, absolutely or relatively, will reduce the redistributive role of the state. Neither does it seem that the pressure on it to supply more and more complex public services in the field of health, education, etc. will be relaxed. So, overall, we may expect more government and not less.

There are three features of this growth that are relevant here. These are (a) the growth of specialisms, (b) the problem of integration of services, and (c) the growing alienation of the citizen.

(a) Specialisms

The growth in the scale and the comprehensiveness of government has made it possible to sort out, within large problems, a number of sub-problems and to break these up into separate functions on which degrees of specialisation can be based. One can see this happening very clearly in the areas of poverty and health. This specialisation has, in general, made for notable progress within the specialisms.

From the middle of the last century the notion of "poverty" has come to be seen as a cluster of specific causes of poverty—unemployment, widowhood, large families, ill-health, handicap, itinerancy, deprivation, etc., etc. From this cluster it has been possible to isolate individual problem areas and to tackle these. Because, considered in themselves, these problems were fairly constant throughout the whole country, each of them could be adequately considered on a national basis and so national levels of specialisation and expertise in relation to each of them could be achieved. One can see the benefits of this kind of specialisation in the hospital services, where the levels of skill, and the cost of the appropriate equipment, required to diagnose and to treat each branch of disease now require concentration of these very scarce resources in as few places in the country as possible.

(b) Integration

However, the pervasiveness of government that follows its growth shows the limits to which the segregation of sub-problems can be carried. This is because many social ills do not exist in isolation: they are intertwined and interrelated. These clusters of interrelated sub-problems are not uniformly distributed throughout the community but are themselves clustered around individuals, families, and localities. To come to grips with a number of these issues it is necessary to find a way to reintegrate the specialised functions. Otherwise, dealing, however efficiently, with one function and ignoring others, or having others dealt with separately and in an unrelated way, will bear the same relationship to social illness as the treating of individual symptoms bears to personal illness. Delinquency, handicap, deprivation, unemployment, bad housing, psychiatric disorders, etc., etc. tend in their own extreme forms to cluster in this way. The individual in trouble often cannot be adequately helped unless he is seen as part of a family in trouble and, as is being increasingly realised, of a community in trouble. In the same way problems of agricultural development, for example, have to be considered in relation to problems of housing, problems of restructuring of decaying communities, problems of the economical provision of public services, etc. So, after the stage of the breaking down and specialisation of functional services comes the second stage of integrating the specialised services that have been developed.

Even within a single branch of these services, this process can be seen in operation. For example, the health services, which have now been put on a regional basis, have within the region been grouped under three broad headings—general hospital services, special hospital services and community care services. The last of these comprises a very large number of personal services aimed at improving the general level of health in the community, but these impinge to a remarkable extent on welfare services, educational services and others.

For them to develop effectively it will be necessary to devise methods of working with these other types of services. Similarly, the special hospital services relate to mental illness, old age and handicap. Here again, at least a part of the solution seems to lie in bringing the services down to a community basis and in integrating them with other community services.

The point of all of this is that while it is convenient for the administrator to think of economic, social, cultural and environmental needs as distinct in themselves, and, indeed, comprising a number of distinct sub-needs, in practice human living is one, and all of these needs are inextricably bound-up with one another; but not to an equal extent in every place.

Perhaps the point emerges when one considers some specially intractable localised problem such as that of the Gaeltacht, which em-
braces needs that are economic, social, cultural and environmental. But
for any one of the thirty or so major agencies providing services in the
Gaeltacht areas the problem of the Gaeltacht as a unique phenomenon
does not take on a life of its own. So, somehow or other, we have to find
ways and means of integrating the various kinds of services so that they
will reinforce one another in their day-to-day activities.[10]

(c) *Alienation*

A further problem is that of the tension between specialisation and
comprehensibility. This is best illustrated in the old dichotomy of "Us"
and "Them". This has not in our society—as in others—led to violent
outbursts against the anonymous and the incomprehensible Them; but
it would be foolish to think that there is not a considerable and growing
problem in this respect. The work of any TD's clinic will bear this out.
The extraordinary private belief amongst the plain people of Ireland
that they will not get their rights except by the use of influence—and
that there are no such things really as citizens' rights—is a disturbing
phenomenon. Nothing like enough research has gone into this issue but
some recent figures about the attitudes of Irish people to administrative
bodies, as compared with those of other countries, are, so far as they
go, disturbing in the extreme.[11] One of the remedies here is to simplify
the system of administration and to bring it down to a comprehensible
scale so that people can see for themselves what is going on and the high
standards that are in fact practised by public servants and their elected
representatives.

This alienation of people from the system of government makes for
difficulties in other ways. First of all, the ease and economy with which
services can be administered depend enormously on acceptance by the
public of the bona fides of what is being done. If there is suspicion and
distrust then the difficulties of administration are intensified. Distrust
and disrespect encourage a sense of irresponsibility, to be seen in fairly
extensive vandalism. The lack of respect for the honesty of purpose of
public bodies encourages a disproportionate number of people to attempt
to defraud them. This in turn leads to building up bureaucratic safe-

---

[10]A point that emerges in the latest Gaeltacht Report, *Gniomh don Ghaeltacht,*
1971.

[11]I. Hart: "Public opinion on civil servants and the role and power of the individual in the local community", ADMINISTRATION, Vol. 18 (1970), pp. 375-391.

guards which themselves tend to alienate the people, and so a vicious circle is set moving.

(ii) Growth of Social Consciousness

The second consideration from growth is that special feature of our age, the growth of social consciousness and self assertiveness. People are now more impatient than they were, more intolerant of poor service, more violent in their reactions to what they believe to be wrong doing. Docility and tractability are now no longer marks of the population at large. With this change has come more determination to have a say in the decision-making which affects the citizens; participation is now one of the vogue words of our society. The very consequences of government itself have contributed to this process. Thanks to the growth of affluence, people now have more leisure, more time, and more opportunity to think, talk, and act about the problems of the community. The rise in education, in nutrition levels, in the level of health—these have meant that people are better equipped and personally more vigorous to take part in community affairs. The notion of representation, that people have moral rights to be represented at, and take part in, decision-making that affects their lives, is now widespread. A striking feature of the significance of this in our society has been the growth of nationally based interest groups and the sort of problems this growth is likely to raise for the future evolution of our society in terms of communications, participation, comprehensibility, and sheer efficiency, and the impact of these on the political system, are sharply, if impressionistically, conveyed in the recent pamphlet by Mr. Xavier Carty of a Tuairim discussion on these issues.[12]

But for our immediate purpose the striking example is the information thrown up by the researches of Messrs Donal Murphy and Gavin in the IPA study of local government.[13] Here we see an astonishing growth of voluntary community bodies based on our towns. The town of Nenagh with a population of 4,500 has 111 voluntary groups, and that of Westport with a population of just under 3,000 has 67 groups. Even two small towns in north Tipperary share, proportionately, in this growth of voluntary and community bodies. If this pattern is replicated throughout the country then one could guess that there would be in our towns as a whole one such body for every 40 of population. We have no precise information but one gets the impression that this is a process still in growth. This is certainly not decay. So, our society is becoming honeycombed with organisations of people participating in

[12]*Government and People: Creative Dialogue.* A report of the 1969/70 Communications Conference by Xavier Carty, 1970.
[13]Para. 4.1.7.

one way or another in various kinds of community issues. That process is certain not to stop there.

The notion that there ought to be people in every community capable of speaking for the community with a fair degree of representativeness fits in with another important democratic need. That is the need to be able to view the operation of the public services in any particular area with some degree of balance and comprehensiveness. The services themselves exist to assist the people in one way or another and it is important, in the interest of the services, in the interest of those who hope to benefit from them, in the interest of those administering them, that there be some good communication system, some adequate system of review, that will say whether or not services are in fact living up to their pretensions. This is clearly an increasing need in our society. In addition there is the problem of opening constructive channels to attempt new initiatives for improving services, for working out new types of services, for devising new systems of social organisation. The system of social service councils that grew up from a powerful initiative in Kilkenny, and is now spreading to other towns, is an interesting example of this; but there still remains a big problem of linking, as it were, the needs as felt in local places and as seen by responsible members of local communities, with those policies and practices operated by persons administering centralised services. Here, too, there is a source of potential tension in our society.

As the services become bigger, more specialised, more centralised, they replace the range of local decision-making and adaptiveness by highly specialised, highly skilled, but remote rule makers. It *is* possible to combine this with a fair degree of local discretion at the administrative level; but this seems to be a skill not possessed by Irish public administration. Everywhere—or almost everywhere—the centralised services fail to give any adequate degree of discretion and scope for adaptation to the local representative of the service.

B.   CONSIDERATIONS FROM EFFICIENCY

These problems of the growth and complexity of modern public administration and of the growth of a more critical, better educated, and better organised set of consumers raises acutely the problem of the overall efficiency of the services provided. Here, to repeat a point made above, we have to distinguish between the technological efficiency and what one might call the political efficiency of the services as perceived at the point at which they are received. For certain services

—for example in surgical hospitals—the technological efficiency service may become, literally, a matter of life and death. But for many other services a high level of technological efficiency may be outweighed by a low level of personal service. Thus for many consumers of electricity occasional failures in the supply of electricity may be much less offensive to them than occasional failures in courtesy in the local branch office of the ESB. The charm of the rural postman may often outweigh deficiencies in the transport of letters and the courtesy of the local telephone operator soften the fury caused by faulty connections. In relation to the technological services one should not, of course, push this argument too far.

But there are also a very large number of services where technological arguments of efficiency do not apply at all or apply to only a limited degree. It is here that the personal factor in relation to efficiency assumes great importance. Basically, the overwhelming mass of the services provided by government end up in services performed by officials for citizens. Where there is a breakdown in the technological services the same consideration applies. When we look to define efficiency in relation to the great mass of public services as they impinge on the citizen and his family we must do so in these human, personal terms.[14]

So we can think of efficiency in relation to these services as comprising (i) responsiveness, (ii) comprehensive structure, (iii) simplicity, (iv) initiative and (v) opportunities for review.

(i) *Responsiveness*

By responsiveness we mean, basically, the ability to react quickly and sensibly to unusual circumstances. This calls for some focus of decision close to the point of service to enable services to be varied in some way. It would be possible to combine this sort of thing with a highly centralised service; but only with great difficulty, a difficulty seldom overcome in the Irish system of public administration. This centralises not only skills and expertise but also even elementary areas of decision-making in the hands of those at the headquarters of the service. The local agents, where they exist, have little or no discretion in varying the rules of the service to meet individual and special cases. Part of the strength of specialised services is uniformity, and the price

[14]This is a particular application of an argument that could be put in more general terms. Thus ". . . to ensure that the organisation and management of R & D is logical, flexible, humane and decentralised, the prerequisites of an efficient system"—Lord Rothschild, *Organisation and Management of Government, R & D*, HMSO Cmnd. 4814, 1971.

of uniformity is absence of local discretion. This absence of discretion leads, very often, especially in the personal services, to a sort of absent minded heartlessness in the application of rules to unsuitable cases. At the local level, nobody can be held responsible for the unsuitability of these applications because no one has the discretion to alter these applications. At the centre, too, the need to adjust or elaborate where the rules operate harshly or inefficiently or wastefully to particular classes of cases does not, for the same reason, get communicated.

Apart from these considerations from the viewpoint of the 'customer', there are significant problems of responsiveness from the viewpoint of the agency providing the service. Every service needs to be in constant communication with the customer, tuned in to the changes in needs and demands, to the changing environment in which the service is provided, to the advance of new knowledge, to varying social and other conditions, to the relationships of the service with other services.

This is a major problem of public administration. Unlike business administration it does not have a ready means of communication where its service tends to fail to meet change in needs. If a business man provides a service that is becoming out of date his customers will go elsewhere and an effective communication will be made by means of falling sales. Partly because most Irish public services are monopolies, partly because they are seldom subject to a profit and loss account, and partly from the nature of the services provided, this method of communicating to the managers of the service whether or not their service is now meeting the need of their customers is lacking to them. Other countries can ease their problems by having a regular system of administrative tribunals for reviewing grievances, but we are notably backward in this. So the establishment of some alternative system of communication is of great importance to the managers of public services to ensure that the services are relevant, vigorous, and adaptive. The attempt is now being made through planning mechanisms to provide public bodies with the kind of communication private enterprises get by profit; but planning itself, if it is to indicate right roads to take and to review the choices taken, is dependent on good communication systems.

Of course, the political system can make valuable, effective, and forceful communications but there is ample evidence that much dissatisfaction is not communicated in this way, and much of it in this country now tends to by-pass the political system.[15] The successful

[15]As emerged with great vividness at the Tuairim seminar on which Mr Carty's paper was based.

running of a highly centralised service calls for a first-class communication system to ensure effective responsiveness. This seldom exists and the problems it poses, as price for the benefits of centralisation, are seldom recognised, much less tackled.

There is, therefore, for the efficient running of a wide-spread but centralised service, great need for good communication and information systems so that the service may be kept constantly up-to-date. Where there is not adequate definition of role between those at the point of service who actually administer the service and those at the centre whose task it is basically to adjust the service to changes in need, this kind of varied information input is extremely difficult to achieve. Where these difficulties are not surmounted, and that is frequently, a form of bureaucratic sclerosis begins to develop and those at the centre of the service, and the service as a whole, become progressively unable to move with the real and changing world. For those at the centre, therefore, who are concerned to ensure that their service is as good as it possibly can be, the very fact of centralisation—to set against its manifold benefits—becomes a liability. There are difficulties here to overcome which, in the nature of the kinds of blanket centralisation practised by Irish public administration, are singularly intractable.

(ii) *Comprehensiveness*

The structural problem also arises because we become increasingly aware of the need to make services more interrelated and comprehensive. This in its full development requires a shift of the bases on which the services are organised from the isolation of functions to the integration of analogous services in a given area. There is increasing need, as the services in the aggregate cover most of the activities of most peoples' lives, to have them based, so far as possible, on a "general practitioner" principle. This principle of a highly trained, highly educated, but *general* practitioner, is one that both in medicine and in the church gives very good service indeed. There are a number of complaints from medical and clerical practitioners about their roles; but one has only to compare their system, whatever its defects, with the absences of similar systems in, say, the agricultural or the welfare areas to realise the advantages of the well-trained general practitioner concept. The general practitioner is able to deal with a large number of problems at his own level, and, where they make demands greater than he can fulfil, his work can be supplemented, either on a more specialised level beneath him by means of medical or religious auxiliaries, or at a highly specialised level above him by means of highly skilled specialists in specific functions. As a result of this type of general practitioner approach it is possible to conceive of services that will take a comprehensive view of the realities lying behind the symptoms that come to notice. So, this may not be an isolated case of juvenile delinquency, but a symptom of a whole family in trouble or that, not just the case of an old person in hardship, but of a whole community in trouble. It is of the nature of the general practitioner concept that he, having diagnosed this more deep-rooted ailment, can get some collective decision-making going to get adequate treatment. If all the relevant services formally relate, not to one another in a given place, but each to an isolated headquarters in Dublin, then the general practitioner becomes virtually powerless. The logic is clear: an appropriate degree of "relatedness" and of decision-making must be lodged in some meaningful and manageable geographical area.

(iii) *Simplicity*

A third aspect of efficiency is that of simplifying the administration of the services. No one who views our system of public administration from the grass roots up, as it were, cannot but be impressed at how extraordinarily complex it is and how difficult to understand. Those of us who feel reasonably at home in the administrative world are often baffled by this complexity. What must it be like for the ordinary citizen, perhaps poor, bereaved and frightened faced with this Kafka-esque world? This situation is in nobody's interest, least of all in the interest of those who provide the services. So one of the principal aims, from the point of view of efficiency, is to simplify the structures and make them comprehensible to the ordinary citizen. From this one may hope that once he understands the way the system works, once he understands the altruistic motives of the providers of the service, the whole system will become more acceptable to him and to his friends and no longer an object of hatred, fear or contempt.

It is necessary to simplify, also, in order to try to achieve some clarity of purpose in the services as a whole. Where the services are complex, where they have grown up at haphazard and without much regard to the growing up of other services, there is much crossing of the lines, much over-lapping, and much under-lapping. In these circumstances it is very difficult for those managing the services to have clear, comprehensive purposes in operating their services in the general interest. This almost invariably leads to waste of money and of human effort.

(iv) *Initiative*

This and the communication problem underlie the need for building into each service room for local initiative and discretion within the broad national framework of each service. In this way services in their local administration can be kept relevant and a means is provided for bringing to light, as seen locally, the needs for new developments on the national front. The problem of reconciling central control with genuine local initiative is no small one; but a greater problem still is when no local initiative, no local communication, can effectively take place.

(v) *Review*

This leads on to the fifth issue of efficiency, which is that of review. This has already been touched on. It is of the nature of a changing world, especially in a world of accelerating change, that what was relevant last year is rather less relevant this year and will be more irrelevant next year. It is essential to keep the services in constant contact with this changing world. This requires a built-in system of review based on the needs of customers and of local circumstances that will communicate to those at the centre what improvements and changes need to be made in existing services in order to keep them fully abreast of their changing environment.

These arguments are put forward, not to say that centralisation is a bad thing and that decentralisation is better. There are clear advantages in centralisation. There are also severe disadvantages. The general argument here is that the advantages can be maintained and the disadvantages reduced by an administrative structure devised on a hierarchical system with an adequate role for each level of the structure.

I think it is clear from these considerations of the growth of government and the growth of citizen vigour, and from the need for the efficient provision of services, that what is needed is a well-devised hierarchical structure with appropriate powers of decision at each level and that each level be related to a vigorous and relevant representative system. This in turn means that the services should be based on appropriate (and, of course, standard) areas and made as comprehensive, interrelated and integrated as possible so that they will win the understanding, the acceptance and the confidence of those they are designed for. This is, of course, the case for a well-articulated system of local government.

IV. WHY NOT THE COUNTY OR SOMETHING BIGGER?

It would be possible to organise a system of local administration based on the county that would meet most of the points made above. It does not follow that the county would be the best unit for all purposes. Other things being equal, the smallest unit possible is likely to be the best in terms of reducing the provision of personal services to a human scale for the ordinary citizen. Contrary to the popular belief, our counties are not small—a number of them cover very large areas. It is as far from Ballinasloe to the extreme west of Galway as from Ballinasloe to Dublin. It is farther from Waterville to Tarbert than from Belfast to Dublin. The very fact that a large number of the personal services have to be organised on a district basis shows that the county is, in practice, too large for convenient working. The point is that unless the technological requirements call for larger size, the human requirements should take precedence, and they quite clearly call for small size—not large size. This is the point about roles made at the beginning of this paper: that there are certain services that are best performed at different levels of the hierarchy of authority. Where the personal services are concerned they should be pushed down as low as possible.

The same sort of argument applies, only with more force, to the regional levels as the evolution of the new regional health boards clearly shows. Here it has become necessary to push the community care services down to the county level, and below, even though the boards have been so recently organised on a regional basis. An important feature of these services is not only physical but psychological propinquity.

It seems, therefore, that the White Paper in proposing[16], however tentatively, to reverse the trend towards the county and towards bigger units has recognised a real need of our community to bring some services at least down to sub-county areas. Where personal services are concerned there is little or no question of technology or of economies of scale arising from substantial capital investment; but a problem does arise of providing adequate personnel to staff these services. It is hard to get and to keep good people for very small authorities. Hence the proposal in the White Paper, which is elaborated in the IPA proposals, for a single county staffing structure, which would make personnel available for the district. In this way the benefits of scale as far as the county is concerned can be obtained and at the same time the districts can be adequately staffed. There is a fair amount of

[16]White Paper, para. 11.15.1. IPA proposals, para. 4.2.

experience of the provision of high level administrative staff—for example county managers—and professional staff—for example county engineering staffs—by the county to urban districts to show that this expedient, while not ideal, is a reasonable solution to the personnel and staffing problem of the sub-county local authority.

V. PROPOSALS

The IPA proposals involve a three stage representative system. There would be the elected county council, the elected district council, and the community council. The proposals involve the election of county councils by county electoral areas—which would be identical with the district areas—in the same way as at present. In addition there would be election to the district councils by the same areas. The district councils would have on them representatives of the community council from the district, but in such a way that they would be a minority of the district council. The district council would consist of the county councillors elected for the district area, the district councillors, and the representatives of the community councils. In this way there would be a representative link with the county council upwards and with the community councils downwards. The district councils would thus be the bottom rung of the formal electoral system. These districts would comprise a significant town plus the surrounding countryside, making up something very similar to the existing electoral areas.

To bring this scheme into operation at the administrative level it would be necessary to have a three stage plan. The first stage would be to group the existing personal services of the county council under the district council and to staff the various offices with county personnel who at the same time would be officers of the district council under a district manager concerned with the full range of services of the district council. A second stage would be to add to these those services that are now partially operated on a local government basis—education, agriculture, justice, health, and welfare. The third stage would be to charge the district councils with the remaining personal services of the various government departments and state-sponsored bodies. Over a period of perhaps some years, therefore, the district councils would be built up into significant administrative units with a wide range of services in so far as they directly affect citizens. It would be the duty of the district council by its various representative and administrative facilities to tackle, in relation to those services, the problems that have been identified above.

VI.   IS IT POSSIBLE TO MAKE PRACTICAL PROGRESS ON THIS PROGRAMME?

The theme is local government, that is, government considered locally. Government is a marriage of politics and administration, with politics in the leading position. It is impossible, therefore, to consider this theme solely from the administrative viewpoint.

To make real progress in this area it is necessary to identify and have tackled five problem areas that are, at least in part, problems of politics. In two of these the issues are mixed, in that while they are primarily administrative, they are almost insoluble without political intervention. In the remaining three the issues are almost wholly political.

The first of these problems is the problem of administrative fragmentation. As we have seen our various public institutions have been established *ad hoc* to tackle problems as they have come into view. The urge towards specialisation has strengthened the sort of inherent urge towards the fragmentation of these services. However, as the state becomes more and more involved, the range of its interests has to widen, and it becomes progressively more necessary to take a view transcending these various fragmented institutions. Unfortunately, none of the institutions, not even the departments, seem to be able to rise above their fragmented condition. They seem to be helpless prisoners of the system. For example, the programme for giving flesh to the concept of district councils that has been outlined above would be quite impossible for the Department of Local Government to undertake for the reason that so many of the functions are the responsibilities of other departments and agencies which would not welcome, and would indeed oppose, any interference in their sphere of responsibilities by the Department of Local Government. It could be that the new Public Service Department will be able to help in this area, but it is inevitable that for a long time to come it will not be strong vis-a-vis the other departments. Moreover, it will be heavily preoccupied with trying to tackle the problems of central government in so far as they impinge on the real heart of the administration. So one must doubt that, at least initially, the Public Service Department will be able to make a direct attack on this problem.

Secondly, any such programme for change lacks a satisfactory intellectual basis. It is a great pity indeed that the Devlin Report, having provided a reasonable foundation for action on governmental institutions from the inside out, as it were, failed to do the corresponding analysis from the outside in.

So, problems of this kind that cut across the responsibility of Ministers and of various kinds of statutory and other agencies are both political and administrative. This is a classic case of the principle that war is too important to be left to the generals: institutions are too important to be left solely to the bureaucrats. The classic solution for this kind of dilemma is the commission of inquiry.

The third problem is a purely political one: it is that of political aims. What kind of society do we want and what values should determine that society? If we want our society to be humane, participative, efficient, and community-oriented, then the issue of the district is crucial. But here again we are appealing to political ideas and it is for the political process to determine whether these are relevant and acceptable.

Fourthly, there is the problem of representation as related to our administrative institutions. It is quite clear that the sort of society that is emerging around us demands a great deal more recourse to the representative system. In the light of this it is surprising that, although the opportunities for public representatives in this country are already very restricted in comparison with other democratic countries, the White Paper proposes to cut their number almost to half. Above all, there is need for the representative system to come to terms with the community and voluntary bodies that are growing up in such numbers throughout the country. The figures of voluntary bodies—111 in Nenagh for a population of 4,500 and of 67 in Westport for a population of 3,000—should be food for serious thought by those concerned with our political system. The same is true of the growth of the national interest groups which seem to be so anxious to by-pass the old political process. If politics does not concern itself about issues of this kind, what else can?

Fifthly, if we want to have a representative system—and some form of representation seems to be essential to the kind of society now developing—ought this system to be an elective one, a nominated one, or a mixture of the two? This also is a question of political choice. I will not hide my own preference. The gains of democracy in the 19th century, which depended on the extension of the representative system over as wide a range of government as was then possible, have been dissipated very largely in the present century. The representative system has been receding both in the number of representatives and in the relative range of duties of government to which it has been attached. I think this is a wholly retrograde movement and should be reversed. This is not to say that there is not room for the ministerial nominee and the professional and vocational representative, but the primacy of the public representative should be, in my view, established as a political aim and should be extended as far as possible.

The immediate problem is, of course, what can now be done? I would urge that while the political issues I have recited are being discussed one practical step could be taken. Just as the setting up of the Devlin inquiry enabled a look to be taken at nearly the whole range of government from the centre out, so do we need a comparable enquiry to look at government from the outside in, from the grass roots upwards.

With the result of these two enquiries we would be in a position to propose, perhaps, a first programme of institutional development for the Ireland of the late 20th century. The setting up of this inquiry—Devlin Mark II as one might call it—seems to me to be the next crucial step in the adaptation of our institutions.

To work out a philosophy of local government, to embody it in an adequate, sophisticated scheme of local bodies, and to implement such a scheme calls for a major heave to build up the kind of society, the type of integrated community, that will make for better living for everybody in this country in the coming years.

Chapter 9

ORGANISATION FOR DEVELOPMENT*

Glendower: I can call spirits from the vasty deep.
Hotspur: Why, so can I, or so can any man.
But will they come when you do call for them?
—Henry IV, part I.

I. THE ORGANISATIONAL PROBLEM

The first point I want to make is that Government is so big, so complex, so ambitious in its aim—or in the things the citizens expect of it
—that nowadays it is not very successful. Think of the last century, and
the tremendous improvements in the health of the people or in the levels
of education. Contrast these with the failures of western governments to
solve the problems of the late 20th century—inflation, increasing crime,
incomes policy and, (dare I say it?) regional development. This contrast
helps us to realise the urgency of thinking about the problems of modern
government. In particular, we should look at the institutions we use for
tackling these problems. Much of these institutions grew up, or were
devised, in the last century. Is it clear that we have a set of institutions
capable of tackling the problems of this part of this century? I think that
this is now one of the urgent problems that this country has to face. It
is striking to go to other countries at this time and to see the efforts that
are being made to adapt, develop and create new institutions for the
problems of our time. We see, indeed, some changes in our own institutions here, but the overall picture is one that is unplanned, *ad hoc,* disorganised—and inadequate.

In a nutshell, we are trying to tackle new, extremely difficult tasks
with inadequate instruments. It is not surprising that when we summon
those spirits from the vasty deep, they do not always come.

Let us look at the various institutions for tackling the problems of
western development. It is 20 years this year since the Underdeveloped
Areas Act to be administered by two Dublin based bodies—the IDA and

*A paper presented to the Western Development Conference, Galway, October,
1972. Reprinted from ADMINISTRATION, Vol. 20 (1973) 1.

an Foras Tionscail—was passed to foster industrial growth in the west. This was followed in 1959 by the Shannon Free Airport Development Company and in 1971 by the regional offices of the IDA, and now by the National Manpower Service of the Department of Labour, also regionally based. The main thrust of the work of the Land Commission has been in the west, together with forestry planting and sea fishery development. Since 1964 the west has had the pilot farm areas scheme of the Department of Agriculture and of the appropriate Committees of Agriculture with in each county a Pilot Area Development Team consisting of the CAO, the District Officer of the Land Project, the Farm Buildings Inspector, the District Engineer of the Office of Public Works and an inspector of the Land Commission. The tourism regions were set up in 1963 and the county councils have helped with tourist amenities, roads, etc. They have also been doing their main job of providing sanitary services, houses and so on. The Department of Local Government has also been concerned in the direct provision of some of these houses as has been the National Building Agency. In 1965 the county development teams were set up, consisting of the county manager, the chairman of the county council, the county engineer, the CAO, the CEO, and now the regional manager of the IDA. The Secretary of each team is, surprisingly, an officer of the Department of Finance and the teams are co-ordinated by a central committee in Dublin, chaired by a Finance official, and with representatives of the 9 government departments concerned with the west, and of the IDA. In 1969 were set up, on the model of a mid-west initiative, the Regional Development Organisations. The Department of the Gaeltacht was set up in 1956 and in 1958 was reconstituted Gaeltarra Eireann, both now under review. In all this period there has been a rising stream of reports, surveys, plans prepared by national research bodies and others.

Well, what are we to think of all of this? Some of these operations have been successful. Some are too new to be judged. But, on the whole, we can safely say that, despite all this administrative activity, the west has not yet been saved.

My main argument to-day is there is not much hope of doing much better unless we try to analyse its extraordinarily intractable problems and to base our solutions on that analysis.

Take "policy" first. Some people may think that the arrival of a regional policy from Brussels—when, if ever, it comes, and the associated funds with it—will answer all our problems. But an overall, international, "policy" of that kind may or may not be appropriate to the particular problems of our under developed regions. Think, for example, of the problems of the Gaeltacht areas within this western region. It

seems to me that a policy to be effective must be based on a close understanding and knowledge of the particular circumstances of the region,
and come up with solutions relevant to those circumstances. Local problems like this need a large number of highly skilled local people to work
out good solutions and to struggle for the resources to carry them
through.

The second problem is how to get the people within the region to
consent to the measures, perhaps some of them disagreeable, and to
give them their full support. In the kind of society we live in now that
kind of consent and support is not got simply by consulting a few wor-
thies. A high degree of involvement with legitimate representatives of
people is essential if the result is to be binding participation. What *system* have we for identifying and involving these local leaders?

The third problem is how adequate a system have we for relating together the various kinds of policies—economic, social, environmental,
etc.—in the regions? These must be worked out within the limitations of
the region itself. What size and shape will the population be? What,
broadly, are the financial and other resources likely to be? What are the
priorities for *this* region that the limited resources will impose? What
balance is to be struck between agricultural, industrial and tourist development? Between water, electricity and telephones? Between schools,
training, police and health? And, of course, as between all of these? This
is basic to any kind of regional policy. At present we have almost no
way, either in the regions or at central government, of answering these
questions—or even of asking them in these terms.

The fourth thing to look for is to see how well we actually do what
our policies say we will do. Have we the means to carry them through
on time? Have we a built-in control system to show us at an early stage
when things are going wrong, or when policies need to be changed? Is
there the discretion and flexibility to change such policies in mid-stream
as it were?

To ask these questions is to see the size of the organisational task
ahead of us. If we look at the administrative structures of Ireland west
of the Shannon we see that we simply do not possess, with one partial
exception, anything that will answer for its area the sort of questions I
have been asking. The exception is the Shannon Free Airport Development Company where since 1960 very substantial amounts of highly
skilled manpower—about 30 in the management grades—and very considerable sums of money—some £47 million, in all, or £36 million if we
exclude the airport—have been mobilised from public and private sources for the development of a relatively small area. In addition, in
SFADCO we have an organisation with a wide range of discretion, free

to move between a large number of different kinds of activities and to relate them together in the interest of overall development. Skills, resources, discretion—only in relation to public participation has SFADCO yet to fully transcend its origins as a body basically bureaucratically inspired.

But, when we contrast what SFADCO has at its disposal with those other attenuated administrative structures throughout the western part of the country—the county development teams, regional development organisations and the rest—then we come to realise how ill-equipped we are to make a success of regional development as a whole.

It may be argued—it almost certainly will be argued—that it is not necessary to have these skills distributed around the west; that they exist in Dublin and that enough can be done there to produce the appropriate policies and to see that they are adequately implemented. We have seen a very impressive example of this in the IDA plans recently published.

Nonetheless, this is not the whole story. This is not the place to debate the advantages and limitations of centralisation, so I shall confine myself to two points.

The first point is: Where on the whole does the national interest lie? You will remember that the basic insight of the Devlin Report on the Organisation of the Public Services was that our governmental bodies were prevented from doing their main jobs by the press of day to day business. One might say that the crucial weakness of Irish administration is that the urgent drives out the important, the special drives out the general, the local drives out the national. This makes for a sort of silting up of our central administrative institutions. There is reason to believe that the same thing is happening to the political and legislative institutions. For example, between 1st April, 1971, and 30th September, 1972, almost 9,000 parliamentary questions have been asked, and about a third of these were on matters of purely local interest. The following is a not untypical example of these:

> Mr . . . . asked the Minister for Education if he will arrange that the school bus will collect pupils of Horestown national school at the entrance to Killineer cottages rather than at Cockle Road, Co. Louth, as at present.

I do not suggest that this is not important to the parents and children concerned, or that this, and the other questions like it, were not properly addressed to the appropriate Ministers. But in the period about 50 hours of parliamentary time was taken up by such questions. When we think that the Dail takes, on average, 2 to 3 hours to deal with a typically short bill we can see how much useful, if uncontroversial, legislation could have been passed in the time that the Dail devoted itself to purely local interests. As we know, questions are but the tip of the iceberg of the vast volume of special representations engaged in by members of the Dail. This great volume of local and special business must be dealt with at the centre because we are woefully short of representative institutions for dealing with local matters at local level. Our local government bodies, by comparison with those in other countries, deal with very few services and we have, relatively, very few public representatives. For example, *after* the present Swedish reforms to reduce the number of local authorities and to transfer State functions to them there will be in Sweden one local councillor for every 1,000 of the population. Here, *before* the proposed great reduction in the number of councillors, we have one elected councillor for every 2,000 of the population. No wonder the press of local and special issues is choking our national institutions to death.

This position is getting worse. If our national institutions are to do those jobs that none but they can do, then they must be freed from detail; the gross and extreme centralisation of public business must be replaced by a more decentralised system. The purpose of this system would be to have a series of filters, so that local matters would be filtered off at one or more local levels, and regional matters filtered off at regional levels. This would leave to come to the top only what is nationally important.

The second, very different, point is this. The proof of all these puddings is in the eating. We have had, in one shape or another over the past 20 years, *ad hoc* attempts to deal with aspects of regional problems. These have been basically centralised efforts with limited local action and discretion. Much good work has been done. Nonetheless, we would not be here to-day had these attempts, overall, been a success.

It is presumably, in some recognition of all of this, that there has been the growing concern to set up regional bodies and to attempt the reform of local government. But these attempts, it seems to me, are inadequate to the needs. In general, these new structures are, overall, just as unplanned, just as haphazard and just as ill-designed to tackle the problems as the structures many of them propose to replace. The system remains essentially one that is centralised, *ad hoc,* hand to mouth. This is not to learn from experience. It is not good enough.

II. SOME SOLUTIONS

However, we are not wholly without resources in this matter. The effectiveness of Irish public bodies is now the concern of a single body, the Department of the Public Service, not yet legally in being but beginning its work. It seems to me that making sense of this whole regional question ought to be one of its first tasks.

What are the issues to be teased out?

First, the issue of decentralisation. The Government have decided on the dispersal of two centralised departments from Dublin. This is of little relevance to our present problems; but if this decision could be transmuted into a policy of decentralisation by engaging in a genuine and general deconcentration followed by genuine and general devolution, the effects could be dramatic.

I have used four terms—"dispersal", "deconcentration", "devolution" and "decentralisation". What do we mean by these? The decision to move the Department of Education to Athlone, without altering its internal structure, and similarly the Department of Lands to Castlebar, is simply to *disperse* highly concentrated and centralised bodies. In Athlone and Castlebar they themselves remain just as concentrated and as centralised as before. However, if the decision were, say, to re-organise the Department of Education on a regional and/or county basis and to give real authority and discretion within the Department to a regional or county director—that would be deconcentration. The further step of transferring these departmental, regional or county functions to a regional or county authority would be *devolution*. Both deconcentration and devolution would be the result of a policy of decentralisation; dispersal would not.

The Devlin Report on the Organisation of the Public Services implicitly recommends *deconcentration* of the departments with local functions to regional directors. The Chubb Report on the White Paper on the re-organisation of Local Government—the report is called *More Local Government*—recommends a massive *devolution* of central government functions to local authorities. These are issues that call for much more public discussion than they have so far been given.

These three problems—to reverse the extreme centralisation of Irish government, to rationalise the areas of field services of the central bodies and degrees of discretion of their regional officers, and to think through the relationships between central bodies and regional and local structures—these are of the first importance and should, in my view, be pressed on the attention of the new Department of the Public Service.

Another big problem—completely avoided in the latest McKinsey Report on local authorities[1]—is the role of the regional bodies. This is discussed in the Chubb Report where separate roles are laid out for regional, county and district authorities over—it is to be repeated—the *whole* practicable range of governmental functions as they operate at regional and local level. The roles suggested are: For the regions— planning, resource allocation, review and the discharge of highly technological services. For counties—the normal discharge of governmental functions at a technological level. For districts—the discharge of the personal services. It will be a great tragedy if the impending proposals for the re-organisation of local government do not address themselves to this problem. It transcends, of course, the range of the responsibilities of the Department of Local Government, Here, again, is an urgent task for the Department of the Public Service in conjunction with the Department of Local Government. The Chubb Report recommended that the assimilation of all the essentially local tasks of government into the local government structure be a task of a special temporary agency of government, serviced by the Department of the Public Service in conjunction with the Department of Local Government and reporting to the Minister for the Public Service within, say, three years.

Inherent in any such programme of deconcentration and devolution is the granting of discretion and freedom of action to the local bodies. Both the Devlin and the Chubb reports propose that they be given the same sort of freedoms as state-sponsored bodies.

A major factor in development is the linking together at appropriate levels of services that affect one another. This calls for 'cross-over' points at the various levels. These cross-over points are important when policies and plans are being drawn up so that the maximum knowledge and skills can be mobilised and committed. They are also important at the action stage so that all will work together in a co-ordinated way. They are important at the review stage so that when things are going wrong in one or more areas they can be readily brought to light and remedied. The cross-over points are of two kinds—within each Department and as between Departments and other bodies. As Devlin proposes, the regional director of each Department and his personal staff would be the cross-over point for each departmental area of responsibility— agriculture, communications, education, justice and the rest. In my Addendum to Devlin I go further and recommend also a general

[1]McKinsey and Co. Inc.: *Strengthening the Local Government Service,* 1972, Prl. 2252.

K

Regional Director and his staff to be the cross-over point as between departmental regional directors.

But this is to talk in purely bureaucratic terms. In these times at least it is essential to face the issue of public representation. Hitherto we have waffled between two traditions—that of the elected public representative with a concern for detailed administration, and that of the nominated representative (as on the board of a state-sponsored body) concerned only with overall control and broad administrative matters. The danger on the one hand is parochialism, on the other bureaucracy. Some middle ground must be found here. The immediate aim is to break down the apartheid that exists in our society—but not in others—between what the Americans call the elected and the appointed officials and to get them to sit down together. This kind of mixed council could be the most effective cross-over point of all. Again in my Addendum to Devlin I propose, amongst other things, a regional council under the chairmanship of the co-ordinating regional director composed of public representatives and regional directors in equal numbers. In addition, each departmental regional director would have the benefit of a representative advisory body of public representatives.

Another proposal that has been made, not in printed form, has been that the problems of regional under-development and economics should be studied under Irish conditions, either here at University College, Galway, or at the new Institute in Limerick. Is it not time that money was spent on getting a deeper knowledge of the adverse forces that have to be overcome, the better to master them?

Here may I make two points? First, all of these are responsible proposals, some far-reaching, some relatively simple. On the whole, they map out the way ahead for us reasonably clearly. They require discussion, examination and, where they are shown to be useful, action. So far as one can see they are getting none of these. Is this inaction important to the cause of western development, or is it not?

III. POLITICAL IDEAS

My task to-day is to talk about organisation, about technical questions that few people, even bureaucrats, are interested in and that, however important some of us believe them to be, are at best dull.

But what do we want to organise for? To bring the development of the west up to that of the rest of the country and so to increase our national rate of development? But what do we mean by development? More factories, more jobs, more motor cars? Or more people, more families, more communities? But why here, west of the Shannon, rather than elsewhere? Because we believe that there are people, values, practices here that ought to be kept here and fostered, that there is something special and irreplaceable in these communities. So we believe that healthy communities ought to be encouraged to grow in this half of Ireland west of the Shannon, to grow and not, as hitherto, to decay. What vision have we got of the kind of life we think should be developing in these communities?

That question is basically one of political ideas and of leadership. It is far outside my terms of reference to-day or my competence such as it is, but we cannot consider this question of organisation unless we have some idea of what it is we need to organise for and some idea of the principles, such as they are, on which organisation has in the past been based. The leading principle has been centralised action. Let us be clear about this. Centralisation as a principle of government does not derive from a dose of bureaucratic original sin. It was a major political idea in this country to which our institutions were required to conform. If it is to be effectively replaced this can only be done by another leading political principle—such as the fostering and growth of healthy and balanced communities that will develop and transmit Irish values. There is a conflict of principle here that must be resolved.

There is plenty of knowledge now to show that benevolent intervention from outside—unless it is very skilled indeed—does not foster community life: it kills it. The overall aim should be to develop and enrich the sense of *community* and *communities* throughout the west. The basic test is: how far does any proposal strengthen community life or weaken it?

This is not just starry-eyed talk. Our society has now reached a stage when we have both the desire and the means to think in terms of strengthening and enriching community life, of encouraging and expecting more people to play a larger part in that life for the enrichment both of community life and their own lives. When we think of public organisations to tackle economic problems, or social problems, or cultural problems, let us keep this aspect of community living in mind. It is clear that limited, *ad hoc* initiatives inspired benevolently from Dublin are in the long run sterile. The sort of administrative tidying up I was suggesting a few moments ago has not much merit unless it can be placed in the light of broad, basically political, ideas about the kind of community we want.

For myself, I am satisfied that one of the aims of our society ought to be the fostering at as many levels as possible of self-governing communities consonant with the maintenance of overall national unity.

In this context the development of local self-government at the regional, county, district and community levels is overwhelmingly in the national interest and it should be the duty of active citizens to see that the survival of out of date centralised and bureaucratic ideas and structures does not impede this development.

IV.   ACTION ON REGIONS

Broadly, what needs to be done about local self-government is, I believe, in the Chubb Report, and I will not refer to that further, partly because it is there to be read. But one facet of this question is specially relevant to our discussions. What needs to be done about regional development as it has come to be understood in this country —the grouping together of three, four or five counties for common action?

If we want to make regions effective I think there are three broad issues that have to be tackled. The first of these is a moral issue, the second is a political one, and the third is an administrative one.

The *moral* issue is to establish a regional consciousness and sense of commitment to the development of the region that can lead people to give up sectional interests and to achieve objectives otherwise beyond their reach. This requires us to define the area and the role —the size and tasks—of whatever region is to be chosen. These must be defined and standardised so that the region will make some sense to people and that their loyalties can grow about it.

The *political* issue is to have representative institutions operating within the region relevant to all the main governmental activities there and related together in some orderly way. This will make for political co-ordination and will give the opportunity for regional leadership in a broad political sense.

The third requirement is the *administrative* one, and this I should like to spell out in some more detail. The first administrative requirement is to define our regions for all purposes, as so many other countries have done. Do we want to have seven, eight or nine regions? Are the county boundaries to be taken as given, or not? I think that whatever answers we give to these questions are not important provided we give the same answers for all purposes. Why should this be? The first reason is to ensure that everyone can work to the same region: it is impossible to create any sort of regional consciousness if the boundaries shift for every purpose.

May I take an example—admittedly an extreme example—of what

I mean? Is Roscommon in the west? Certainly it is west of the Shannon and if I am a Roscommon man and get ill I look to the Western Health Board at Galway to look after me. Similarly, if I have a civil defence problem that is where I go. If I am in the tourist business, I find I belong to the midlands region in company with six other counties all of them *east* of the Shannon and I look to Mullingar as my centre for tourism. My physical planning region, centred on Athlone, links my county with only four of the six that are joined to it in the tourist interest, again all of them *east* of the Shannon. If I am looking for a grant to extend my factory a similar region applies. But if I want to send my child to a regional technical college I find that if I live in the north of Roscommon I must look to Sligo and if I live in the south of Roscommon back I go to Athlone. Add in the varying counties and bits of counties used for other educational purposes, for transport, for electricity distribution, and the rest. See how the confusion mounts. This is administrative bedlam. There may be good reasons for each of these special arrangements. But when we add them all together we see how confused and disastrous is the overall picture. Alas, poor Roscommon! What moral, political or administrative credibility can exist in such circumstances?

These things—health, education, industrial development, tourism, etc.—are all related in terms of planning and they are certainly all related in terms of the individual citizen who is the customer for their services. Surely it is not beyond the wit of present day Ireland to do what the Anglo Normans did in the 13th century here—to define boundaries for all purposes and to stick to these? No doubt even the best defined boundary will create anomalies; but no anomaly is as great as the kind of confusion I have been trying to illustrate. Other instances of this kind can be given from other counties. This is the first, and absolutely basic, step to be taken if we want to make any sense at all of the regional idea. Common boundaries are essential for collecting data for planning and for relating the activities of different agencies. Reasons such as these have persuaded other countries, with more complex problems than ours, to define common regional boundaries. There is no reason why we should not do the same, or why the Devlin recommendation for an immediate inquiry into this issue could not be immediately set on foot. It seems to me reasonable that those concerned with western development should press to have this done forthwith.

The second step is a more difficult one and that is to try to define some sort of a role for the region as distinct from the local government bodies, on the one hand, and the field services of the central bodies, on the other. This is a matter discussed at some length in the Chubb Report. This report sees the regional structure as being basically the planning, resource-allocating, and reviewing body within the region. Below it would be executive bodies at the county level, and personal services at the district level. I think this makes for a logical solution of the problems of the relationship of region to local government. It is difficult to see how there can be any meaningful re-organisation of local government until this issue is resolved. It is still not too late to look at this whole issue of regionalism in the perspective of a central government system stripped of local issues.

The third step is to clarify the relationships between the very large number of field services of central government and state-sponsored bodies, on the one hand, with the various kinds of regional bodies, on the other, and with the local government structures beneath them. Here again the definition of common regional areas would go a long way towards meeting the difficulties. But it would also be necessary to ensure that the field services of the centralised agencies had in fact delegated to them within the regional area a degree of discretion comparable to that of the specifically regional bodies themselves.

Fourthly, it would be necessary to staff the regional bodies in a manner befitting their responsibilities. Again, I would like to quote the example of the Shannon Free Airport Development Company. If this was the sort of organisation that was necessary to turn the tide at Shannon then what kind of very high level skills must be deployed to turn the tide in Donegal, Sligo and Leitrim, to name three counties?

The fifth requirement is that an adequate system of co-ordination exist both at the representative and at the administrative level between all the administrative bodies operating in the region. We are inclined to forget how many of these there are. The make up of some of the regional development organisation boards gives us some idea. If genuine regional policies are to be devised a great deal more bodies will have to be included. There are in this country operating in any given area some scores of administrative agencies. Basically, some kind of regional body representative of the political and administrative sides of the bodies operating in the region would have to be established over the whole range of these agencies. This, by any standards, will not be easy.

Finally, regionalism makes no sense unless the regional bodies have a substantial say in the allocation of large sums of money. If there is to be regional policy there must be some sort of regional plan. If there is a regional plan the broad plan, once approved, must be backed by whatever resources can be made available to implement it. The regional bodies will have to have some degree of discretion about how those resources are to be allocated as between the various local priorities.

These, very broadly, are the problem areas that must be tackled if anything is to be done to make a reality of regional policy, regional planning, regional development—call it what you will—in the interest of reviving the west of Ireland. The demographic, social, economic, cultural problems of the area are simply staggering and will be accentuated if the east of the country participates in the economic dynamism of the EEC. Unless there is some evidence that these problems are going to be tackled on the scale that their magnitude requires, then there will be plenty of ground for severe pessimism in the middle and the long terms. The clarifying of minds on this scale, the assembling of the necessary political and administrative institutions and the study and analyses needed to prepare fully comprehensive plans for regional development will all take a good deal of time. There is none of that time now to be wasted.

What do I suggest? I think the first issue is to make up our minds what it is we want to do about this regional question. If the decision is to go for development on a regional basis then it is essential to settle issues about areas, representation, powers and resources for regional bodies. Serious deficiency in one of these will seriously hinder the rest. I think the first stage is to give some sort of political and administrative credibility to the regional development organisations and to give them a comprehensive remit. I think the second stage is to campaign to get the inquiry, recommended in the first Devlin Report, underfoot into the field services of the centralised agencies and, as I would add, into the tying in of these regionalised field services into a comprehensive regional structure.

These things do not stand still. Apart from the local government re-organisation, changes will be occurring in relation to the agricultural services, and, probably the educational ones. Something is afoot about part of the welfare services. Have the health boards reached their final form, especially in relation to community and special care services?

The Devlin Report on Public Service Re-organisation looked at our administrative systems from the centre out, as it were, and produced a rational scheme for them. When we look at the chaotic system or lack of system on which so much of western development depends, we see even greater need to clarify, to standardise and to democratise the system from the ground up. The whole geographical system of Irish administration needs a thorough examination in the interests of efficient government overall. It seems to me that those attending this Conference might reasonably press for this.

V. WHAT HAVE I BEEN SAYING?

I said, first, that modern government has been tackling special 20th century problems without much success because the instruments it uses have not been designed for these new jobs.

I said, secondly, that if the west has not been saved it has not been for want of agencies of one kind or another aimed to save it, but that these agencies, with the one exception of SFADCO, were too specialised, too weak, too controlled to achieve much success.

I said, thirdly, that the more comprehensive efforts—such as with the RDOS, and the local government reform and the so-called decentralisation of two Departments—suffer from the same weaknesses.

I said, fourthly, that now with the Public Service Department and the various reports—Devlin, Chubb and the rest—we have the means and the knowledge to tackle these problems on a scale that offers some hope of success.

I said, fifthly, that we need some political ideas of the kind of society we want to see here west of the Shannon, and that the administrative means of achieving this society should be directed to the need to foster self-reliant, local, self-governing communities.

I said, finally, that the Devlin proposal of a limited study aimed at standardising the regions and at rationalising the field services of central bodies should be implemented, and that the whole problem of the operation of the machinery of government at the regional and local levels should be the subject of an inquiry comparable to that given by Devlin to the central machinery.

A slow old business, you will say—and rightly. But another 20 years could be lost if we let slip this chance of hitting the iron when it shows *some* sign of heating up.

Chapter 10

SOME PROBLEMS OF REGIONAL DEVELOPMENT*

I should like to make two preliminary points. The first is that what I am going to talk about is not that for which I have been billed. The title of my paper was agreed with the organisers of this Seminar in a moment of aberration. I am not able to talk about *Principles* of Regional Development. I doubt if we yet know enough about the science and art of national development to talk in terms of *principles,* if by principles we mean some sort of rules for decision and action that should result in successful operations. In national development a small part, and a relatively new one, is regional development. This has not, so far as I can discover, so far produced anything that one could dignify with the name of *principles.* So, what I propose to talk about are some *problems* of regional development.

The second preliminary point is that I think that Galway is a suitable place in which to discuss these problems because the surroundings here illustrate a number of the problems of regional development—as you will be discovering during this week. Galway is the capital of what we in Ireland call "The West". In this very room a few months ago a representative of the European Commission in Brussels told us that the West of Ireland, that is that part of Ireland substantially west of the river Shannon, is the most underdeveloped of the areas in the enlarged European Community. I think most of what you will be hearing and seeing over this week will be addressed to the sorts of problems that, while manifest in this area, are not, of course, peculiar to it.

Problems of regional development fall into two very broad classes. The first class is the one we can illustrate here, the problems of *under-development* or non development. But there are also acute problems of over development. These problems we cannot illustrate in Galway or, indeed, in any part of Ireland to any significant extent. To use a medical analogy, the problems of regional development are in some places acute and in some places chronic. On this basis, the problems

*A paper presented to a seminar on Youth and Regional Development in Europe, Galway, February, 1973. Reprinted from ADMINISTRATION, Vol 21 (1973) 1.

we can illustrate for you here are chronic problems. But even here, we can show you only part of the story. One of the intractable problems of regional development is the declining industrial area—the sort of problem one sees in the mining districts of Wales or the ship-building districts of Scotland, structural problems faced, and successfully solved, by the European Coal and Steel Community. I mention these not to fill you with remorse that you cannot personally visit this week examples of every kind of regional development problem, but to try to illustrate the remarkable complexity of the subject.

I. ORIGINS OF REGIONAL DEVELOPMENT

"National Development" is one of those activities that has grown up in recent decades, largely as a consequence of the success of the economists in showing how economic development can be brought about. There are inded many who would deny that a metaphysical concept like development has any rationality at all. But if one takes a pragmatic view and looks at the amount of activity that goes on in practically every country under the name of development, and considers the fair degree of success there has been in a number of places, one may be prepared to concede that it must have some degree of significance.

The problems posed by development apply in most, if not all, countries. If one has too little development one tries to induce it; if one has too much one tries to control it; and if one has unbalanced development one attempts to arrive at some optimum "mix" of the various kinds of development. It is for reasons like these that most countries now engage in some form of planning—economic planning, environmental planning, social planning, etc. It is as a by product of central planning that attention has come to be paid to the issues of regional planning and development. If I may quote from a United Nations paper on this issue:

It has been realised more and more that national development plans formulated only at the central level, usually on a sectoral basis, have important implications for regions and localities and that sectoral co-ordination at regional levels is indispensible to effective implementation. Through planning on a regional basis, the central (and, if existent, the regional) government is enabled to devise policies, programmes, and projects immediately geared to problems and needs which are being experienced at the regional and local level. Furthermore, regional plans in whose formulation regional governmental units and interest groups have participated are far more likely to generate co-operation with and support for the central government than are plans simply imposed from above by higher authority. Indeed, imposition of plans and projects ill-adapted to local conditions may produce opposition sufficiently strong to frustrate their implementation.

But there are other origins of regional development ideas—for example, river basin developments involving hydro-electric power generation, flood control, and provision of irrigation water; one thinks here of such a body as the Tennessee Valley Authority. Or the regional development may be to facilitate the exploitation of economic resources such as petroleum, bauxite, iron ore, and forest products. It may also —and this is the one perhaps most relevant to Irish conditions—aim to raise living standards and provide new employment opportunities in economically and socially depressed areas, as in the Mezzogiorno. It is undertaken to try to slow down growth in already overcrowded national capitals, as in France. And it is availed of to achieve a more balanced distribution of economic growth within national boundaries, as well as supra-national ones such as those of the EEC.

II.   WHAT IS A REGION?

One of the problems is to define what we mean by the word "region". There is great ambiguity both about the area of the region and about its function.

Areas

There are supra-national regions such as the EEC, Comecon, and, to take an example outside Europe, Central America. There are in federal countries regional structures grouping a number of states for various purposes—one can see this emerging at the present time in the United States.

Within a unitary state one can see the development of fully fledged regional governments, as in Italy and, up to very recently, in that part of Ireland which is incorporated in the United Kingdom.

There are large areas sharing common problems, but often no common regional structures, such as northern and western Scotland, western and south-eastern France, the Federal Republic of Germany along the zonal boundary, and the Mezzogiorno. The representative of the EEC to whom I have already referred similarly divided Ireland into three economic regions running north and south, the eastern strip being a modern society, the middle strip being in an intermediate stage of development, and the western strip being underdeveloped.

However, when we in Ireland talk about regions we mostly think of something smaller than these—in effect the grouping of two, three or four counties together in seven, eight or nine groups of typically a quarter of a million people. In more populous countries the region will have a bigger population—the Italian constitution suggests a minimum regional population of a million. Most states seem to have something like 10 to 15 regions—in some countries more, in some countries less— these being usually groupings of existing local government units.

Geographically smaller than the region proper is the special region. One can think of three kinds of these, the most spectacular being the city-region around great conurbations, such as London or Paris. Then, we have in Ireland two other kinds of regions—both of which you will be hearing about—which are a good deal smaller than a single county. There is the region around Shannon Airport where successful attempts have been made to establish industrial development and, despite considerable disabilities, tourist development. There are also scattered cultural regions—one of them not far from here—where the last remnants of those who speak the Irish language as their native tongue are living, often in conditions of considerable poverty. In Scotland, in Wales, in Brittany, similar problems exist.

So it is difficult to give geographical precision to the term "region". It has irreverently been described as a name for something bigger (or smaller) than the last area we have been talking about. However, it would greatly help discussion if we all make clear what kind of geographical area we have in mind when we use the word.

Functions

The development functions given to the regions vary widely, depending on the extent to which government in the country tends to be centralised or decentralised, to give priority to areas or to functions. This country, for example, is a very centralised one, and gives priority to functions over areas. So, various questions arise. Is this development induced or controlled or co-ordinated *within* the region, or by some outside body? If within the region is development generally the responsibility of the regional body, or of a number of *ad hoc* bodies? What range of powers and initiative do the regional bodies possess? And so on. From the UN document I have already quoted from I have extracted a table—which is the appendix to this paper—showing the range of options for institutions for regional development. It would be tedious to go through these in detail. For now it is enough to say that the range of options is very considerable.

So, just as it is difficult to give geographical precision to the term "region" so also it is difficult to give it any kind of institutional precision. This country can provide some good examples of both these failures.

III. TASKS OF REGIONAL DEVELOPMENT

One of the snags about development is that it raises a number of basic questions—and by "basic" we mean questions that are most difficult to answer. For example, the question of equality. It does not seem to be in the nature of the development process that it operates equally in all places. It is, of course, influenced by the location of natural resources, or of special transport facilities, or of special hindrances such as natural frontiers. But whatever the circumstances, uniform national development does not occur. It has its own inherent logic that (I think) even those who study the economics of location do not fully understand. In the same way, economic growth of itself does not evenly distribute its benefits to the population. For both of these reasons, a great part of modern governmental activity is concerned with the re-distribution of resources as between the better off places and people and the less well off places and people. Not all the less well off people are in the less well off places, but as a general rule those who are in the less well off places are also themselves amongst the less well off people in the community. This unevenness of the growth problem—its perhaps too great ebullience in some places and its reluctance to start at all in others—poses the tasks of regional development.

These problems are not only economic, they are also environmental, social, cultural, political and administrative. Many of them are very tough problems indeed, and I think it would be far too optimistic to say that there has been much success anywhere by governments in coping with them in all their complexity. Nonetheless, this is becoming an increasing pre-occupation of modern governments and everywhere one looks one sees some attempt to tackle this regional development question. Perhaps we could leave to one side for a moment why governments should be worried about these problems, and have a look at the problems themselves.

Economic Problems

If we look at the economic problems of underdevelopment, we are struck at once by the question of waste, especially of human resources. Unemployment, under-employment, wasteful employment—these are all the marks of underdeveloped areas. In addition, there may well be many unexploited natural resources in these areas that would be of value to the whole community if they could be made available. Sometimes these are known; sometimes they are not known and have to be sought out. So, actual and potential waste are the striking economic features of underdevelopment.

On the other hand, if we look at the economic costs of over development we see that these are very considerable also. The sheer cost of maintaining great cities seems to be becoming quite insupportable. The waste of time and energy involved in the problems of getting large numbers to and from work in congested areas are very striking. Many critics of the consumer goods society would say that it is based on a quite remarkable adherence to the standards of conspicuous waste. It is said that the use of natural resources per head in the developed part of the world is about twenty five times that in the underdeveloped parts of the world. If there were to be a levelling up without a levelling down then the world simply would not have enough resources to support its population at the present levels of what we call the developed world.

Overall, therefore, there seems to be a strong economic case—if we think of "economy" as the wise use of resources—for trying to achieve some levelling off in economic welfare between the economically vibrant and the economically stagnant areas.

Environmental Problems

If one looks at the problems of the environment one sees a similar maldistribution. Means of transport and means of communication, as well as such services as piped water and sewerage, tend to be scarce in the underdeveloped areas and the standard of housing in many of these leaves much to be desired. On the other hand, in the over developed areas there are also great problems—housing and water and sewerage problems are often worse in the slums and shanty towns than in the rural areas. There are the great problems of congestion and pollution. There are problems of the conflict of the means of wealth with the environment, acute in some places, emerging in others.

To take two local examples: the three principal Irish cities of Dublin, Belfast and Cork are set in surroundings of great natural beauty. How can they be got to develop without in fact destroying their environment? This is the sort of problem that arises also in underdeveloped areas. For example a dispute is arising in this country now about whether there should be an oil refinery in a very underdeveloped, but very beautiful, place in the south west of the country, at Bantry Bay. How does one balance the opportunities for direct and indirect employment offered by such an investment against the danger to the natural beauty of the area, its recreational value and its tourist potential? There are issues here that are not easily resolved.

Social Problems

If one looks at the social problems they tend to be even more acute. There is great inequity in a system where people in one part of the country can enjoy well paid employment and a standard of living many times higher than those in other parts of the country where employment is scarce. What happens, of course, is that people are sucked out of the underdeveloped area—at least the young and active ones are. This is a very striking feature of the western part of Ireland. The lack of industrial opportunity in Ireland and the demand for labour in the growing industrial areas of the United States and the United Kingdom have brought about a situation that the people were attracted out of the country and the population of the whole country was halved in less than a century.

The effects of this on the communities that are left behind are very considerable. I am sure Dr. Scully will give you some of the startling social statistics that apply to agriculture in this part of Ireland[1]. Apart from the poverty of the people, apart from the very high level of unmarried ones, apart from the large number of old people left on small, semi-derelict farms, one has, in addition, the breakdown of many rural communities. These have not been replaced in the west of Ireland by the growth of any significant urban structures. And the absence of these, of course, makes the task of getting economic development going in these areas much more troublesome than it might otherwise be. But the breakdown of the rural communities has caused two significant social problems.

First, the selective emigration of the most vigorous and active has meant that those left behind were those in greater need of shelter and of strong community. The absence of this community and family support, the leaving of old people, of old unmarried people, in isolated

[1]Scully J. J.: *Agriculture in the West of Ireland: A Study of the Low Farm Income Problem,* 1971.

conditions, has contributed, according to the psychiatrists, to the extra-ordinary incidence of mental disease in this country. It is often said that the Irish are a mad people. They are not; but as compared with other countries, disproportionate numbers of them *are* mad.

Secondly, there is a very high dependancy rate here—that is to say for every working man or woman there is a large number of dependants, both the very young and the very old.

So, underdevelopment makes for very intricate social problems, and it becomes very difficult—or at any rate extremely expensive—to do any-thing about them. These conditions can be seen in many other parts of Europe.

On the other hand, if we think of the social problems of the over-developed areas we find to an increasing extent in the modern world another kind of breakdown. This is, substantially, the breakdown of law and order, the rising incidence of crime—violent crime, theft, etc. In this part of Ireland one can go out and leave one's door open and house unlocked and have little fear that anything will be taken from it even during a considerable absence. At the other extreme, many people in New York—and now, it seems, in London—have reason to be fright-ened about being on the streets after dark. We have been accustomed to think of civilisation as the product of cities, where people went for security, for human relationships, and for convenience. Now, to an in-creasing extent, the city is dirty, dangerous, and inconvenient. The city used to make for greater community bonds. Now, in many places there is an increasing tendency to alienation and to rejection of social rules.

Cultural Problems

One of the arguments *for* underdevelopment may be the cultural one. Here in Galway we are very close to part of what is called the "Celtic Fringe". In this fringe, scattered mainly along the Atlantic seaboard, are the last remnants of those who speak the Celtic languages—in Western Ireland, in Western Scotland, in Wales and in Brittany. Everywhere, these places are culturally under siege—so much so that one prominent Irish writer has said that the only way to save the Irish speaking dis-tricts in Ireland is to build a high wall around them! These are perhaps special problems, but they are shared by a number of countries. Per-haps, the cultural problems of the regions may be eased by greater con-cern on the part of the government for regional development problems, but it would be idle to deny that there can be conflict between, say, economic and cultural development unless very great skill is exercised.

In a slightly different context one may echo what General de Gaulle said about the EEC—that it did not mean that some future Dante would write in Esperanto. Nonetheless, when one looks at how modern cities affect the cultural life of those who come to them from traditional societies, when one sets against the curious greyness of modern suburban living, not to mention the acute cultural problems of slum and shanty areas, when one sets against these the growth in the dissemination of cultural values by easily available education, by cheap books, discs and broadcasting—one cannot be sure that the rich cultural texture of life in the traditional areas will, on balance, always be replaced by something better.

Political Problems

If one thinks of these problems in terms of political systems one sees how taxing they are. To induce development where there is under-development, to control development where there is over development, and to co-ordinate development where there is unevenness of development—these pose tough political problems. These problems are basically those of what kind of a society, or what kind of a world, do we want? How can we create within our society a greater sense of community, of community sharing and of community participation? How important, for example, is the pursuit of equality within the society? And so on, and so on. This calls for long term political thinking which is not readily done in the hurly-burly of normal political life.

Administrative Problems

Related to the kind of political society one wishes to see, are the structural or administrative problems that arise in consequence. How far is it possible to have reasonably comprehensive government at the regional level? How can there be evoked regional and local participation? How can we have systems for co-ordination? How can we ensure effective management at all these levels? This is an area where we in this country have done nothing like enough thinking. We have a good deal to learn from a number of other countries in this respect. Nonetheless, the overall issues have not been fully thought through anywhere, I think. The problems of the relationships of central government and administration with subordinate regional and local government and administration—the relationship of vertical government as it were, with horizontal government—these problems have nowhere been satisfactorily solved. Yet they are an essential part of the total problems raised by the concept of regional development.

L

Another facet of these problems is the increasing interest of the ordinary citizen in what is going on, his greater awareness that he may have something to contribute, the remarkable growth—in this country at any rate—of voluntary, community and vocational groups, the rising demand for explanation, consultation and participation in decision-making that affects the citizen's work and his community—all of these suggest that the techniques of centralised and bureaucratised government will need to be adjusted to new ideas of regional and local representation and participation. As Aristotle said, man is a political animal and regional development at both the political and administrative levels is going to have to cope with an increasing number of these animals. That is to say, institutions that will take full account of the complexity of the problems will have to be adapted or made anew.

IV. PROBLEMS OF OBJECTIVES

We are faced here with some pretty tough political problems. These are, basically, what do the different societies think necessary for the good life? One could, of course, spend a long time on that subject; but here may I touch on two problems especially relevant to regional development—migration and quantification?

In practical terms, if we look at an underdeveloped area, we think first of all of a job for those who want to work, and then of reasonable pay and satisfaction in that job. In present day Europe this is not a general problem, but a local or regional one. On the whole, the techniques exist for providing full employment over very wide areas. But does it follow from this that one should not have to migrate, that it is necessary or desirable that one find a job in these districts or in the neighbourhood of where one was born and brought up?

For example, there is a slogan in this part of Ireland called "Save the West". Why should the West be saved, in the sense that those people who are now living here should be aided to live here at a reasonable standard of living? I suppose it is at the heart of the whole nationalist argument that those who wish to live within their own country should be able to do so without great sacrifice. But does it follow that those who wish to live within the same region, or the same locality, within their own country should also be able to do so without great sacrifice?

If to avoid, or reduce, internal migration is the objective, a number of other factors come into play. One becomes concerned with maintaining an existing form of community life. One becomes concerned with maintaining existing cultural patterns which themselves may conflict with, say, economic development or be disrupted by it. One becomes concerned to provide environmental, health, educational services over perhaps a much wider area than would otherwise be necessary. One is, in effect, taking a view that rural or village or small town life is in some way better than life in big towns or cities. There is often a severe clash between progress and amenity. In Ireland, for example, many of the underdeveloped areas are very beautiful. How much of this beauty should be sacrificed so that existing settlement patterns be maintained?

But perhaps these issues rest on deeper assumptions still? One is perhaps assuming that present day patterns of communications and of transport will not significantly affect the readiness of people to commute very considerable distances between their homes and their work—this assumption may well not be well-based in this country at least. One is assuming that traditional patterns of industrial settlement that grew up before transport became speedy and communications so vastly improved will continue. For example, is there still an economic necessity to crowd in the same place people who do business together? Is it still necessary (it clearly is not in many large cities) for people to live near their work? Are the disutilities of extending services out into these remote areas greater than the disutilities of trying to improve, for example, the flow of traffic into, through, and out of large modern cities? Or of policing them? In short are the gains from enabling people to live in their traditional neighbourhoods worth the costs?

For example, the Swiss share a different pattern of living from most other rich people. They have no really big towns. Their small towns and factories are scattered through the countryside but without spoiling it. Does their example suggest that one *can* have a high standard of living without the strongly developed urban structures that are to be found in the "Golden Triangle"? I don't know the answers to these questions; but they seem to me that they are the sort of questions that any programme of regional development must address itself to. They are, of course, the stuff of politics.

Quantification

In the modern world many problems have been solved by being quantified. Many decisions have been eased because we could quantify inputs against outputs and so decide which course gave the better return and which a less good one. One of the most useful concepts in getting the whole notion of development underway has been the system of quantification known as the gross national product. But it is clear that gross national product only measures those things that are quantifiable in money terms. If I pay a housekeeper her work is included in the gross national product; if I have a wife doing similar work, that is not included in the gross national product. A rise in gross national product by 4 or 8 per cent means that those things that can be measured in these money terms have grown in this way. But what about those other things that cannot so be measured? What about the quality of life? As a consequence of the rising GNP has it risen or fallen? The products of the Ruhr are included in GNP but not their by-products in the Rhine. So the trivial thing that can be priced contributes to growth and development, but not the priceless thing. So the GNP, from becoming a useful tool, has tended to distort our whole system of values.

One is back to the old problem of a monetary system. Money can measure a number of things; but it cannot in fact measure the most valuable things in life. One is familiar with the sneer about the man who knows the price of everything, and the value of nothing. So we find that vigorous Dutchman, Sicco Mansholt suggesting that we should replace the concept of gross national product by the broader one of gross national utility. And we find his equally distinguished compatriot, Jan Tinbergen, in Dublin last year controverting the conventional wisdom of the economists who say that utility cannot be measured, by proposing to do just that. So, perhaps the issues will become clearer in the future. But for now we are faced with the clash of unquantified values, a clash that can only be resolved by the political system.

V.   PROBLEMS OF INSTITUTIONS

The way to resolve these problems is to try to agree on certain values for the society we want to have and, having agreed on those values as far as we can, to create political and administrative systems that will translate the values into effective action.

I suppose you young people can look forward to the day when the basic problems of food, shelter, employment and well being of every member of your community can be assured. (May I as an old man express some pessimism about this. The way the world seems to go is that the important things of life such as food and shelter become increasingly expensive and difficult to obtain, while the largely irrelevant and often useless gadgets of modern living become cheaper and more plentiful. We see an increase in leisure, but the opportunities for recreation diminish. However, let me not entertain these dangerous thoughts). Let me repeat—it comes back as always to the question of the values we have.

Depending on those values, it is relatively easy to think of systems of politics and of institutions that will give effect to these values. But to create these institutions, as we so ofen do—or worse, to proliferate them—without getting our values, our objectives, what it is we want to see the society doing, without getting these things clear in our heads, is a recipe for muddle, confusion, and failure. So, if we can design the good life, it will not be too difficult to translate it into objectives to be achieved in a measurable period, and to create the institutions, public and private, to achieve these objectives. Once we have defined the objectives and have sketched out the institutions for achieving them, then we have to tease out the various problems of the roles of the different kinds of institutions—what each should do, how it can work effectively with the other bodies—how to have representation from the people and to involve them in a participative way—how to finance these bodies whether by local, regional or central taxation—and how to achieve effective management within the institutions themselves.

You will, I imagine, hear during the week a good deal about these latter matters. I think that if I have anything useful to say here this morning it is that you ought to bear in mind these other more general, more fundamental and more difficult issues.

VI. NEEDS OF YOUTH

In the very explicit instructions given to me by the organisers of this Seminar—which they were good enough to repeat in the programme —I am to do something to provoke discussion on the needs of young people and the role they can play in relation to regional development. I approach this part of my task with a certain wariness. Who am I to say what are the needs of youth? The young people in my own family politely, but firmly and insistently, make it clear to me that I know nothing about this subject. So I fall back on one general point and for the rest content myself with asking a few questions that may stimulate discussion. The general point is one made by the English economist, Lord Keynes, that few ideas enter the minds of politicians or civil servants much after the age of twenty-five so that the kind of society that these people bring about in their latter years tends to be formed from ideas absorbed at that early age. Was it not Goethe who said "Young man be careful about what you want, because by thirty-five you will have it"?

I pose, first, a few questions about values. How would we rate gross national utility as against gross national product? How important is equality in society, and, in particular, how important is geographical equality? Should cultural and emotional values loom large in our decision-making processes?

Then another set of questions. How significant is the pursuit of politics? How responsible do we feel for providing leadership for our own community, locality or region? How important do we think it to be to adapt and rationalise existing, political and administrative structures in the interests of regional development? How do we see the injection of skills into these structures—for planning, for organising, for co-ordinating, for managing? Do we favour a basically centralised, or a basically decentralised, society?

When all is said, the world is your oyster. We have here in Galway, for all our underdevelopment, some of the world's most delicious oysters. My last word is how do you propose to prize open and savour that succulent bivalve?

EXHIBIT A

CLASSIFICATION OF REGIONAL DEVELOPMENT POLICIES AND FORMS OF ADMINISTRATION FOR REGIONAL DEVELOPMENT

Regional Development Policies	Forms of Administration
Single or limited purpose programme for a specific limited area	Special task force or study group in local institution
Multi-purpose programme in specific limited area	Development responsibility assigned to local jurisdiction or a ministry
Multi-purpose programmes for one or more wider areas characterised by special resources or problems	Single or limited purpose authority or corporation attached to local or state jurisdiction
National focus on major development area with wide range of programmes supported by special national policies	Limited or multi-purpose authority or corporation under national jurisdiction

	Multi-purpose authority or development corporation involving participation by both national and local or regional jurisdictions
Use of regional approach to information collection and data analysis	Regional study and research centres and data banks attached to national or local jurisdictions
Encouragement of development planning by local authorities within a region	Planning offices created within local jurisdictions with national encouragement and support
Use of regions for planning purposes within context of national plan	Co-ordinating offices for supervision of sectoral plan implementation on regional basis
Co-ordination of national plan implementation on regional basis.	Creation of basic planning units at regional level, but attached to the national planning office
Development of regional plans within guidelines of national plans and the execution of such regional plans	Basic planning units at regional level in which both national planning office, national ministries, and local authorities participate
Co-ordinated planning and plan implementation of both national and local government development programmes in each region	Regional authorities organised with substantial autonomy and authority
Same as above with private sector involvement	Creation of regional governments

Chapter 11

A NORTH CLARE DEVELOPMENT ORGANISATION?*

May I be excused for beginning, on a personal note, what will otherwise be a dull presentation?

My father was born on a small farm two miles east of Ennistymon, that is, four miles east of here. He was one of ten children. His father died almost 50 years ago, a hard driving, hard drinking man with, when he died, much to show for his life's work. Of the ten children, five emigrated, two married away from the farm, and three remained unmarried on it. Last autumn we buried the last of these on the hill above the town. The Land Commission had taken the now much neglected farm and the family house was falling into decay. That, last autumn, was the end of the Barringtons in this part of the world. As a boy I spent many happy periods on that farm amongst relatives and neighbours that seemed to me to be the salt of the earth. Now, when I came back, nearly all that world had fallen into sterility and decay.

So, to be invited here to this meeting today, so soon after that burial is, for me, a very special experience indeed, psychologically, a re-birth.

What I propose to talk about is this. First, are there any general ideas that support the idea of local development? Indeed, what do we mean by local development, and what conditions must be met if we are to have effective local development?

Secondly, what are the special issues that arise when we think about organising for development in North Clare—possible objectives, special problems and planning needs.

And, thirdly, based on all this can we outline some sort of design for a North Clare Development Organisation?

I. GENERAL ISSUES OF DEVELOPMENT

I should like before we get down to more specific questions, to run over a few general ideas.

*A paper presented to the North Clare Development Group, Lahinch, March 1973.

Why local development?

The first is, why should we have local development? I can think of at least three *general* reasons why we should be interested in the development of this remote corner of Europe. It might be objected that it is enough to have the overall development of the greater European Community of which we are now a part. Against this, the logic of the argument from Irish nationalism, which I accept, makes us want to preserve Irish society, and Irish people within Ireland.

But does it follow from this that, for example, all the people west of the Shannon should be helped to stay there if they wish? Or that we must preserve even the weakest of our counties—as the people of Leitrim have so significantly asserted? Or that the people of part of a county such as North Clare should likewise be preserved? Clearly, there are limits to that argument. If one is devoted to North Clare but wants to operate a first class kidney unit or be a commissioner in Brussels, it is not reasonable to expect these facilities to be provided hereabouts.

But if one wants to be a farmer, or a housewife, or a business man in a moderate way, in an area such as this, then the argument is a different one. It is that, other things being equal, each of us has a reasonable claim on the resources of the community to help us to spend our days in the places where we were born, if that is what we want to do. This argument is being urged throughout large areas of Europe at this time, and it was in effect accepted at the Paris summit conference on the EEC last year. It is increasingly accepted that economic growth of itself is not enough. In any event, it tends to concentrate, of its own accord, in certain centres making these too big, too inconvenient, too top heavy. It has become an interest of government—both international and national governments—to spread this growth around. They try to do this so as to raise or preserve the quality of life and to try to give equal opportunity to all the people in their community. So, we are here today not just because we are a little mad or pig-headed. We are here because we share a belief with very many people in large tracts of the EEC—a belief that this district of ours (like similar districts in Holland or in Italy, in Brittany or in Bavaria) ought to be preserved from depopulation and ought to share in the prosperity of the whole community. This belief is the foundation for the new impetus being given to regional and social policies in the European Community. A general argument for our local patriotism is, therefore, that the principle of geographical equality is now generally agreed in Europe.

A second argument is the democratic one. In the world that is growing up more people want to have a say in the way their lives are run. Inevitably, great technological forces make for larger and larger areas of operation and more and more centralised decision-making. But very many decisions do not need to be centralised and these are often the ones that most directly affect our daily lives. To an increasing extent, all of us are determined to have a say in these. So, as a counter-balance to the inevitable centralising, technological forces there is, everywhere, the drive to develop the decentralising, participative, democratic forces. If this participation is to have any real meaning for most of us it must take place in small areas, near where we live.

A third argument follows from this. One of the definitions of efficiency is that it makes the most effective use of all the resources that exist. This can only be fully done on the basis of local knowledge, local initiative, local commitment to development.

There can be splendid national, and indeed international, plans for development but these will not mobilise all the resources available (including all the knowledge) or be effectively implemented unless there is full local input into them and commitment to their carrying out.

So there is no need, therefore, for us to feel at any disadvantage in the argument about local development. In terms of both national and international commitments to equality, democracy, and effectiveness local development scores high marks.

What is local development?

But what sort of meaning can we give to the term "local development"? It can be considered under a number of forms. We can think of it as regional development. We can think of it as a task of local government. We can think of it as the development of a district, such as North Clare. This last is what is relevant to us here today. We can see it on a smaller scale still in terms of community—and, even, parish —development.

Ireland is a very centralised country. One reason for this—most important in the early days of the State—was a political one : to make sure that the Government in Dublin really was in charge of the government of every part of the State. That is one reason why our local government system is so tightly and centrally controlled, more so, perhaps, than that of any other democratic state. Another reason for our centralised system is the belief that to make organisations bigger is to make them more efficient. That is why there has been a steady shift from small local authorities to the county authority, to regional authorities, to Dublin. Efficiency may well go with bigness where large capital plants are concerned. But when it comes to human, personal services almost the exact opposite is true. This is because the efficiency of *personal* services is to be measured mainly according to their human qualities of compassion, promptness, flexibility and common sense. These are qualities that large organisations find it almost impossible to display. That is why the tide has, perhaps, at last begun to turn in this country and we see the drift back to the idea of giving our local authorities a more human scale.

The white paper on local government re-organisation[1] dipped a wary toe in these waters by suggesting that county councils might open district offices with district committees and district officers to bring the local services into direct contact with the people. It also envisaged encouraging community bodies on a smaller scale still. The McKinsey Report on strengthening the Local Government Service[2] supports this idea of district offices. The recent report by Messrs. Roche and Christopher[3] on consumer protection proposes that local government should have a programme concerned with Community Services, covering consumer protection, citizens' advice, libraries, local amenities and the like, and that this should be based on the district.

However, it is the Chubb Report, called *More Local Government,* that in 1971, went furthest along this road. It accepted that the traditional local government services, so far as they directly affected people, should be grouped at district level. But it went much further. It urged that all the *personal* services included in the general health services, the education services, the agricultural services and the justice services should be grouped at district level, and then went on to say that *all* the personal services supplied by other government departments and state-sponsored bodies should be grouped together at that level. If this were done we should have a vastly expanded system of local government. Local authorities would become big, not by having their areas increased, but by being given much more to do. District councils would, as far as personal services are concerned, be mini-government offices. In this way every citizen could have the administration of these personal services within easy personal reach.

But the argument here for bringing all these personal services within easy reach of everyone was not only to make things easier and more comprehensible for the citizen. It was also to bring the administration

[1]Prl. 1572, 1971.
[2]Prl. 2252, 1972.
[3]D. Roche and R. F. Christopher: *Consumer Protection—A Role for Local Government,* 1973, Prl. 2916.

of these various services under local, democratic control. It was also to overcome the problems of fragmentation that result from the specialisation of these services, and to relate them together at or near the point of service.

In the arguments about the efficiency of large, centralised bodies this last point was wholly overlooked. It is that when you centralise many services, you make them more fragmented and inflexible at the point of service. Parts of many services that ought to be related together —even in a single field like education or housing or agriculture—go their separate ways because there is seldom a way of relating them together at or near the point of service. The major argument for the district type of organisation with the widest range of personal services at its command is that the services can be grouped together in the overall interest of the people of the district. This grouping and co-ordinating would apply not only to parts of a single service, such as those I have mentioned; these can at least be co-ordinated at or near the top of a single government department. It would also tackle the problem of those distinct services, administered by several departments, which whether they overlap (or, more usually, under-lap) can at present be co-ordinated by no one other than the whole Government itself. Woe betide the man with a problem that falls between several departments! The great argument for the district is that it permits sensible co-operation and flexibility of diverse services at the local level. At least it would, if there were a genuine degree of decentralisation to these bodies. There are some glimmerings of hope that at long last the tide of centralisation that has made us perhaps the most centralised of all democracies is beginning to turn, its own inherent inefficiences having become increasingly obvious.

District

I have been using the word "district". What do we mean by this? Briefly, two things. First, a community area centred around a town— perhaps five, six or seven of them in a typical county—with a total population in the range of 10 – 20,000. Secondly, a council, mainly elected, but partly containing representatives of community organisations in the district. This council would supervise, through a district manager, as many as possible of the personal services—whether supplied by county, regional or national bodies—that are provided in the district. A tall order, you may say, and perhaps only the youngest of us here will live to see its full flowering; but the logic of the situation is, I believe, bringing us, however slowly, in that direction.

If we do move towards a district form of local government, there will be nothing exceptional in that. That is what we had in this country up to 1925 and what nearly every other country has still. It is this country that for the past 50 years has been the odd man out. This is a way by which we can enable local government to mean what it says —the operations of government carried out in a local area.

Conditions for development

I should now like to say a few words about that much used expression "development!" What are the conditions for successful development?

The first point to remember is that development is a very complex process. On the national level we have had an object lesson in this. Our national planning began with the idea that economic development would by itself bring about development as a whole. It then became clear that this had to be supplemented by physical or environmental development. But, as the unseemly scramble for the proceeds of economic development showed, it became necessary to get involved in the further process of social development. This is not, I believe, the end of the story. There are, I think other sides to this—especially the cultural side—that have not yet been recognised. The point is that development is a thing of many facets—now one of them requires special attention, now another, but all of them must be considered in relation to one another so that the development of one helps with the development of all and vice versa. This is the first condition for successful development.

The second condition is one that has as yet been most inadequately grasped. It is the crucial importance of good organisations to the success of whatever kind of development is required. I think that our failure to grasp this fact is the cause of many disappointments. Even where the need for administrative reform has been grasped, we have been very slow in carrying through the necessary reforms. For example, I think we are due for some pretty bitter disappointments over regional development unless we try to hack our way through the local and national administrative jungle that will otherwise engulf most of our aspirations there.

The third condition is what I might call the political one. That is to say, the problem of how to bring the people along with whatever it is planned to do. How do we have adequate consultation, how do we evoke the consent of the interested parties, how do we get their commitment to the steps, sometimes disagreeable ones, that have to be taken to achieve objectives? And, overtopping all of these, how do we establish fully representative and participative institutions for these purposes?

II. SPECIAL ISSUES OF DEVELOPMENT IN NORTH CLARE

Objectives

Now, to bring things nearer home, what ought to be the objective of development in North Clare? This is a matter for you yourselves to decide. It is for me to mention a few possible choices.

One possible objective would be to aim to preserve the existing population of the district. A difficulty here is that merely preserving the population is not sufficient in itself. Any such objective, even if people were willing to stay, only poses a further question. In effect, what would they be preserved for?

Another possible objective would be to provide enough jobs for all the people of the district who come on the labour market. This turns out to be a tall order. Let me explain. Each year 200 to 250 young people become available in this district. Retirements from existing jobs might leave as many as 150 vacancies; but it is unlikely that the existing number of jobs on the land will be maintained. Allowing for all the factors, it would be necessary to provide about 100 to 150 new jobs a year. The plans for the *whole* mid-west region provide for some 1100 new jobs a year. As the population of North Clare is less than one-twentieth of the population of the region as a whole, its share of the planned new jobs would be about 50 if these were distributed on the basis of existing population; but this itself is unlikely. So there remains a substantial gap to be filled. The likely decline in employment on the land, coupled with the extremely small amount of industrial and service employment in the district, would call for a major development of the industrial and service employment-giving opportunities of the district. So this objective, at least in the short run, does not seem to be feasible. To say that the surplus of job seekers should be found employment, if necessary outside the district but within striking distance of it, is merely to point to what are the objectives of the IDA and SFADCO.

If one wishes to think what might be the special objective of a North Clare district, therefore, one may be forced back onto an objective that is both narrower and more generalised than either of those I have mentioned—namely, to preserve and enrich the texture of life in the eight (or ten) parishes that constitute the district. This is to assume—an assumption that is inherent in the whole operation here today—that the people of these parishes constitute, or can be brought to constitute, a sub-society of their own.

Clearly this question of objectives is one to be teased out in much more detail after whatever discussion may be necessary. But in the end, some objective or set of objectives must be chosen around which efforts and an organisation can be built.

Constraints

Given that there will be an objective, whatever it may be, it is useful to look at the constraints, the difficulties, there may be in achieving it. These constraints and difficulties do not so much hinder action as tell us the kinds of action that must be taken to achieve the objective.

The most important of these constraints is the demographic one. The detailed figures for ages etc. from the 1971 census are not yet available, but it is clear from the 1966 figures that there are severe demographic problems. The first of these demographic problems is the very high proportion of old people in the area. The second demographic problem is the heavy preponderance of jobs in agriculture, which, in terms of employment, is a declining industry. In the district there are about 4,750 jobs. Almost two-thirds of these are in agriculture. Events are likely to bring about circumstances in which about half of these jobs will go. The third demographic problem is the extraordinary weakness of the manufacturing sector which, with 300 jobs, represents only about six per cent of the total.

A main constraint is that of physical resources and facilities. This is a question of surveying what is and is not available—of course, a great deal of this has been done, and very valuable contributions have been made here this afternoon. From these surveys close study will be needed to settle what are the crucial, or as we say the *strategic,* factors, and how can they best be combined together.

For example, if we are thinking about jobs we have to think also about the various systems for preparing, training and identfying people for those jobs—the schooling systems—secondary, vocational, regional technical, university; the training systems of AnCo and CERT; the employment promoting systems of IDA and SFADCO; the placement system of the new Manpower Service; as well as the source from which new jobs can come, and including the unorganised job demands of the employment market. Against this must be put the outflow from agriculture. So, to develop both the demand for jobs and the supply of suitably equipped people, and to marry these at the highest possible level, is work requiring a high level of professional expertise across existing institutional boundaries.

The same sort of thing can be seen in relation to farming jobs. The detailed soil survey done by the Agricultural Institute—so far as I understand it—suggests that the livestock carrying capacity of Clare farms could almost be doubled; but this is occurring here more slowly than in other counties. If farms could be enlarged and cattle stocks increased farmers here could enjoy a good livelihood. The re-structuring of farms will depend, at least in part, on the willingness of old farmers without successors to give up their farms in favour of their younger and more active neighbours. The older farmers will do this, if at all, only in return for suitable compensation and facilities. Here is a problem for the various branches of the Department of Agriculture, the Land Commission, perhaps the various housing authorities, the Health Board, the Department of Social Welfare, and so on. Again, a complex operation right across departmental boundaries. As of now, we seem to have no way of dealing with this kind of issue in a planned, co-ordinated, humane and efficient way.

This leads one to the problem of the various kinds of institutions we have for solving our problems. If one looks at these from the viewpoint of the district one sees three separate sets of problems.

The first set of problems can be solved largely *within* the district itself because they are matters within the control of the people here. Examples are: local, voluntary and community organisations, local recreational facilities, credit unions, etc.

The second set of problems is concerned with the relationships *between* the district itself and those outside bodies—they are mainly official bodies—that operate within it—the county council, or SFADCO, or the regional health board, the Department of Agriculture or whatever. There is an extraordinarily large number of these bodies, all with different interests, structures, temperaments, and so on. To evoke their co-operation and commitment in a continuing way is a task of great complexity.

The third set of problems raises issues of a general nature—such as what is to be done about the price of land—that have to be tackled and settled far *outside* the district.

Then there is the ever-present problem of finance. The purely local issues are not too complex. But when we turn to mobilising the various forms of public aids that exist so that joint attacks can be made on the problems of unused resources and inadequate facilities, then we are in an area of considerable complexity that calls for skilful planning. There is also the question of evoking wholly new forms of financial aid. For example, a study in another not dissimilar district suggested that the deposits from the district in the banks exceeded the investments of the banks in that district. If that were to be true of this district, what steps could be taken so that the imbalance be righted?

Overriding planning considerations

In any planned approach to these problem areas there are, I think, three overriding considerations.

The first, as I keep on insisting, is the complexity of the development process. I think the whole justification of the district approach to development is that it looks at personal and family life in the round, as it were, and considers not only jobs, or houses, or roads, or health, or telephones, or old people, or schooling or bus services, or recreation, or the thousand and one other things that impinge on each person's life, but all of these things—or at least related groups of them—together. It may be (just) tolerable for official bodies in Dublin or Cork or Limerick or Galway or Ennis to pick up their telescopes and look at some individual in, say, Doolin as a congest, with a farm needing drainage, the father of a handicapped child, the recipient of unemployment assistance, needing home help, etc. etc. But the whole sense of a district organisation is to see him and his family primarily as a unit, and to pull all these official viewpoints together so that he can be helped as a person, and not as a bundle of unrelated social and economic symptoms.

The second overriding consideration is the need for participation, participation by the local people and participation by the various kinds of institutions that exist to serve them. Local participation in the earlier stages must rest on a basis of local community groups in parishes or in groups of parishes, vocational bodies of farmers, etc. and on other interest groups. In the longer run this group participation would have to be supplemented by a broader democratic participation via properly elected public representatives. Another crucial form of participation is that of public bodies and their officials. Somehow the institutions have to be bound into any district structure, and this means that the local official representatives of these bodies, with the full backing of their superiors, must be involved in the operation of the enterprise. Otherwise its whole purpose will be lost.

The third overriding consideration is the administrative one. There are four main elements in this. First, it is crucial to define as soon as possible the *area* of operation of the district. In North Clare this means deciding what area should be covered by the district—eight or ten

M

parishes, for example? It means sorting out the district in relation to some of the traditional areas—for example, the old Ballyvaghan and Ennistymon rural districts, or the current Ennistymon county electoral area, and so on. Not very difficult, but important. Once the area is defined it becomes possible to align the various official commitments in and to that area. This question of definition is a relatively simple matter which in this country we find excruciatingly difficult to decide upon.

Equally excruciating to get defined, but equally important, is a clear *role* for the organisation. By this we mean that one makes clear what is the job of the organisation and how much freedom it will be allowed in doing that job. This will be the result of bargaining with various bodies, bargaining to get some freedom of action on the one hand, and, on the other, to get defined degrees of commitment on their part.

Then there must be an effective *planning system,* and a means by which the various interests affected by any plan can be fully consulted, can be fully committed to the carrying out of their part of the operation in a co-ordinated way, and can be subject to systematic review of their performance in relation to that commitment. This brings one back again to the continuing role of a body truly representative of all the principal interests.

Then, again, there must be an equally effective *management system* to ensure that the plans, once accepted, are actually carried out—this does not always happen.

III. A POSSIBLE ORGANISATIONAL DESIGN?

Can we now sketch out a design for this organisation? A probable objective is to preserve and enrich the texture of the social life of the district. For this task it would be necessary to involve all the relevant interests, local, personal, representative and official. There are four broad areas of operation:

First, there is the *environmental* area, which would include roads, houses, water and sewerage, communications, transport, power, amenities, etc.

Secondly, there is the *economic* area, which would include agriculture, lands and forestry, fisheries, industry, labour, services (including tourism) and finance.

Thirdly, there is the *social* area, which would include health, welfare and justice.

Fourthly, there is the *cultural* area, which would include education, recreation and such interests where North Clare has outstanding resources such as archaeology, botany, music, etc.

If one draws up even a reasonably inclusive list of the official bodies concerned in these areas, one finds that they are very numerous indeed. When one takes into account, in addition, the various voluntary, professional, and vocational groups that must be involved, one is conscious that, progressively and by the middle term, provision must be made for the involvement of a large number of persons. Perhaps what might be done is to set up four main panels—one for each of the areas suggested —that is, one for environmental problems, one (or perhaps two) for economic problems, one for social problems and one for cultural problems. For the more complex issues arising under each of these broad headings there might be sub-panels. Clearly there would necessarily be a good deal of interlocking between the various panels and sub-panels.

One of the tasks here to-day is to set up an interim organisation; this is basically a task of giving support to a selected working group. So much for the short-term. In the long-term we might hope that what is being started here to-day will help to bring about a whole new look and a democratisation in the relations of government to local areas; but that, to repeat, is for the long-term. The problem now is to give some thought to what might be done in the middle term. How to get things launched with such a degree of skill and professionalism that we can look forward with confidence to a widely representative system in the longer term?

The following is a possible administrative structure for that middle term. I just throw out a few ideas for discussion. First, it would be necessary to set up a company limited by guarantee, so as to have a legal entity, capable of holding property, etc. It would be necessary that this company should command wide support through having a large number of individual members paying an annual subscription, and it should aim to have some sort of significant income through having corporate members—these would be vocational, official and other interested bodies— paying a very much larger annual subscription, depending on their size and financial strength.

Secondly, there could be a council representative of all these members which might meet quarterly.

Thirdly, this council would establish an executive committee of perhaps eight to twelve persons. This committee would be crucial to the whole enterprise and should consist of highly skilled persons competent to master what seems to me to be the really daunting technical and administrative problems that would face them. One would like to think that this committee could be made up of the ablest and most skilled people that can be found.

Fourthly, this committee would appoint a well-qualified manager for the organisation and secure—perhaps through the benevolence of SFADCO—a highly skilled research and planning facility. Fifthly, the committee would also set up the appropriate panels and sub-panels so as to involve the various interests in an orderly way. Two crucial interests here are the county development team and, of course, SFADCO. One would expect to see the special skills of these bodies being heavily called upon when the panels are constituted and set to work, called upon indeed in relation to underpinning the whole organisation.

It may be too soon at this stage to be thinking of such formal structures, and, in any event, there is plenty of room for argument about the details of any such structure. What is important, I think, is, nonetheless, to keep some such overall design in mind. It is essential to ensure that the interest and the enthusiasm for this venture are not lost because sufficient skills were not mobilised to get the whole venture off the ground.

Clearly, a major step once the organisation was established, would be to ensnare, as it were, those public institutions that already have a direct and close commitment to North Clare. One thinks immediately of the county council, and their officials working in the district, particularly the assistant county engineer. One thinks of the mid-west health board and their officials who also work in the district. One, perhaps, particularly thinks of the various educational interests ranging from the school headmasters to the departmental inspectors who might find it convenient, within the overall umbrella of this organisation, to tease out and rationalise the educational problems of this district and see how far they could specially help towards solutions for some of its economic problems.

One thinks too of how, perhaps, the housing (including water supply) problems of the district might be the result of a joint plan to which local groups, the county council officers, the officers of the Department of Local Government, and the officers of the Land Commission, might all make valuable contributions. If there were a comprehensive programme by which houses to buy, houses to rent, and re-conditioned houses were provided through co-operative, county council, and group activity, an important injection might be made into the district. If this should set up a demand to attract back to the district those who had left it and acquired skills elsewhere, so much to the good.

One thinks of the committee of agriculture and their advisers in the district, as well as the local officers of the Department of Agriculture on the land project, farm buildings, and other schemes, as well as other interested parties involved in a study of methods of overcoming the relatively slow growth in Clare—or at least in this part of it—of the build up of livestock numbers that would inject so much extra purchasing power into the district. To ensure that this benefit was retained so far as possible in the district, it might be possible to foster the development of service and distribution facilities in, say, the three main towns.

These are, of course, just a few samples that occur almost at random; but you who know the district well will be able to think of many more.

CONCLUSION

Well to finish, what I have been saying is this. There are strong general arguments for the sort of local development we are interested in —arguments based on equality, democracy and efficiency, arguments that are now accepted as part of the social and regional policies of the EEC. The more one looks at the nature of the problems of local development the more one sees that they can only be overcome by a whole new approach to government and to local government at the district level. We need local democracy, local co-ordination, local planning, local management. Perhaps what is happening here to-day is the beginning of a brave, new initiative of this kind?

I think we may see emerging here to-day something that will be of great significance to North Clare, something that will be of great significance to the country as a whole. Just as a whole new interest in local structures grew out of the pioneering surveys of Muintir na Tire in Limerick in the 1950's, and new conceptions of development and the scale of the efforts needed to achieve it, from the work at Shannon in the 1960's; just as out of these roots grew the notion of the mid-west regional development organisation in the late 1960's, a concept now spread to the country as a whole; so also, at the other end of the spectrum as it were, we may see evolving in North Clare, out of the same roots, a new conception of how to humanise and make comprehensive, at the personal level, the whole vast fragmented miscellany of governmental institutions in this country.

Is it too much to hope that the powers that be who have accepted the idea of and given special aid to designated areas, and special areas, and pilot farm areas, might come to look on this as a most exciting experiment, also entitled to special consideration? Could we think of it as a Pilot Local Development District? Its nature would be to combine experimentally all the governmental services provided in the district and reduce them to local, flexible scale in the interests of the comprehensive development of North Clare.

In the interests of North Clare, in the interests of the country as a whole, a great deal depends on *your* making a success of this experiment. I have no doubt but that you will.

Chapter 12

LOCAL GOVERNMENT REFORM*

This is a time of change in our administrative institutions. They begin to occur in central government following the implementation of the principal recommendations of the Devlin Group. We have had substantial changes in the health services in the setting up of the new regional health boards. We are seeing the evolution of regional development organisations, and other regional institutions. We have had in the past couple of years two White Papers about the reform, respectively, of the structure[1] and finances[2] of local government. We can discern the beginnings of change also in those services that have part of their activity in the local government sphere. In education, restructuring is taking place at second level where local bodies, the vocational education committees, have major interests. The agricultural extension services, the special job of the county committees of agriculture, are in the melting pot. In social welfare, plans are being made for the future of another local government service—home assistance. Changes have been occurring in the administration of housing, and others are due in relation to the principal roads.

In this process of change and adaptation one cannot discern any overall plan or pattern. There is to be seen, however, a significant drift, a drift away from the small, local, democratic and compendious body to larger, more specialised, largely nominated bodies—or to completely centralised ones. The White Paper on the Reorganisation of Local Government gently suggested favouring the development of community bodies, of embryonic district organisations and of regional development organisations, all on a more or less informal basis.

At the same time the White Paper turned its face against the smaller statutory bodies and public representatives. This has meant in effect, a further retreat from the representative system which is the distinguishing mark of local government. The proposals, if implemented, would have reduced the number of elected local representatives by about half. If this should occur with the green wood, what indeed of the dry? So, it is not

*Cork University Extension Lecture, April, 1973.
[1]*Local Government Reorganisation,* 1971. Prl. 1572.
[2]*Local Finance and Taxation,* 1972. Prl. 2745.

175

surprising that the ordinary observer is a bit confused about what is happening. Is it possible to identify any rules, principles, guidelines that would help us to judge the picture overall and decide whether individual changes add to or substract from that?[3]

I think that in any approach to considering local government reform in the broad sense, ranging from regional bodies through county bodies, through district bodies to community bodies, some eight questions might be posed. I think the answers to these questions may help to throw light on the adequacy or otherwise of the steps that are being taken to bring about local government reform. These questions are:

1. Why should we have a system of local government?
2. What is its purpose?
3. What should it do?
4. How many tiers of local authorities ought there to be?
5. What should be the areas of each type of local authority?
6. What kind of management system does a local authority need?
7. How is local government to be financed?
8. What ought to be the nature of central-local relations?

These are all far-reaching questions and it is possible in the time only to suggest summary answers to them.

1. Why local government?

In this country we have three broad systems of government. First, there is *central* government, concerned with the overall problems of the community. As it happens, it is also concerned with a very large number of the detailed problems of special areas. Secondly, we have *functional* government, where a single body is concerned with a single function— as the ESB is with electricity, Bord Failte with tourism; and so on. Thirdly, we have *local* government which is concerned with a number of things that occur in a particular area.

There was a time when, given the restricted range of governmental activities, some people thought that central government might be confined to the great affairs of state—overall finances, foreign policy, defence, and so on; and that all the rest of the governmental functions could be discharged at the local level. That is not now the system that we operate in this country. Only vestiges of it remain in the compendious nature of much of our local government system. This is the first mark of local government, that it tends to group together a number of not necessarily related functions except insofar as they occur in a particular place.

[3]The general and international framework of local government systems is well set out in A. F. Leemans: *Changing Patterns of Local Government,* 1970.

However, now that government touches the individual citizen at so many points it is a major advantage to have an easily accessible "crossover" point where the impact of separate services on the same individual can be related together. This is a major inherent efficiency of a local government system with broad functions.

A second feature of local government is its pervasiveness. Because local authorities are spread throughout the country, and because they all have similar functions, the various local government activities are carried out in a singularly pervasive way.

The third mark of local government is that the controlling body is elected by the citizens of the area.

The net effect of all this is that the system is democratic and, in relation to those jobs for which it is adapted, highly efficient, as well as adaptable. One does not need to be too starry-eyed about the merits of local government; but it is a fact that pretty well every kind of country has a local government system. In many other countries, a number of them notably better governed than this country, it plays a bigger constitutional, practical, and emotional part than it does with us. There seems, therefore, to be some inherent instinct towards a local level of government, and it embodies a number of values, democratic and efficient, that cannot otherwise be realised.

2. What is the purpose of local government?

The purpose of local government is admirably set out in the White Paper:

"The existence of local authorities is due only in part to practical considerations. From an administrative point of view, it will readily be conceded that certain public services must be organised on a geographical basis—these are services requiring local knowledge for their administration, convenient means of access by the citizens of the area, or the actual carrying out of operations in the area. But practical, economic and administrative considerations do not necessarily require that the local organisation required to provide such services should be an independent entity with a directing body elected by and answerable to the residents of the area; it could, for example, be a local branch of a State body. The real argument, therefore, for the provision of local services by local authorities (in the sense in which the term is generally understood) is that a system of local self government is one of the essential elements of democracy. Under such a system, local affairs can be settled by the local citizens themselves or their representatives, local services can be locally controlled and local communities can participate in the process and responsibilities of government."[4]

"Local government exists, therefore, for democratic as well as practical reasons. It is in a special position for—

'it is the part of government that is most accessible to the average citizen, that most closely touches him and presents the most opportunities for public service. It is a school of citizenship. It associates many citizens with the actual business of government and has a peculiar function as the arena in which men and women can graduate as public representatives. It fulfils a higher purpose in a democratic State than that of a mere provider of roads, water, sewers, hospitals and all the rest and its success must be judged by the manner in which it fulfils its dual role.' "[5]

"Because of the importance of the public services provided by local authorities and their contribution to economic and social development and because of the substantial proportion of national resources devoted to the services, it must be a basic objective of any reorganisation of local government to create conditions in which the services can be provided effectively; in other words, each unit of local government must be capable of providing an acceptable standard of service in an efficient and economical manner. But, as pointed out in Chapter 2, local authorities are more than the providers of important services—they exist because of democratic as well as practical considerations. It must, therefore, be an equally important objective to foster responsible and live local government, to create conditions in which there is maximum scope for local discretion and initiative, to encourage to the fullest possible extent involvement and participation in local affairs, to make membership of a local authority interesting and attractive; in short, to ensure that the local government system fulfils the democratic purpose it is designed to serve."[6]

The main comment one can make on these admirable sentiments is that they are not very well translated into action in the proposals in the White Paper. One might also make the point that the inherent efficiency of the relatedness of services, their pervasiveness, and their democratic control, already referred to, do not seem to have been fully grasped.

[4]Para. 2.1.1.
[5]Para. 2.1.2. The quotation is from John Collins: *Local Government,* 2nd ed., 1963.
[6]Para. 4.2.1.

3. *What should local government do?*

This is the heart of the problem. Quite clearly the extraordinary patchwork of central, regional and local agencies that we have at present is neither democratic, in a local sense, nor, in any overall sense, efficient.

To see what local government might, or ought, do it is necessary to look beyond the traditional local government bodies, and to relate them to the whole system of government. This involves us specifically in trying to relate local authorities to the existing and developing regional bodies and to the field services of the central government departments and of the central state-sponsored bodies. Is it possible to differentiate particular kinds of functions that are appropriate to each type of organisation? Do we need a new conception of the roles (or jobs) of central, regional, county, and district government to supersede the existing complex and confused non-system? This raises major issues of deconcentration, and devolution, of government and the means of participation in governmental activities by the citizens. This kind of approach involves us in being more sophisticated in the way we look at governmental functions. At present we tend to look at them almost exclusively on a *vertical* plane, as a confrontation between central government and the consumer of governmental services. But any rationalisation of the present non-system requires us to look at them also on a *horizontal* plane so as to try to relate, on some principle of congruity, the various kinds of services together, irrespective of the kinds of organisations that at present supply them. If one does this one can begin to see emerging a hierarchical system. We know that, if a hierarchy is to work, the jobs of each level of the hierarchy must be clearly differentiated on degrees of generality. Thus the more specific services, especially the personal ones, would become, irrespective of what kind of organisation now supplies them, the tasks of local government.

4. *How many tiers of local government ought there to be?*

One of the striking features of modern Irish life has been the growth of voluntary organisations. These are for various kinds of social, cultural, sporting, etc. activities and tend to be special in themselves. I understand that the village of Sneem with a population of 250 has 25 such organisations centred on it. In the Fermoy area there are about 93. In Nenagh with a population of 4,500 there are 111. In Westport, with a population of about 3,000, there are 67. And so on. Out of these specialised groupings has been emerging a new sense of community where common interests in the development of community facilities and

resources have been beginning to make their presence felt. The same
is to be seen in the suburbs of the cities. We are now witnessing the
growth of an extensive network of community organisations. It is not
clear that these community organisations can have any very significant
administrative role, but they clearly have a representative one. This
obviously is the first tier of a local government system keyed into the
dynamics of Irish life.

Above that one can see the need, recognised, if inadequately, in the
White Paper, for some form of local office where at least the personal
services of government can be administered in a manner that is close
to the people, that can relate one service to another, and that is democratically controlled. So, here we have both a representative and an
administrative tier.

Thirdly, there are the significant technological services—similar in
many ways to those provided by existing county councils—which require
a larger area of operation. Here we have the third tier of representative
government, and the second administrative tier.

Fourthly, we have above the existing counties the emergence of
regional groupings, the special functions of which are emerging as the
overall review of development within the region, planning for the future,
and the administration of those special, highly technological services
that require a larger area for their operation than the county—acute
general hospitals are a case in point. Here also, if planning is to be
effective and to be acceptable to those who are planned for, there must
be a representative system. So here we have a fourth tier of the representative system, and a third tier of the administrative one.

All of these, are, of course, subordinate in their appropriate ways to
the top tier of the whole system, that of central government.

5.   *What should be the areas of each type of local authority?*

This, like the other issues arising out of proposals to reform the
structure of local government, is discussed in the Chubb Report.[7]

Given the pattern of Irish life a basic community area will be something like one or two parishes.

The basic district area will be a significant town and its hinterland.
The dichotomy that now exists in our local government system between
towns and rural areas is something that has survived from the walled
towns of medieval times, where conquerors had to protect themselves
from the people in the rural areas who resented their intrusion. That is

[7]*More Local Government: A Programme for Development*, 1971.

all long since past, town and country now live in partnership, and our institutions should recognise that fact.

Clearly, the area of main technology is likely to remain, for some time at least, the existing county. Whether some rationalisation should be made of county boundaries, and whether some of the weaker counties should be amalgamated with their neighbours, are questions that ought to be tackled. There should be a system for ensuring that this is done after full public enquiry and discussion.

Finally, the region. This has worked out in our system as, typically, two, three, or four counties grouped together. One of the problems is, of course, that for different services the regional groupings are sometimes of different counties. But at least there is not much breaching of county boundaries and it may be possible to bring some order and sense into the definition and standardisation of regional areas.

6.   What kind of management system does a local authority need?

It is clear from the experience of private industry that an efficient way of getting things done is to appoint a board representative of the owners, who themselves appoint a chief executive who has very extensive powers of initiative and implementation but who is held accountable to the board. This is the system that we have in our state-sponsored bodies. It is the system that has also been introduced, with endless debate, into our local government system. One of the most notable features of that system has been, by means of the Local Appointments Commission, to build up a corps of competent officers selected solely on merit. This laid the foundations on which an effective management system could be established. There is not much doubt, after all the debate, that an essential feature of the management of any public organisation is the existence, under a representative board, of a powerful chief executive flanked by a competent staff. That issue has been settled in public debate, and its implications ought by now to have been more generally applied.

7.   How is local government to be financed?

On the problem of local finances one does not get much help in the most recent White Paper on this subject. The debate during the recent general election has left the issues extremely confused. However, a few points might be made. First, local government is a substantial consumer of capital, and a very efficient method of supplying capital to local authorities from central sources, through the Local Loans Fund, has been established. On the whole, this system of finance works very well and does not call for significant discussion, except insofar as the central controls on the details of capital works are still, in places, carried to absurd lengths.

When one looks at the system of current taxation of local government the situation is, of course, otherwise. If local government services were to be developed and extended a number of issues will have to be clarified. The first is that it is not inherent in our system that local government should only do what it can pay for from its own resources. In practice the state has been contributing about half the expenditure of local government in recent years. But there is nothing mystic about that half. If the most efficient way of financing a service is to provide it from central taxation, then there is nothing wrong or embarrassing in that. If Bord Failte Eireann or Coras Trachtala or the Industrial Development Authority can get all their funds from state resources, there is no intrinsic reason why local authorities should not do so. It all depends on what is the most efficient way of raising funds for the financing of public services.

The existing system of local taxation bears all the marks of a taxation system that has, for generations, been crying out for reform, and has not got it. In the first place, the national taxation system ought to be seen as a whole and the contribution of taxes on property (i.e. rates) in that system considered in that light. Secondly, the grotesque system of valuation by which houses are valued according to letting values that were, at least partly, current in 1852 makes for gross inequity and inefficiency. I believe that there is a great need in this country for a review of the total taxation system from the point of view of efficiency, equity and its re-distributive effects. Local finances are an outstanding candidate for first attention here; but, again, in the context of the whole system of financing governmental services.

8.   *What ought to be the nature of central-local relations?*

We have in this country probably the most subordinated system of local government that exists in western democracies. This is justified—as in the White Paper on Local Government Re-organisation—because the state contributes so much to the current expenditure of local authorities. But this is a rationalisation. A system of control that was devised for the boards of guardians in 1838—when the first major experiment in creating Irish democratic institutions was begun—has, notwithstanding the strength of Irish democracy, been spread to the whole of the local government system. This cribbing of local discretion contrasts extraordinarily with the degrees of discretion given to state-sponsored bodies where, in the majority of cases, all or virtually all of their finances comes directly from the state and there is no system of local representation or taxation at all. It was this anomaly that made the Devlin Group suggest that local authorities should be given the same degree of administrative discretion as state-sponsored bodies have—that they might all be seen as comparable types of executive agents of the total system of government. Both in comparison with how we treat the newer established forms of government and in comparison with other countries abroad, we run an absurdly subordinated system of local government.

The problem here is that we have not thought through any principles on which administrative autonomy ought to rest. In some instances—and local government is the glaring one—we have been so frightened of the possible abuses of autonomy that we have virtually abolished it. In others, we have been so frightened of the abuses of lack of autonomy that we have granted it on an almost lavish scale, as some state-sponsored bodies can illustrate. We need to look this issue in the eye and see is there not a middle way, or a series of graduations of autonomy appropriate to various types of organisations, that will enable free, flexible and responsible initiative to be be combined with overall national control. This is inherent in the whole Devlin system now being applied, and local government ought not to be an exception to this.

Problems of Reform

Can we draw any general ideas from these rapid observations?

I think the first requirement is to see government as it operates in geographical areas in the widest possible perspective. We should not allow our ideas to be limited by historical accidents or by departmental frontiers. Let us think, when we are discussing local government reform, of the meaning of the words "*local*" and "*government*"—that is government as it operates in a locality of some sort whether that be a community, a district, a county or a region. If we take this wide perspective then it is possible to make sense of the systems of government we have.

The second point is to clarify in our minds how far we wish the democratic processes to go. It is an essential feature of local government that it be carried on under the surveillance of the elected representatives of the recipients of the services. Notwithstanding the growth in public awareness and the desire for more participation, the drift in our governmental institutions has been away from that kind of democratic system. Are we happy that this should be so? Is not a condition of effective action in the future likely to be a great deal more of public participation, public assent, local democracy?

Thirdly, we must be concerned with the effectiveness of government. A large number of bodies dealing with bits and pieces of problems—bodies fragmented within themselves (e.g. the field services of several departments), and fragmented as between themselves and other bodies concerned with similar activities, cannot make for efficient, flexible or adaptable administration. It is an old rule that what is simple is efficient. There is scope for a vast simplification of our systems of government and administration as they apply in relation to the individual citizen and consumer.

Are such things as more democracy and more efficient government in the overall interest of our society? I have no doubt that they are, and that a comprehensive overhaul of the geographical operations of central, functional and local government would contribute greatly to the quality of life in this country and to the effective meeting of the needs of the citizen.

What are the barriers preventing this kind of approach to the problems of the reform of local government in the broad sense in which I have been indicating? I think the issues as to what ought to be done are clear enough. What is needed is an essay in persuasion so that the people can see that some such ideas as have been sketched out here will be in their overall interest. This is a problem of informing the public as to what they might reasonably expect of those who are concerned with improving their governmental machinery. It is, of course, a political question in the sense that whatever is done must in the last analysis be decided by politicians, and they, in turn, must be satisfied that there will be public assent to what the politicians decide ought to be done. Thirdly, there is the question of persuading the vast number of administrative bodies that a rationalisation of their activities "in the field" is in the public interest.

It would be foolish to underestimate the difficulties that lie in the way of overcoming the obstacles to a genuine reform. Nonetheless, I for one get the impression that the public themselves are now coming to a greater degree of concern about this problem than either politicians or officials have so far brought themselves to express.

The classic way of at least beginning to tackle this problem is to set up a wide ranging inquiry into the system of government at what has been described as "sub-national level". This might well be an inquiry similar in scope to the first Devlin inquiry, but taking its perspective from the local area rather than from the central one, concerned with how best to meet the needs of the ordinary citizen in a rapidly democratising society. One might expect such an inquiry to lay out the general principles on which a genuine local government reform could be achieved, and the ways and means of doing this in a manner that will be compatible with the overall needs and aspirations of our society.

In the same way, the problems of local taxation ought to be viewed in the context of the taxation system as a whole. Here, again, there is a rising public awareness of the need to rationalise, to simplify, and to make more equitable, the various methods of raising public taxation.

N

Chapter 13

THE WAY WE LIVE NOW—DEVELOPING OUR DEMOCRACY*

The way we live now is a product of three factors:

the past, to the extent that we have inherited its ideas and institutions;

the present, with its strains and stresses; and

the future, insofar as we discern its problems and take steps to prevent them.

The way we live now and in the future depends greatly on how we develop our democracy. This is not just something we inherit from the past, regard respectfully in the present, and pass on unchanged to the future. It needs as much concern, anxious thought and careful development as any great inheritance.

Our democracy is a number of ideas or values that we hold in common and a set of institutions established to maintain those values and to give them increasing relevance to our daily lives, now and in the future.

My present purpose is to say something about problems of some of our important public institutions. The development of our democracy depends on how these public institutions translate our values into our daily lives now and in the future, so that in our daily lives we shall be increasingly free, increasingly equal, increasingly responsible, and increasingly playing a part in the events that shape our lives.

What do I mean by the term "public institutions"? For now, the Houses of the Oireachtas, the departments of government, and the various regional and local bodies insofar as they relate to this general theme of the development of our democracy, of increasing the democratisation of our society.

I want to say that the vigour and adaptability of these institutions are crucial to all our lives; that there is a particular need for our

*Lecture at Adult Education Centre, Kilkenny, January, 1975.

Houses of the Oireachtas to adapt themselves to the great national needs of the present and the future by shedding detailed work to subordinate institutions; that we need to plan for better government, and to think critically about developing our democratic system.

I. THE PROBLEM OF ADAPTABILITY

This country is at one of the turning points in its history. Economically, we have now begun to be a part of the modern world. Politically, we are now members of the European Community. Socially, nearly all the forces of the modern world can be seen operating amongst us. Our public institutions were devised for a simple, under-developed, agricultural, politically and socially isolated society fifty years ago. Can they now cope with this changed world without themselves undergoing significant change? Can we be sure that our institutions are well geared to guide us safely through the dangers that exist and that lie in front?

The public sector in Ireland—as is common in most other western democratic countries—deals with about half the business of the country. This is often the better half of that business, because of the importance of the decisions taken in government. The tendency is for both the proportion, and the importance, to increase rather than decrease. For example, in all countries, an increasing responsibility of government is to redistribute more fairly the results of economic growth—by means of greater financial support for those who are weak and ill, by means of greater help towards the development of educational and health services, and so on. I don't argue that this growth in state activity is good or bad: it is simply a fact of modern life.

You may say that, whatever about the role of the state, what is important are the people we elect to govern us, and not the institutions of which these people are in command. This is to take too simple a view. No matter how much care is taken in the selection of the driver, he is unlikely to reach his destination on time if the car he drives breaks down, or its steering, or brakes, or accelerator do not effectively respond to his commands. There is no conflict between good governors and good institutions. Good institutions can contribute considerably to good government; bad institutions can seriously interfere with it. Good government is the child of the marriage between good governors and good government institutions.

It is commonplace to say that things nowadays change very fast and that we, if we want to keep abreast of events, have to do a fair bit of changing too. This is no less true of institutions than of individuals. But it is harder for the institutions. Let me give an example. A private firm has a fairly clear motivating force to make changes—so that it can continue to make a profit. If it does not adapt it will go out of business, as many do. Public institutions seldom have single, clear-cut objectives, and usually lack the sharp annual discipline of the balance sheet. It is often possible for them to continue for long periods to fail to adapt to changing circumstances.

A number of issues arise when one looks at our institutions in this way. The basic one is can we organise the flow of public business so that what is nationally most important is dealt with at the highest levels of government and what is least important nationally is dealt with at the lowest levels?

So much for generalities. Let me now try to be a bit more specific.

II. THE PROBLEM OF PARLIAMENT

A major problem is that of the development of the most important of all our public institutions, the Houses of the Oireachtas. In a democracy parliament must, necessarily and rightly, be a central part of the whole governmental process. There is a danger that this may not be wholly true of our country. If this is so, the fault is, I believe, a failure of adaptation and development.

Our directly elected house, the Dail, plays, of course, its part in the great occasions of state. But there are important occasions on which it plays little or no part, such as the origin and development of the planning process of this country, to which I will be referring later. This was one of the most important episodes in the history of our independence; but the Dail has been so pre-occupied with the *details* of administration, especially the personal details of the constituents of the members, that its procedure and the time of its members have not been geared to such general issues. The Dail was originally designed for a small, rather poor, mainly rural society where the role of government would be minimal. In those days it was feasible to have a highly centralised system of government, and to have the members of the Dail as the moderators, as it were, between the central government and the citizen. The huge volume of constituency work now falling on deputies is at least in part due to this policy of extreme centralisation.

By comparison with modern legislatures our Dail is woefully under-equipped in relation to staff, research facilities, private members' time, committee procedures, even library services. The members of the Dail are themselves becoming more articulate about these problems, and they need the encouragement and support of the ordinary citizens to get the process of parliamentary adaptation underway.

But deputies will not be able to find time to think about the more general problems of Irish government unless some method is devised for easing the enormous burden of detailed constituency work that is thrown upon them. I will come back to this later.

The situation of the Seanad is even more disturbing. It clearly has great difficulty in finding a role in our system of government. So do second houses in many legislatures; but our situation need not be as bad as it is. The notable feature of our Seanad is that, constitutionally and in practice, it plays a very small part in legislation, it exercises very few review functions, and, although it is composed on a vocational principle, seems to have few vocational links.

Contrast the Seanad, and its role, for example, with that of the National Economic and Social Council, which, one expects, will be heavily involved with the big economic, social and regional questions of the community and which is, of course, so strongly representative of the significant vocational interests in the community. There are many other, more specialised, bodies, with substantial vocational interests, attached to the system of government. But there is a big cleavage between these kinds of bodies and the Houses of the Oireachtas.

What has been happening is that the big questions confronting the community as a whole are handled by vocational, nominated, and non-elected bodies. Members of the Oireachtas seldom or never are members of these bodies, and there seem to be no other effective links between these bodies and the deputies and senators. There is something curiously wrong here.[1]

It would be very much in the interests of democratic practice if our two Houses of the Oireachtas were brought more clearly into the main stream of national life and some form of working partnership established between elected representatives and expert advisory groups.

III. THE PROBLEMS OF SHEDDING THE LOAD

But only part of the remedy here is the strengthening of parliamentary institutions. Another part is to devise ways by which the great load of

[1]See Informal Committee on Reform of Dail Procedure: Report, 1972, esp. para. 5.
For a recent critical review of Oireachtas procedures see Alan J. Ward: "Parliamentary Procedures and the Machinery of Government in Ireland", *Irish University Review* 4 (1974) 2. See also Senator Mary Robinson: "The Role of the Irish Parliament", ADMINISTRATION, Vol. 22 (1974) 1. See also B. Chubb: *The Government and Politics of Ireland*, 1970, ch. 8, and *Cabinet Government in Ireland*, 1974, ch. 7.

detailed and particular business can be shed by the members of the national parliament. There are two main steps that could be taken. The first is to have a system for dealing with the grievances of the citizen against the administration. The second is to reverse the wholly exceptional degree of centralisation that we practise in this country.

Grievance Procedures

As the state interferes in more and more of the activities of the community the individual citizens will have grievances about individual decisions taken in relation to them. In this country there are a number of ways of dealing with specific grievances, but the overall system—outside constitutional rights—dates from the era of state prerogative. If the King's servants have done me a wrong, or denied me a right, I will appeal to the King to exercise his clemency to remedy my grievance. Only, nowadays, we substitute an elected minister for an hereditary monarch. This it not now the system that applies in most democracies.

In developed democracies the citizen has certain rights that he can establish against the state, and special institutions have been created to ensure that he can do this fairly easily. Hence the system of administrative courts that exists, for example, in most of the European countries. To pick up the relatively few cases that fail to be dealt with by these courts, the Scandinavians, as we know, have supplemented the system by the institution of an ombudsman. This is a far cry from writing to your TD to see if he can exact a favour from a minister on your behalf. In fact such intervention is unusual in other countries.

That is why the Devlin Report reviewing governmental organisation proposed institutions to regularise the relationships of the citizens with government, relieve a cruel burden on public representatives, and help to allay the widespread, if unfounded, suspicion that "fixing" is the order of the day in Irish government administration.

Decentralisation

We in this country have not grasped how centralised is our system of government. We have concentrated great powers in ministers, great volumes of work in central government departments, great numbers of public servants in the capital city. In consequence, there have been at least three major drawbacks.

The first is that the centralisation of the public services means that when they meet the citizen they are fragmented, rigid and remote. This has made the citizen bewildered and distrustful.

Secondly, we have very few elected public representatives outside the national parliament. Those we have—in the local government system—are concerned with a small part of the business of government. To an increasing extent our representatives are nominated for us by ministers, not elected by us, the people. This, to my mind, is not democratic advance, but its opposite. A great part of the work of local representation about local matters is now thrown on the over-burdened shoulders of national elected representatives. My argument is that it should be disposed of locally by representatives elected by local people for that purpose.

The third drawback is that central government has become clogged up with a vast mass of detail. This seriously interferes with the really important business that only central government can do. This problem has begun to be realised and some limited experiments are now going ahead.

But the real issue will not be tackled until we produce an effective system of local and regional government, until we decide to have a thorough going reform of the run down system of local government that we have, until we decide what to do about the spontaneous rise of community and district organisations, until we make sense of the fragmented ad hockery of our regional bodies, until we move back again from nominated representatives to elected ones.

In the interests of the efficient operation of the public services, in the interests of involving more people in the processes of government, in the interests of freeing central government from the crushing burden of detail so as to let it get on with its own special job, it is vitally urgent that an intelligent programme of decentralisation be adopted.

And by that, I don't mean the haphazard scattering of bits of government departments around the country.

IV. THE PROBLEM OF PLANNING

What would be left for the central government to do? Two things, basically. To plan, and to see that the plans are made to work.

A Planning System

When, in 1958, this country last faced serious economic difficulties, the self-confidence and the spirit of the people were mobilised by means of an economic plan—called the First Programme for Economic Expansion. This plan set out in lucid terms a set of priorities for achieving economic growth. It was, as we know, successful. Since then we have had two other plans, or programmes, each less successful. Now, the process seems to have come to a stop. Both the present government and its predecessor seem to have lost faith in the planning system.

It can be conceded that national planning everywhere has its difficulties and its disappointments; but our experience shows that a stagnant, dispirited economy can be marvellously revived by the application of intelligent formal planning.

Planning is not a mystique. It is an attempt to get one's ducks in a row. This is done by rationalising what we do in the present, by rationalising what we shall do in the future, and by establishing accountability for what has, or has not, been done in the past.

First, the present. The volume of state intervention is now so great and has been arrived at in so *ad hoc* a way, that many of the things the state does with its right hand conflict with those it does with its left. For example, the overall aim of social policy is to redistribute more fairly the resources of the community. But many policies for taxation, education, health and other services in practice do the opposite of this. For example, the child who gets only a primary schooling has devoted to him very little of the resources of the community although he is likely to come from a poor home. If he finishes at the end of secondary education he has had a great deal more of these resources although his home is likely to be reasonably well off. With a university education he gets vastly more of those resources although his home is likely to be the best off of the three. This unplanned favouritism continues into later life. Future income depends almost entirely on level of education. To him who hath. . . . The same sort of thing can be seen in many other areas of policy. The point is that there is need for *some* form of social planning to ensure that when we redistribute the national resources we give most to those who need it most.

Secondly, the future. If the process of economic growth continues there will be a steadily increasing volume of resources to be redistributed in the community. Would it not be a good thing to try to agree on the broad outlines of priorities for spending these resources? How much for investment, how much for increasing general standards of living, how much for the poor, how much for the development of our cultural values, and so on? This would not be easy, but the results ought to be better than from just drifting along.

Again, big operations take different periods to complete—a few months for a grain crop, five to seven years for an atomic power station, 50 years for a forest, and so on. Within projects something similar occurs —in the case of the atomic power station perhaps three years for one piece of equipment and, if one were starting from scratch, perhaps ten years for producing highly qualified atomic engineers. It is crucial to good management to phase these "lead times", as they are called, so as to make sure that all the parts of the operation are started, and finished, in time. This is even more true, if more difficult, in the management of the national business. To do this with as little waste, delay and confusion as possible it is essential to have forward planning.

The need for planning becomes the more urgent if we are heading into serious economic difficulties, in common with much of the rest of the world. It may be that, by taking thought, one cannot add to one's stature one cubit; but one can often avoid a lot of unnecessary trouble and suffering.

Implementing the Plan

But it is not enough to plan. It is also necessary to make sure that the plan is made to work.

Much of the disappointments that have been met with here and in other countries in the practice of planning have arisen from three failures—first, the general failure to equip the official bodies—especially the government departments—with planning units and, in consequence, planning skills; secondly, the failure to get commitment to the plans; and, thirdly, the failure to have an adequate system of accountability for bad performance.

It is a striking fact that, in this country, seventeen years after planning began and notwithstanding several official announcements, our government departments are, with a few exceptions, not yet equipped with the instruments of planning, that is, units whose tasks are solely to tease out objectives, to elucidate the success or failure of existing policies to achieve those objectives, and to study alternative ways of achieving those objectives. These units need to be staffed by demographers, economists, statisticians, sociologists, and so on; but, in general, the public service lacks these skills.

The failure to get adequate commitment to the plans comes partly from these lacks. Insofar as the department or the public agency is not equipped to plan in a meaningful way, it is unlikely to be totally committed to the practical realisation of the plan.

The failure to have a system of public accountability has had a similar effect. How can one expect, in real life, great commitment to realising the projects in the plan when no-one in public life seems to care whether the projects are realised or not, and there seems to be no way by which the plan could impact on the system of parliamentary accountability?

So, here, is another way in which the rational ordering of our affairs makes for the development of healthier forms of democracy. One great advantage of a planning system is that the quality of the stewardship of the public bodies gets brought to notice. If the plan shows that certain things were to have been done by a certain time, and they have not been done, then it is clear who is to blame. Again, if an important input is missing from the plan, then responsibility for the failure can be fixed.

These ideas were central to the Devlin proposals that all public bodies should be adequately equipped to plan their affairs, that each government department should rationalise the plans in relation to its own sphere of responsibility, and that the Department of Finance should rationalise the plans overall.

Here is a classic example of how members of the Oireachtas, by means of special, joint, or mixed, committees would have the crucial information on which to base an effective supervision of the adequacies or otherwise of the various parts of the governmental machine.

V. THE PROBLEM OF DEMOCRATISATION

Central to what I have been saying is that the need to deepen the democratisation of our life should make us think critically about our public institutions, parliamentary and administrative.

The basic task of government is to bring about overall national development. To enable government to get ahead with this task it is essential to free our system of central representation and government from the overwhelming mass of detail that engulfs it at present. In this way parliament and central government can be raised from the disproportionate concern for day to day business so as to equip themselves to take comprehensive and long-term views about our national needs, and to ensure that these are being met to the limit of our abilities. If parliament and government do not perform this task, then who can?

But let me not be misunderstood. Of course day to day business is important. For most of us in our daily lives it is highly important. But there are other institutions that, if developed adequately, could relieve the central ones of much of this load. Our system would then be not only more efficient; it would also be more democratic.

If we want to develop the quality of our democracy we must strengthen both the representative and the administrative structures below the national level. So, to communities, to districts, to counties, and to regions we must give appropriate levels of the work of government. This will enlarge the role of the public representatives, bring the citizen into closer contact with the public services, and rationalise those services in the interests of humaneness and efficiency.

Thirdly, there is, to repeat, the need to establish a rational system for the remedying of individual grievances about those services.

I propose, therefore, a three-pronged programme for increasing the democratisation of our society. First, to free and equip central government for the high level work that only it can do; secondly, to decentralise to strengthened subordinate and democratic bodies the great mass of the detailed work of government; and, thirdly, to provide an orderly system for the redress of grievances. This is precisely what a number of highly democratic countries, such as those of Scandinavia, have done and are doing in the interests of making their societies more democratic as well as more efficient.

Why should the individual citizen concern himself with matters of this kind? I think there are a number of reasons why he should. First, in a very real sense, his material well-being will depend on how effective government is in coping with the increasingly difficult problems of the modern world. Secondly, a big part of the quality of our life here depends on good government. By "good government" I don't mean only the quality of the members of whatever government we may have in power at any given time. I mean also, and particularly, the quality of the institutions—or if you will, the implements—that are available to these men to organise the resources of the society in the way we wish them to do.

There is another reason, probably in the long run more important. That is, the kind of society that we want to become. Do we have a vision of a society where men are reasonably equal, where those who have legitimate grievances will have them speedily—and of right—remedied, where these equal men have a significant say in what is done on their behalf, where there is the freedom and the ability to engage in real initiative and effective government at a number of significant levels? If these things are important to us—and they are likely to become more important as we become better off, better educated and have more leisure—then the problem of how to adapt our institutions to meet the needs of our developing society will become increasingly urgent.

There is a well known saying of Lloyd George that war is too important to be left to the generals. General de Gaulle, taking over power in France, is reputed to have riposted that politics is too important to be left to the politicians. Whatever about this, the institutions of government are too important to be left as the *sole* concern of politicians and public servants.

VI.   CONCLUSION

So, what I have been saying is this. Government in our society is very big business. It needs a similar degree of passionate commitment to its efficiency as is taken for granted in relation to private business. But, beyond all this, we must be concerned with the quality and richness of our society not only in material terms. We need to work not only for economic growth but also for democratic growth.

Chapter 14

CENTRALISATION, CONTROL, COMMUNITY*

What I propose to say is that the principle of centralisation applied to the running of this state over 50 years ago has led to the subjecting of our local government system to an extraordinarily tight network of controls. In consequence, the central authority has been obsessed by detail to the neglect of broad problems of organisation, finance and, above all, political values that need to be spelled out for the rising needs of a participative democracy. It is crucial to get the central authority to grasp the need to discharge its overall duty. That duty is to give the necessary leadership to enable local government to play a large and significant role in the remorselessly rising tide of Big Government.

I.   CENTRALISATION

May I begin on a personal note? My first job in the 1930s was in a small manufacturing firm. The boss of that firm worked a nine to six day, five and a half days a week. He occasionally took a few days' holidays. Otherwise he was always on the job. He opened the letters coming in in the morning, he supervised the dispatch of the goods in the afternoon, he checked invoices going out, and he signed all the letters. There was nothing that went on in that firm that he did not have his finger on. He was completely in control of it. It was by many standards an extremely efficient firm, and, so far as he was concerned, a very profitable one. However, it has now been taken over by one of its rivals, and survives as a vestigial name in a multi-national group.

I mention this personal experience because it seems to me to sum up the attitude of mind of the founders of our State. The Minister in a government department—which was to be kept small—was intended to be like the boss of that firm. By being in complete control of what went on he could be held, according to the constitutional system adopted under the Ministers and Secretaries Act of 1924, personally responsible

*Paper to Community Government Movement Seminar—Dublin. 7th June 1975.

197

for everything that occurred. If he did not open all the letters coming in he did attempt at the beginning—certainly in the case of the Department of Local Government and Public Health—to sign all the letters going out. When the rise of business made this impossible he still remained personally responsible for everything that went on in his department. Because he was personally responsible he could be held accountable in detail to the Dail and therefore democratic control could be asserted over the whole system. That is to say, the democratic control would be a central and centralised one.

II. CONTROL

As part of this centralising tendency the activities of local authorities were brought under tight central control by means of the Local Government (Temporary Provisions) Act of 1923. The origins of Irish local government are diverse, but one origin was in the setting up of Boards of Guardians under the Poor Relief (Ireland) Act, 1838. This was an extensive experiment in democracy for that period, and was, not unreasonably in the circumstances, accompanied by an extraordinarily tight central control over the activities of the Poor Law guardians. Other branches of local government experienced nothing like this kind of control. However, when we got our independence and notwithstanding that the practice of local democracy was well established, it was the model of the Poor Law branch that was applied to the whole of the local government system. As a result, there was little or nothing that could be carried on by a local authority in any part of the country of which the then Minister for Local Government and Public Health could not be aware and, thus, be held accountable if something went wrong. So there was erected, on the model of the small business and the small farm, from which most of our founding fathers came, a most remarkable degree of central control over local government, perhaps the tightest that exists anywhere in the democratic world.

The origins of Irish local government all lie in the power of the State. The origin of the State in many other countries lies in the cohering of self-governing communities on which the State itself was founded. When we in Ireland adopted our two Constitutions we saw no constitutional role for local government. Again, this is in contrast with a number of our continental partners who have provided within their constitutions for a specific place for local government. Irish local government is, accordingly, not only the creature of the State but is to a quite remarkable extent subservient to it.

There are two main kinds of control, general controls, and ministerial ones. These latter tend to be controls in detail.

General Controls

The general controls fall into three kinds—legal controls, financial controls, and popular controls.

The legal controls require that the local authority must act, like the rest of us, in accordance with the law. However, this is supplemented by a specially restrictive version of the general doctrine of *ultra vires* which means that nearly always a local authority can only do what it is specifically authorised by law to do, or which it may reasonably claim is inherent in such authorisation. The freedom of action of local authorities is thus circumscribed by the need to get specific statutory authority for any new function, "function" itself being taken, usually, in a very restricted sense. So, the individual, as well as most corporate bodies, may do anything that is not forbidden by law —that is may display initiative and flexibility. On the other hand, a local authority can act only on authorisation. That is, its scope for initiative, flexibility and ready response to changing conditions is severely restricted. In the past, local authorities used to acquire extra powers by special private bills sponsored in Parliament on their behalf. Nowadays ministers have a monopoly, for all practical purposes, of such legislation. To relax any legal control, or to acquire new powers therefore, a local authority—or local authorities generally—must in practice persuade a minister to initiate and carry through the necessary legislation.

The second kind of general control is the financial one. This requires that local authorities should manage their financial affairs with probity and prudence. However, as they have virtually no means of raising fresh sources of revenue, this usually means that for any significant new initiative they are dependent on financial help from the State.

The third general control is that of popular control, the responsiveness of elected members to the needs and the wishes of the electorate. Their ability to respond is, of course, limited by the legal and financial rigidities to which I have referred.

All of these forms of general control demand adherence to *standards*. These standards are respect for law, respect for financial probity and prudence, and respect for community moral values.

Ministerial controls

The second broad range of controls comprises the ministerial ones.

These are financial, staff, appellate, and general administrative controls.

The financial controls relate both to capital expenditure and to a large part of current expenditure. The main reason for control over capital expenditure is the need of the State to keep control on the aggregate of all capital spending and, as virtually all the capital spent by local authorities is borrowed from the State, to ensure that resources are available to meet these demands. Moreover, it may be necessary to guard against unduly mortgaging the future: heavy capital expenditure now may arise from the desire to avoid current expenditure and to throw undue burdens on posterity. Thirdly, capital expenditure has been controlled as a method of ensuring that the standards of the works on which the capital expenditure will be spent are adequate—neither too low nor too high. It is here that perhaps the most detailed controls of all have been applied, for example, in the design of housing schemes. However, there is some significant relaxation now going on here.

There is extensive ministerial control in relation to the staffing of local authorities. A minister is concerned with the internal organisation generally of local authorities, with the methods by which the most important appointments are made, and with overall control of pay.

Another area where the minister has extensive control is in the right to receive and adjudicate on appeals against decisions of local authorities. The most notable of these relate to planning controls, proposals to acquire land compulsorily, and staff of local authorities. There is general acceptance of the idea that there should be a right of appeal from the decisions of local authorities. That the minister should adjudicate on these appeals is more controversial, and there is a tendency—notably in relation to planning appeals[1]—to hive off this function to a quasi-judicial body.

Apart from these specific powers of control, the minister has general administrative powers—indeed duties—of control. These are basically the duty to supervise the overall conduct of local government, and to provide remedies for such failings as may emerge. So, the great changes in Irish local government associated with the Local Appointments Commission, the management system, the county engineering system, derived from this general administrative power of control. But this duty has been carried further, as when the minister has removed elected councils from office for failure to exercise financial and other responsibilities, the most recent example being the removal in 1969 of the members of the Dublin City Council for failing to strike a rate adequate to meet its responsibilities.

[1]For example in the Local Government (Planning and Development) Bill, 1973, now before the Dail.

Overall, it adds up to a formidable body of controls. There is probably nothing like it. This is borne out by a comment by the Maud Committee in Britain where they point out that of the seven countries they examined, Ireland had quite the most stringent system of central control over local government[2]. The Devlin Report, also, said that local authorities ought to be given the same degree of freedom as are given to state-sponsored bodies in our system[3]. Since then, there have been some improvements at the margin, as it were, but, basically, the main structure remains untouched.

One may mention here the contrast between local government and the state-sponsored bodies, between what one very distinguished figure in local government, the late John Collins, called "the Bond and the Free". The state-sponsored bodies are also a response to the excessive centralising tendencies of our system of government, where these tendencies, as applied to the civil service, broke down in the face of the need to develop a developmental role for the State. One of the remarkable contrasts in our system has been that while local government tended to be ever more securely bound by the central administration, these functional bodies—that is, the state-sponsored bodies—were given such a substantial degree of freedom.

III. CREATIVE CONTROLS

However, it is not enough to bewail these difficulties. It is necessary to think clearly about the issues that they raise. The first issue is the great importance, as the business of government and of local government grows, of achieving the transition from the particular to the general, from interference in detail to guidance and leadership in major matters. It is necessary to effect the transition from the negative scrutiny of proposals made by local authorities, to the positive or creative use of controls as a feedback. In this way there is achieved an understanding of the overall problems that need to be solved in the general interest, whether by way of legislation, financial changes or otherwise. So, one can see the useful role for controls in relation to

    (i)   the setting of standards,
   (ii)   general problem solving,
  (iii)   research, and
  (iv)   leadership of the system as a whole.

[2]Maud Committee on the Management of Local Government, H.M.S.O., 1967, Vol. 1, Page 13.
[3]Para 13.3.10.

o

(i) *Standards*

To discuss adequately the issue of standards would take me far outside my present purpose. There are tough problems of defining what standards should be applied in local government—perhaps less passion might be applied to the definition of the size of bedrooms and more to the definition of the legitimate relationships of personal and public interest. There is the problem of the *levels* of these standards —for example, the design standards for main roads. There is the problem of the degree of *uniformity* to which these standards should be applied. Should everything be the same throughout the whole of the country, or should there be room for diversity and experiment from place to place, even if this means that some people are worse off in one part of the country than in another? If so, how wide should be the range of that diversity? There is the problem as to which standards should be *mandatory*—as in relation to honesty—and which *advisory* —as in relation to aesthetic matters.

(ii) *Problem Solving*

The second broad area is in relation to *problem solving.* There are many areas where problems need to be identified and solved, but I will touch here only on two. The first is that of the organisation of local government. It really is disconcerting that in the publications we have had from both governments on this issue[4] there is evidence of so little thought about how local structures are to fit in to the future of our society, where the role of government, both absolutely and relatively, grows at a startling pace, and where the rise in the concern of local people to participate in that government is such a notable feature. Is it not necessary to tease out what are those things that are special to central government, what are those that are special to the functional or state-sponsored bodies, and what are those things that are best handled on a geographical basis, and within that geographical system how best to differentiate the various levels of local and regional government?[5]

The other great neglected area here is in relation to finance. Virtually all the capital expenditure of local government is raised from the State. Is this necessary or desirable? As economic resources grow, the oppor-

[4]*Local Government Reorganisation*, Prl 1572, 1971; *Local Government Reorganisation,* Discussion Document, Department of Local Government, December, 1973.
[5]This is attempted in *More Local Government: A Programme for Development,* 1971.

tunities for raising capital by a diversity of means tend to increase. The older ones amongst us will have seen the remarkable growth of building societies in our society, or of the way that the Agricultural Credit Corporation has been able to raise funds. It is not essential that the State have a monopoly of the capital raising duties for local authorities. Could not, for example, the Local Loans Fund be transformed into a Local Government Bank which would not only lend money to local authorities, but would encourage local people to invest funds in the development of their own communities? Moreover, given the remarkable success of our local authorities in meeting their capital commitments, there should be little difficulty in such a Bank raising funds in the European market for necessary and desirable capital works. We need to transform our thinking from the notion of controlling profligate local authorities into one of a Bank prudently raising and lending funds in the interest of local development.

There is evidence of the same degree of lack of creativity in relation to the current expenditure of local authorities. About 40% of the current expenditure of local authorities comes from grants from the State. To these grants are usually attached precise and restrictive conditions. The extent of these conditions is quite remarkable by any standards. But the most striking contrast is between the panoply of controls erected on this 40% contribution and the remarkable freedom given to state-sponsored bodies who often receive 100% of their current expenditure from the State. The more one raises one's own income the tighter the controls! Again, the Bond and the Free.

While this passionate pursuit of detailed controls is engaged in, occupying a great deal of the time of those employed in central administration, we have endured the quite extraordinary and (it seems to me) reprehensible neglect of the taxation basis of local government. We are still operating the system of taxing for local government on a valuation system based on letting values appropriate, in part, to the year 1852. The result is the gross inequity, inflexibility and unpopularity of the rating system.

It has been said that "men pay their taxes in sorrow but there rates in anger". Why so? Basically, I suggest because our rating system has been so neglected as a system of taxation that it has become highly inefficient. There is a striking contrast here between the twenty years of modernisation of our central taxation system, the great overhaul by the Revenue Commissioners and successive ministers for finance of all the main taxation systems of central government, and the paralysis that seems to exist in relation to local taxation systems.

If the problems of sorting out the system of valuation and rating are insoluble, then another, more efficient and equitable, system of financing the current expenditure of local government should be found —it is not absolutely necessary to the notion of local government that there should be a local taxation system at all. If a balance of disadvantage must be struck, then let freedom be traded for taxation powers. Bord Failte Eireann or Coras Trachtala are able to carry on their promotional operations without being bedevilled by the preoccupations of an out-moded and inequitable taxation system. They get 100% grants for their current expenditure from the State. If there is good reason why they should have relative freedom, in a general sense, in spending those grants, then a similar degree of freedom should be given to local authorities.

(iii)   *Research*

Thirdly, a great deal more research needs to be done to find out what are the problems of our rapidly changing society. An Foras Forbartha has been established to do research of this nature in the environmental sector. But there are a number of fundamental research services that need to be supplied if any adequate system of local planning is to be engaged in. The one that strikes me most vividly is the need for demographic research. How can effective plans be made about sewers or houses or any other environmental service—indeed almost any public service—unless we know how many people are likely to be living in any given place and what the likely structure of the population is to be—how many children, young people getting married, old people, etc. etc.? In addition, with the growth of community consciousness in our society we need to know a great deal more about how people see government, what they need from the various forms of governmental systems, and how the deficiencies they identify can be remedied.

(iv)   *Leadership*

The fourth broad area is that of leadership. We can see this very vividly in relation to housing. Successive ministers for local government have seen the overall as well as the local problems of housing the people and have stimulated local authorities and have provided great capital resources to tackle this problem. One would like to see this leadership on a somewhat more sophisticated basis. Leadership would be more effective, if perhaps less charismatic, if a little more thought were given to understanding the emerging social problems of our society. For example, it has been obvious to a number of people for a long time that the remarkable rise in young people of marriageable age in our society would provoke a housing crisis. If steps had been taken sooner to identify and specify the size and distribution of this problem, much human suffering could have been avoided.[6] But this is merely one example. There are many other areas where a legitimate role for the central controlling authority imposes responsibilities of thoughtful leadership.

IV. MANAGING BIG GOVERNMENT

We are forced back continually to a central problem. How can the system of government be adjusted so that it will respond adequately to the needs of the latter part of the twentieth century? The sheer size of modern government, both absolutely and relatively (it is now heading towards two-thirds of all the activity of the community) imposes tough responsibilities for the overall management of our system of government. Any modern big business handling the huge resources now handled by the government of even a small state like ourselves, which continued to behave like the small business I described at the outset, would, as that did, find itself unable to survive. Something *must* be done to transform the overall government of this country from its peasant and petty bourgeois origins to the conditions of the late twentieth century. The methods of the 1920's are now totally inappropriate to the methods of the 1970's. So, while conceptually we stand still, all sorts of *ad hoc* solutions are being tried on a short-term basis. The result is great confusion of purpose and inefficiency of operation.

It is essential that we devote some thought to the proper roles of the various levels of modern government. Not only in relation to the rather restricted system which now comes under the label "Local Government"; not only in relation to the fields of health, of agriculture, of education; but also in relation to what should (I believe) be happening in many other fields of government. Coherence and order need to be brought into the various systems that operate below the national level, whether these are regional, county, district or community systems. We need to give a good deal more thought than we have been giving—this of course is the purpose of the discussions here to-day—to the conditions for the healthy operation of these systems.

[6]e.g. "if the present inventory of housing is regarded in terms of historical behavior, if the present state of new housing construction is judged on the basis of previous demand curves, then a housing crisis of immense proportions is predicted within a decade." Paul A. Pfretzschner: *The Dynamics of Irish Housing*, 1965, p. 17.

I could not hope to deal adequately with these here now, but a few points can be made. First, the various traditional systems we have inherited for local government need to be given a *wider range* of duties. For example, in other countries most cities the size of Dublin would be responsible for education, municipal police, municipal transport, welfare and substantial cultural functions. I would, of course, press much further this question of extending the range of local government functions. Secondly, the various levels within that system need to be given a much greater degree of *autonomy* in that range of operations. Thirdly, in order to free the creativity of our people much wider ranges of *initiative* must be given within those defined degrees of autonomy. Finally, to ensure that there is responsible management following the exercise of that initiative, a great deal more *responsibility* should be pinned on those whose task it is to discharge the duties at each level. All of this is something that can be learned from the practice of modern business. Even more striking, it can be learned from the successful operation of state-sponsored bodies within this country. We are extraordinarily slow in transferring the fruits of successful experience from one area of our State operations to another.

A second need is to learn how to link the functions of central government with those functions—regional, county, district, or community— that can be dealt with by means of local participation. It is a commonplace of government in the European countries that there be in each local area an administrative and political "cross-over" point between central and local government. There are various forms of this linkage. Here again, we could learn from the experience of other people.

Thirdly, we might give a little bit more thought to the idea of "Development". This has meant, at the national level, basically economic and, more recently, social development. At the local level it has tended to mean environmental development. But there is another broad area, crucial to all of these, and that is political development. Our people need to operate a democracy which takes account of the extraordinary ramifications of modern government on the one hand and, on the other, of the willingness and desire of ordinary people to play a more active part in the decisions that govern their lives. In Britain and Ireland the great struggle from the 1920's onwards was to get the State to fulfil its responsibilities to the people in relation to economic and social development. It seems to me that the big problem that is now emerging —and the root of our present discontents—is how to create the political conditions for a richer and more participative democracy, that is, for political development. In any such discussion the roles of the various levels of local government—from community up to regional—are of crucial importance. The inescapable responsibilities of central government are to create a coherent local government system from the disorderly, fragmented, *ad hoc* structures that have been created, especially since the 1950's.

What is needed at the national level, therefore, is a form of high level management of the society as a whole—the teasing out of objectives for the society, especially political objectives in the sense I have been using the word, the careful development of systems that will enable these objectives to be achieved, the discharge of the overall legislative functions that only those at the centre can engage in, and the ready review of the operations within the system.

V. PROBLEMS AND SOLUTIONS

Well, what does one do?

I think the first thing to do is not to behave like a bull rushing at a gate. It is important to understand what the problems are, before propounding solutions to them. Much discussion tends to be about solutions to problems that have been inadequately defined, and have not been generally accepted as problems. Science, it has been said, has advanced not by propounding solutions, but by progressively clarifying the questions. What questions are relative to us here?

I think the first question is one of *perspectives*. What kind of society are we aiming towards? This is not solely a matter of aspirations, it is also a matter of the forces that are operating within the society already. Just as in sailing, one must not only know where one hopes to get to, but one also must understand the effects of winds and tides that are part of the environment of the journey. We need to do a good deal more thinking about, achieve a higher level of understanding of, and engage in more dispassionate discussion on, all of these things.

Secondly, we need to engage in a good deal more definition of the requirements of a coherent set of governmental systems in our society, of the roles of the various levels within that system, and of the essential requirements of autonomy within those roles.

Thirdly, it is not enough just to resent the interference of the central authorities in local autonomy. We must also see what are the proper roles and responsibilities of central government in relation to the problem we have on hand. In my judgment, the Department of Local Government should be active not *only* with the admittedly important problems of housing, roads, or sanitary services. Another part of its role concerns the overall political richness of our society. This is not, of course, peculiar to that Department but, at the sub-national level with which we are concerned, it should be possible for that Department to pull the various threads together and weave them into some sort of acceptable pattern. Other departments are also concerned—Health, Agriculture, Education, to name but three—but above all it should be clarified that the lead role lies with the Department of Local Government and that Department should be judged on its overall effectiveness as to how it discharges that role. There is also a task here for the Department of the Public Service, but that should be an ancillary one, unless the Department of Local Government declines what I see as its crucial responsibility.

As to the community, at all levels and according to all groupings, it must try, as a result of thought and discussion, to arrive at a reasonable consensus about what the issues are if we are to have a more democratic and a more efficient society in this country. I think a good deal of progress has been made in some quarters, but it is obvious from the level of discussion on the White Paper of the previous Government and the Discussion Paper of the present one, as well as from the general public apathy, that the public mind is still conditioned by the out-dated ideas of the past and by those who express those ideas. So, if we wish to get anywhere, we must define our market, produce a good product, package it acceptably, and be persistent and skilful in selling it.

I think that if we are to create structures within our society that will help us to liberate ourselves and to raise our communities to greater levels of self-awareness and freedom, there is a long, stony road to be trodden. Nonetheless, the sheer force of events increasingly demands action. Perhaps the strength of that force will overcome the mindless adherence to the ideas that have formed our local structures, ideas that were out of date at the time they were implemented, much less now, fifty years later.

VI. CONCLUSION

What I have been saying is that those of us who are concerned with the future of local government must devote much thought—as we are doing to-day—to the challenges that confront local government and the problems that they pose. Above all we must analyse the old modes of thought, the out of date ideas that bind us, so as to arrive at solutions and proposals relevant to the future, not the past. A major fetter on such fresh thinking is the system of centralisation and control, devised when government was small business, now wholly out of date when government is very big business indeed.

Chapter 15

POSTSCRIPT: INSTITUTIONAL DEVELOPMENT

These are the best constituted bodies, and have the longest existence, which possess the intrinsic means of frequently renewing themselves . . . .
—Machiavelli: *Discourses* III 1.

In the minds of thinking people the issues that arise in relation to the operations of government outside the capital city, and the problems of local and regional representation, have begun to clarify themselves. Nonetheless, these issues are not easy to grasp, partly because they have been overlain with assumptions that have been inadequately examined, partly because what used to be called "introspection" in relation to administrative systems has only in recent years gained any degree of respectability, and partly because we lack appropriate intellectual tools. There is now, however, a rising tide of interest especially in the problems of how government can be decentralised, brought closer to the people, and democratised.

One does not have to think long about these diverse, but related problems before one begins to see the need for a coherent structure into which the individual solutions can be set, and this leads one to consider how such overall structures can be adapted, or adapt themselves, to the changing times. In a developing world, thought needs to be given to the development of public institutions on whose successful working so much of national development itself depends.

If we wish to understand the cluster of problems in the context touched on in this book, we must see them in the light of, first, a developing democratisation of our society, and, secondly, that itself in a context of Institutional Development. Here we might reasonably ask ourselves five questions. The first is: what is Institutional Development? The second: what is the level of Institutional Development in this part of Ireland? The third: can we identify any values and principles of Institutional Development? The fourth: what are the dynamics of Institutional Development? The fifth: can we identify what might be the elements of a programme for Institutional Development, with particular reference, as here, to the issue of decentralisation for democracy?

I. WHAT IS INSTITUTIONAL DEVELOPMENT?

So far as the institutions of the Republic of Ireland are concerned the year 1958 was notable for the publication of the first Programme for Economic Expansion and Dr Whitaker's study *Economic Development*. These had three important administrative facets. The first was that conscious planning for development became a major administrative tool of government. The second was that the development then seen as of crucial importance was *economic* development. The third, of course, was that economic stagnation was replaced by economic growth, that this growth induced many changes throughout the society, and called for, amongst other things, significant administrative adaptation. Comprehensive change, it became slowly apparent, was both a consequence and a condition of the new departure.

It was soon demonstrated, if that was necessary, that economic development does not occur in isolation and that economic progress must depend, to an important extent, on environmental or infrastructural development; in consequence planning of some sort was at least as necessary in the environmental sector as in the economic one. So, in the same year as the second Programme for Economic Expansion was introduced, there was also passed the Local Government (Planning and Development) Act, 1963. This involved a commitment to planned development as a means of meeting some at least of the environmental or infrastructural needs of the society.

A further consequence was that it came to be realised that a limiting factor on, and a major contribution to, growth was a cultural one – the adequacy of the educational system to produce educated and skilled people. Hence (note the title!) *Investment in Education* by an OECD team under Professor Patrick Lynch in 1965, and the big advances in second and third level education that followed. A degree of planned development in the cultural sector had begun.

It then became clear that there was need, also, to have planned development of the methods of distributing the fruits of the economic progress that had made themselves manifest. Indeed, this need had something to do with the introduction of the third programme before the second had run its course. Significantly, this third programme, introduced in 1969, was called the Third Programme for Economic and *Social* Development (my italics).

Whether planning for development should restrict itself to "the commanding heights" of the society, or whether it should be pervasive, is a debate with which we are all familiar; but it is, I think, less important than that our experience over a period of 15 years shows us that development is a many-sided thing and that development on the economic, the environmental, the cultural, and the social sectors are all related to a quite remarkable degree. This experience has also shown us that a planning approach to development must, if it is to extend over a period, take this complexity into account.

In a pragmatic way, feeling the ground before us cautiously as we go along, we get some glimmering that these separate, but related, roads to development are leading towards a single objective, that of national development. We strive not only for the development of more employment, or better roads, or fairer shares, but, it seems, for the improvement of the whole many-faceted society in which we live, so far as governmental action is relevant. As soon as this overall conception of national development begins to emerge, contributed to by *concurrent* streams from the economic, social, environmental, cultural sectors, we begin to discover that we cannot shake off the questions: "what is development for?" "what sort of society are we aiming to develop towards?" From that perspective the answer to these questions seems to be: a better "quality of life", to use a well-worn phrase. This often tends to be limited to concern with such problems as pollution, amenity, the destruction of natural beauty, and the like. But behind these we are concerned with the development of human beings in our society, the enrichment of the human personality, the creation and strengthening of the bonds within the various communities and the society as a whole, as well as, of course, striking a balance between people and the natural environment. That is to say, we become faced with the problem of political development, taking "political" in its broadest sense. We are brought back to the issues continually raised by Professor Ivor Browne: the need to extend the sense of responsibility of individuals, to open up to them the possibility of useful individual, social and collective action – in fact, to accept the logic of the dictum of Aristotle that man is naturally a political animal.

One does not have to argue that the problems posed by the interrelationships, and the interlocking nature, of economic, environmental, cultural, social and political development are exclusively the problems of government. Even where a major objective of government is to create self-sustaining activities towards these ends solely within the private sector, and it is successful in achieving that objective, there still remains a large area of governmental activity, typically, in the western market oriented society, some 50% of the business of the whole society, a proportion that seems remorselessly to rise.

Considered even in political terms, the tasks of leading the community in the directions indicated by the diverse needs of development, of reconciling the conflicts set up by such changes, of getting agreement on new goals, of achieving consensus for new or altered institutions to achieve those goals, of allocating resources between them—these call for increased skills in politics itself and for new and adapted political structures.

Again at the level of administration, the sheer complexity of the tasks of planning for development, the wide range and interrelationships of these tasks, and the difficulties of striking balances between them pose severe problems for the institutions of government. Yet, insofar as governmental activity is crucial to many forms of development on a national scale, the effective working of the institutions of government, political and administrative, is of the first importance. If we think of public institutions both as essential contributors to the various facets of national development, and as a consequence of the successful achievement of a high level of national development, we see how important they are to the whole enterprise. They underly the activities in each of the five streams contributing to national development. Moreover, new developmental tasks bring about new or altered institutions, e.g. for health services or educational services. Institutional development becomes a crucial contributor to the whole development process.

Each of the sectors—economic, environmental, cultural, social, political—not only contributes to, but can also impede, the development of the others. The problem is to get them, at each stage of the process, in the appropriate "mix". For example, highly educated people may be both a precondition of economic development and a consequence of it. But highly educated people who are frustrated or unused may make for political instability. Political stability may be crucial to social development and, again, a consequence of it. And so on. But underlying all of these is the effectiveness of the institutions charged with the task of playing government's role—whichever that may be—in all of the processes leading to national development.

The institutions of government in this sense are both political and administrative, tightly interlocked. They can, in some degree, be considered separately. Here we are mainly concerned with administrative and executive institutions.

Because these are *public* institutions the study of their behaviour and potentialities is in effect the study of public administration. Unfortunately, this study is not well developed anywhere. Within that broad area of study there is the question of how institutions can themselves be developed to discharge the new and interrelated roles posed for them in the five substantive sectors of national development.

II. LEVEL OF INSTITUTIONAL DEVELOPMENT

Over the whole range of government, we can think of institutions as falling under the three familiar headings of political, juridical, and executive. For our present purpose we can leave the juridical institutions to one side, though I believe the problems in the juridical area are at least as pressing as those in the other areas. If we take the political and executive institutions together we arrive at what we mean by "government". Government itself can be seen as having two facets: representation and administration. It is extremely difficult to assess how effectively these institutions do their jobs, but one can assess, without too much labour, how well developed they are as compared with similar institutions in well-governed countries. The approach from the standpoint of institutional development in the governmental sphere enables us to make a preliminary judgment as to how far our representative institutions, and how far our administrative institutions, are well or ill-developed, at least by comparison with other models. It is part of my general argument that, looked at in this light, Irish institutions, both representative and administrative, are, with exceptions, reasonably healthy but poorly developed.

This is not the place to do more than sketch the general outlines of any such survey, but a couple of obvious points can be made. Some of the headings under which a full survey of our representative institutions might be made might be: fewness of public representatives; lack of adequate organisation or equipment for the tasks at hand; lack of independent sources of information; lack of discretion; lack of power; lack of respect. I think if we examine our representative institutions under some such headings we will see a significant degree of under-development. One of our houses of the Oireachtas is extraordinarily weak and under-equipped in many respects. The other is powerful collectively but, by comparison with other parliaments, is extraordinarily under-equipped for bringing an independent mind to its job—it lacks committees, staff, research facilities, independent sources of information. It is, in effect, still geared to the problems of the simple agricultural community for which it was first designed: in this what is special is of too much interest and what is general is of too little.

Outside the parliamentary sphere the picture is worse. Public elected representatives are, by comparison with almost any other country, extraordinarily few on the ground, and the proportion of public business with which they are concerned is small and becomes a steadily declining one. On present trends the future form of representation is with ministerial and vocational nomination on a centralised body; the popularly elected public representative, outside parliament itself, will become increasingly scarce and irrelevant. This is an odd evolution for a democratic society. It is hard to see how these trends can be squared with the modern movement towards more participation in government and the evolution and freeing of the citizen to perform his natural function as a political animal. In particular, can one reconcile it with the increasingly difficult task of obviating dissent, distrust and conflict between administrative bodies and their 'customers', a basic function of the elected representative of those 'customers'?

The picture on the administrative side is not so depressing, but nonetheless it also shows evidence of underdevelopment. We see a large number of administrative bodies grown up in an *ad hoc* way, cumbersome, remote from the people governed, and hard for them to comprehend, hard also for the public representatives to control. The very *ad hoc* nature of this growth has made for great confusion of roles amongst them and there is little evidence that any real progress in defining these roles is being made. There is much confusion as to the degrees of autonomy and discretion that they ought to exercise. There are most inadequate means for the orderly hearing and redress of grievances. There are some alarming indications that the people whom these institutions exist to serve dislike and distrust them.

The significant problems here come from this phenomenon of the rapid and perhaps haphazard growth in the business of government as well, of course, as the growth in the complexity of social organisation generally and its articulateness. Arrangements that worked well when government was small business are no longer adequate. The growth in the number, speed and size of vehicles has led to a remorseless rise in road deaths and injury and to increasing congestion, so leading, in turn, to a vast increase in the extent and complexity of activity and skills for roads and traffic engineering. A similar challenge is posed for those whose concern it is to see our public institutions developed to meet the consequences of the growth and complexity of public activities. But we start with great handicaps. That these are important problems is realised by few, and we are woefully short of the tools and skills for tackling them successfully.

One of the major tools in the achievement of an effective programme for economic development was the invention of gross national product, a measure of the success or failure of the economy to achieve acceptable levels of growth. Efforts are being made to devise "social indicators", which ought to have the same effect in their appropriate spheres. In the institutional sphere, however, we have no such measures for levels of achievement, for ready comparison with other countries or for measuring success or failure from year to year. Necessarily, there-forefore, any survey of the present position and of comparative pro-gress tends to be subjective.

Subjective survey is, of course, not good enough, especially when one considers the importance of the institutions and the vast resources, human and financial, they dispose of. There is a formidable case for scientific research in this area to produce facts in place of hunches, quantities in place of opinions, concepts in place of prejudices. A modest beginning has now been made in this area, but there are vast empty spaces.

Nonetheless, there is from common observation enough indication of confusion of purpose, and by comparison with other countries, of weak institutions, to show the need for an extensive programme of institu-tional development. The formal establishment, from 1 November 1973, of the Department of the Public Service should begin to remedy these problems; but there is a long, stony road to go.

III. VALUES AND PRINCIPLES OF INSTITUTIONAL DEVELOPMENT

If the pace along that road is to be an acceptable one some aid must be given by identifying guiding lines along which institutional develop-ment can work. These guiding lines might be divided into two classes—values and operating principles. Words like "value" and "principle" are dangerous ones. Let me try to set out the sense in which I use them. "Values" as used here fall into two kinds: first, objectives or goals on which there is a consensus that they ought to be achieved in some sense —these might be called "terminal values"; and, secondly, general rules of behaviour, or "instrumental values". By "operating principles" I mean those rules for action that experience and study have shown to lead, where other things are also conducive, to successful results.

When one is dealing with a subject such as institutional development, still in its early stages, it is not always possible to see clearly which are the major values and operating principles and which the less important ones. Nonetheless there are certain values and operating principles, in the sense in which I use them here, that, whenever one studies the problems of institutions, keep on cropping up. So, greatly daring, I venture to put forward a tentative list of values and operating principles that seem to me to be relevant to the achieving of institu-tional development.

Values

When we come to consider values we are on slippery ground. Nonetheless this is an issue that is essential to any scientific approach to the problems of institutional development. We must try to define and clarify the values that are relevant to this area of thought. Here is a tentative, perhaps personal, list of values, taking the long term or terminal ones first.

The crucial long term value of relevance to this discussion is that institutions are a good thing—not just a " necessary evil." They are good in that they embody some part of the social consensus and of the popular will. As society becomes more integrated and its personality becomes more articulate we are likely to see more and stronger (though not necessarily bigger) institutions even if these institutions at times conflict with one another.

A second long term value is that national development is crucial to the survival of the community and its enrichment. The purpose of the operation is to improve the quality of life of the society by making more effective use of, and enhancing, *all* its resources in the common interest. In this the most important objective is the development of *human* resources in the widest sense of that term.

The instrumental values are less esoteric because they are mainly the familiar values of democracy. I think that the first, basic, one is that the people are to be trusted and to that end there must be more public participation in the administration of government. There are many problems in public life to which there is no ' correct ' or ' scientific ' answer, and it may be that these problems will become more numerous as the range and complexity of public action extend. The solutions to these problems must depend on the values of the people, what they are prepared to accept as right and necessary. It seems clear that, if the channels for communicating the applications of those values are to be improved, the representation of the people should be strengthened and increased, and that the representatives should be, as far as possible, chosen by the people they are presumed to represent. For a democratic system, at least, the great danger to avoid is the alienation of the people—after a certain stage of that process has been passed government itself becomes increasingly difficult and, in the end, impossible.

Secondly, it follows from this that public control insofar as it relates to general issues should be strengthened, and the systems for remedying individual grievances should be made more orderly, more pervasive and more effective.

A third main instrumental value is, I think, efficiency. What we mean by this term needs to be defined with a very cool head indeed. The constraints on government action are very different from those of, say, engineering or, in many ways, business; hence efficiency by public institutions in transcending these constraints is, in practice, very different from what is commonly meant by the term. As I see it, efficiency in this context means good service to the people by the right use of all the resources of the community. It means, above all, that what is proposed to be done by government in alleviating the needs of the people in accordance with their terminal values will be accepted by the people and will get their support. In a more special sense, of course, it means the use of the best modern techniques and the development of new ones in the interest of the best use by public bodies of the resources of the community. It means institutions well adapted and responsive in their needs and wants and capable of meeting these at the minimum cost in time, men and money. It means skilful use of an appropriate array of operating principles.

Operating Principles

This third instrumental value of efficiency helps, therefore, to identify the operating principles. The great problem for efficiency in this context is, given the special constraints on government action, how to cope with the consequences of the growth in the size and complexity of the work of government. Because that growth has been haphazard and unplanned it is necessary to have some operating principles for re-patterning the increased volume of work and the institutions that have been engulfed, or made irrelevant, by it. There are two processes in this re-patterning—that of *differentiation* into new or altered categories, and that of *integration* of these new categories. The first two of our sets of operating principles are concerned with differentiation, the remaining three with integration.

The first operating principle, I suggest, is that on which the report of the Public Services Organisation Review Group was based, namely that there should be a clear differentiation between the policy making process and the process of execution. There is, however, a danger here of over-simplification. One can differentiate roles fairly simply— responsibility for policy with one body ; responsibility for execution with another. But whatever about final decision on policy, the *formulation* of policy involves both kinds of body. This is because a big part of the formulating process is a cybernetic one ; it requires continuous feed-back from the process of execution. This does not

P

invalidate the overall principle but it does call for sophistication in applying it.

Secondly, there is the set of principles, commonplace in the discussion of management problems, concerned with *standardisation.* These are that objectives, priorities, roles and levels of expectation must be defined, and that efficiency (however it is to be defined) should be a guiding rule.

A third set of operating principles—on which considerable reliance is placed in the papers in this book—is concerned with integration after these differentiations have been made. It is that the work of government and, therefore, the set of institutions for discharging it should be grouped in a coherent system by means of an orderly *hierarchy.* The effective working of a hierarchy depends on a high level of co-ordinated action. There are two enemies of such a hierarchical system that must be guarded against. The first enemy is excessive vertical 'draught' to the top of the hierarchy, so destructive of initiative and responsibility at the lower levels. Hence the need, in the vertical sense, for the right use of the operating principle of *subsidiarity* that will provide for each level of the system an appropriate range of autonomy. Arrangements must be such as to facilitate the proper filtering of the flow of business in a vertical sense—that is, from the top to the bottom of the hierarchy and back again.

The second enemy of a hierarchical system is the barriers to the horizontal flow of business, producing another kind of frustration of initiative, of flexibility and, above all, responsibility. So there is need, in the horizontal sense for the operating principle of *co-responsibility* as between different bodies and sub-systems within the system to permit free horizontal movement, so that affairs can flow smoothly between corresponding levels of different hierarchies, avoiding the twin dangers of dams on the one hand and leaks on the other.

These operating principles call for the establishment within and as between hierarchies of *cross-over points* in order to facilitate communication, provide foci of decision, and opportunities for democratic input and control. In this way the pace, the comprehensiveness and quality of decision-making are enhanced. It is a major part of my argument that the fragmented, inadequately differentiated, inadequately integrated, centripetal and over-centralised nature of Irish administration frustrates this aim.

A fourth group of operating principles relates to the importance of *representation* as a means of integrating special interests with the general interest, or at least for an identifiable part of it, and for establishing credentials so that it is clear who it is speaks for the general interest, or at least for an identifiable part of it, and what is the degree of support he enjoys amongst the people. It is also important for the purposes of meaningful consultation with the special interest groups. Consultation itself is of little use unless it involves participation ; this brings us into the areas of instrumental values touched on above. At the level of operating principles one must stress that crucial to real participation is understanding by the public of issues and operations. This is one reason why it is so important to simplify and clarify to the greatest extent possible what the institutions are and what they are trying to do, to remove so far as is possible the elements of mystery and misunderstanding. Equally crucial at the operational level is prior information so that there be informed public input into the decision-making—and decision-accepting—processes. That is to say, the bias should be towards open government.

A fifth group of operating principles relates to *review* and *accountability*. If freedom to use discretion and autonomy in working are essential for the effective discharge of business by the institutions, then there must be systems for judging effectiveness (e.g. input to, and implementation under, a planning system; full use of human, financial and material resources) ; of accountability for significant failures—not failures of detail ; and an adequate system for the hearing and redress of individual grievances.

IV. INSTITUTIONAL DYNAMICS

A main aggravation of the problems we have been considering is the growth of public institutions. Can we identify, and attempt to understand, the forces making for this growth and, if so, harness them to the process of institutional development ?

If we think of political development as substantially the achievement of wider fields of consensus, then it is necessary to have some forms of public activity and, in consequence, institutions to translate that consensus into effective action. If the institutions are to be appropriate instruments for serving the consensus that has been achieved, there must be, at the very least, a passive response within the institutions to the needs of the time.

In the private sector the balance sheet and at least an annual profit and loss account are powerful adaptive factors for institutions ; notwithstanding this, many of them fail to adapt and cannot get the support to continue. In the public sector the political cycle is much longer than an accounting year and the institutions can go unadapted for a long time before the need for reform bursts out in some kind of political discontent. Even then, public institutions rarely go into liquidation. Hence, as a general rule, institutions in the public sector are not noted for their adaptiveness.

But the translation of consensus into the realities of a rapidly changing society involves more than passive response: it calls for a positive, creative, dynamic spirit within, and as between, institutions. How to achieve this spirit, and maintain it, is at the heart of the problem of institutional dynamics.

Nonetheless, public institutions do change. What are their inherent dynamics?

There is, first of all, *momentum*. When an organisation is newly established the problems it has to face are relatively clear-cut and the members of the organisation are keen to devise workable objectives in relation to those problems. As they settle down to their jobs their skills increase and their capacity for discerning and devising schemes for achieving further objectives and sub-objectives increases at a fairly rapid rate. Generally, this initial momentum and the personal dynamism of the original members of the organisation can expect to keep things going perhaps for a decade or two. The external sign of the success of this is growth, and thus opportunities for enhanced responsibilities, and promotions, for those within the organisation.

As the organisation settles down and gets a clear grasp of its problems it begins to lose its initial momentum. Instead, it has learned how to respond effectively to stimuli coming from recognised sources. It passes through the phase of *adaptedness*. Because, however, the organisation is having some success in achieving its objectives, either the sources of stimuli dry up or change. If the organisation is too well adapted to its original purpose, its activities become less and less relevant to current problems. Because people in an organisation will always find something to do, even if it is not strictly relevant to the situation, the organisation will find itself proliferating into a number of activities, perhaps relevant to its original purpose, but no longer really relevant to the world in which it is operating. Hence, simple proliferation.

If, on the other hand, the organisation is able to move from a situation of being adapted to its original purpose to one of being *adaptive* to a continually evolving situation, the organisation is likely to be distinctly more dynamic and to have a longer life expectation. The dynamic will come from the continued relevance of the external stimuli on the organisation. However, these stimuli can themselves be a source of danger. If the organisation, while being ready and able to respond to these stimuli, has lost its original clarity of purpose it can easily succumb to the weaknesses of Stephen Leacock's horseman who, it will be remembered, galloped off madly in all directions. If an even more acute attack of proliferation is not to be suffered by the adaptive organisation over that of the adapted one, it is necessary to control the adaptiveness within some intellectual framework.

This framework is necessarily a *cognitive* one, basically internal to the organisation. That is to say, the main task of leadership in the organisation becomes to think through the current objectives of the organisation and to recast its methods of operation to take into account the stage of development both the organisation and its environment have reached. This recasting is a difficult and painful operation for any organisation. The conclusion, as a result of the thought, may be that the organisation has served its purpose and should be wound up. This is a conclusion seldom reached from the inside of any organisation. But even if the conclusion is less drastic than this, the re-thinking can lead to significant and, in the short run, always disagreeable change. What happens is that a kind of dialectic comes into operation. On the one hand the adaptiveness of the organisation makes it differentiate in a biological sense. On the other hand the strength of the cognitional input from its leaders brings it up against barriers that require the differentiation to cease for the time being and for the activities to become consolidated in a new scheme of organisation. In public organisations, for the reasons given, the pressures to engage in this kind of re-thinking seldom come from outside—or if they do, come only at long intervals ; this imposes a very heavy responsibility on the heads of the organisation to keep this dialectic in operation.

It is not unknown for external pressures of this kind to be exerted ; but when they occur it is more probable that the organisation literally falls apart. This is very often how new government departments tend to get born. At other times, public disquiet leads to the setting up of a commission of inquiry which from the outside, as it were, may make proposals for organisational change that, occasionally, are adopted. Finally, there is the attempt, as in the Devlin Report, to build into each organisation and for public organisations as a whole an orderly external source of stimuli in the shape of the Department of the Public Service. In addition there was the attempt to build in a cybernetic capacity, in the shape of an organisation unit, to underpin the overall management of the organisation. The techniques of programme budgeting are also intended to make a similar contribution in this internal sense. The purpose of these three innovations is to build a close cognitive link between the needs of the situation, whatever it may be, and the response of the organisation.

If one moves from a single organisation to a group of related organisations constituting a system, much the same sort of forces can be seen to operate, though under much enhanced difficulties. The management of a system—the civil service, local government, the health services, perhaps the state-sponsored bodies—is, of course, much more difficult than that of an individual organisation. Often, there is in practice no overall management at all. If this is attempted —for example, the relationship between the Department of Local Government and local authorities—it tends to bring the individual organisations into severe subjection to the managing one. This in turn erodes their autonomy and, accordingly, their adaptiveness. It may be possible for the system as a whole to be adapted even though its constituent parts are not themselves adaptive, but this is very difficult to achieve. It depends, basically, on the cognitive quality of the central organisation and this, all too readily, becomes swamped in a mass of detailed work. In these conditions the system becomes not adaptive but adapted. In the long run, in consequence, it tends to become irrelevant.

The problems become almost insoluble when one thinks of a set of systems built into a structure, such as the set of local, regional, and field service organisations that constitute the areal or geographical structure of government. In Ireland, so far, this " structure " is solely an intellectual construct : it has no operational meaning. It lacks, therefore, any dynamics of its own. This situation is not, of course, a necessary one.

One of the striking signs of proliferation is fragmentation—the fragmentation of individual organisations, the fragmentation of systems and the failure of those systems to transcend their fragmented condition and to cohere into structures. It is not easy to illustrate these points, but perhaps an illustration not irrelevant to the theme of this book may be used—the solutions adopted for the accommo- dation problems of certain civil servants. This is, of course, to describe symptoms. It is well known that there is a sub-system for dealing with accommodation in the civil service. It results in, as we shall see, fragmented solutions, and it itself involves the fragmentation of management responsibility for reaching coherent solutions. So the symptoms may well have a significance beyond that of the relatively trivial example that is given here.

As a general rule, it is highly desirable that where headquarters staffs are not too numerous they should be accommodated under the same roof. This helps to establish overall unity of purpose within the organisation ; it greatly improves communications, especially informal ones ; and it helps to develop an *esprit de corps* in the organisation. The old Department of Local Government and Public Health broke up in 1947, and the new Department of Local Government then had a staff of 358 persons while the new Department of Health had a staff of 126. By 1961, half way through the lives of the two departments, the staffs numbered 357 and 244 respectively. As the first half of the lives of the two new departments did not show significant aggregate growth, notwithstanding the development of various new services, it was still possible to accommodate both departments in the Custom House. However, in the second half of their lives to date significant changes occurred. In 1974 the numbers in the Department of Local Government had risen to 882 and of the Department of Health to 319. The core headquarters staffs of both departments remain in the Custom House, but the Department of Local Government now also occupies three other Dublin locations (Conyngham Road, O'Connell Bridge House, and Lower Mount Street) and the Department of Health two other Dublin locations (Hawkins House and Phibsboro). Neither department is so big that it could not be accommodated under the roof of a single modern office block, but that is not how the accommodation problem was tackled.

These departments are not untypical in the solution adopted. For example, the Department of Local Government shares O'Connell Bridge House with elements of the Department of Social Welfare, the Department of Transport and Power and the Department of Labour. The Department of Health shares Hawkins House with elements of the Office of the Attorney General, two branches of the Department of Education, two branches of the Revenue Commissioners and part of the Civil Service Commission staff.

It is clear that whether one considers, from the accommodation point of view, the departments as individual organisations, or civil service departments as a system, proliferation in numbers and fragmented locations are the order of the day.

What may be more significant is the nature of the growth of the two departments. If we separate the cognitive parts of the departments from the rest—in effect the administrative grades from the advisory and executive grades—we get an inkling of the nature of this growth, especially in the Department of Local Government.

Department	1947	1961	1974
Local Government			
—administrative staff	19	29	73
—executive and advisory staff	339	328	809
TOTAL	358	357	882
Health			
—administrative staff	11	26	51
—executive and advisory staff	115	218	268
TOTAL	126	244	319

These figures are no more than indications of trends. On the one hand, the advisory staffs, while in practice mainly executive, have some administrative input. On the other hand the administrative staffs have grown in some measure because of the growth of executive work. What is apparent is that the Department of Local Government has become, by Irish standards, a big executive department at a time when its *raison d'etre*, the local government system, languishes and is in confusion. Executive work has taken over from cognitive work.

If one thinks of regional bodies as a structure—but this for reasons already given is probably too ambitious a thought—proliferation in numbers, sizes, roles, constitutions, etc., is also the order of the day. Whose business is it to have a cognitive input to the solution of these problems ?

There is, clearly, among public institutions a factor making for growth because, reasonably in the official's mind, despite one's best efforts, there always seems to be more and more to do. This is allied with the general belief that prudence dictates that things ought to be allowed "to develop naturally." So the growth of institutions tends, other things being equal, to be *ad hoc* and unplanned. Where this occurs we have the common organisational diseases of proliferation, fragmentation, and confusion of roles. Where it occurs amongst a number of related organisations we tend to have considerable confusion and rivalries of purpose. This, overall, leads not to adaptiveness, but to its opposite. The point is that the " natural " tendencies conflict with adaptiveness. A function of institutional development would be to strive to avoid this common disease, to seek something more positive so that the institutions individually and collectively will become adaptive.

It is apparent, therefore, that individual public bodies are not un-dynamic : the problem is the relevance of the dynamism that operates. It is equally clear that there is little or no such dynamism in the integrating, or synthesising, process : individual bodies proliferate, but systems and structures do not adapt and develop. This has happened for 50 years with much of the civil service *system,* and is now happening with much of the local government *system.* One is tempted, for emphasis, to put the contrast with too much force : dynamism in the *differentiation* of individual institutions; paralysis in their *integration* into systems and structures. The cognitive dynamic, if it exists, has not been harnessed to this task.

Within proper limitations, institutions, systems and structures should be not only dynamic but become creative as well. That is to say, they should be farseeing about the evolution of new roles within the overall consensus and be capable of producing consistent solutions to the problems that arise. The primary task of the institution may be development in the economic or the social or the environmental sphere. But there is a corresponding need, if that kind of development is not to be impeded, for development in the institutional sphere itself. By the nature of the institutions this must be planned development. This planned development calls for a conscious drawing together of the three dynamics, that is, those deriving from internal growth, external stimuli and cognitive leadership.

V. ELEMENTS OF A PROGRAMME FOR INSTITUTIONAL DEVELOPMENT

To prepare a programme of institutional development it is necessary, first, to get an agenda of issues reasonably defined and agreed upon. I think the Public Services Organisation Review Group Report, the Devlin Report, adequately covers the issues as they had emerged from discussion in the 1950s and 1960s. It is already clear that there are other issues emerging in the 1970s that must be added to this agenda. That report was, however, predominantly concerned with issues arising from the problems of the role of the civil service in our system of administration. It almost totally ignored the problems of parliament, and of regional and local government. It barely scratched the surface of the problems of the state-sponsored bodies. Of necessity it could not deal with the problems arising from our joining the European Communities, or ones that may emerge from whatever settlement there may be in Northern Ireland. Other problems, such as the need for

Q

the effective co-ordination of issues that arise within and as between the broad sectors, economic, social, etc., discussed above, as well as within the functional areas of individual ministers ; the problems of juridical institutions; the provision of adequate administrative under-pinning for parliamentary institutions; the extending of participation in the business of government to larger sections of the population ; the simplification of the services that impinge on the individual citizen ; and the democratising of our institutions generally—all of these have barely been thought about. However, to discuss this further would bring me far outside my present purpose.

The second element of the programme is adequate machinery for dealing with these issues. Again, the Devlin proposals for the establishment of the Department of the Public Service, which has now been formally adopted, and the establishment of staff units within the various institutions—especially of organisation units— are major advances along these lines. However, when one considers the work that is going on about the restructuring of the health, hospital, educa-tional, agricultural, assistance services, or the various proposals about local government reform or regional development, one sees that over large areas of our administration little or no " machinery " in this sense has in fact been assembled. In default, this restructuring is necessarily being tackled largely in a spirit of enlightened amateurism. Of course, life cannot stand still while we attempt to build a science of these things, but that very fact underlines the urgency of getting organisational units properly equipped with relevant skills. These, given a reasonable intellectual under-pinning, could harness the natural dynamics of the organisations and systems in an effective process of institutional development.

The third element is the winning of support amongst the public, amongst the public representatives, and amongst the administrators for the programme so that the institutions will agree with it and translate its aspirations into effective operation.

VI.   DECENTRALISATION

This book is basically an attempt to bring some thought to the study of one, reasonably popular part of a programme of institutional development, that of decentralisation. What do we mean when we discuss " decentralisation of government " ?   What sort of machinery ought to be established ?   What values, terminal and instrumental, are appropriate for fitting the issue of decentralisation into any programme of institutional development ? Again, what operating principles are useful for considering this issue ? The reader of these papers can decide for himself how far these questions have received at least tentative answers.

At this moment perhaps one could touch on one big problem area. That is the clash between centralisation and decentralisation as two operating principles. As I see it, a general argument in these terms is substantially meaningless.

If we assume that the political arguments for centralisation are not now pressing, then the objective (as opposed to the subjective) arguments mainly rest on the proposition that centralisation makes for "efficiency." This brings us back to what we mean by the instrumental value of efficiency. Thinking on this has been largely vitiated by what seems to me a simplistic view of this term, a mechanical view based on an engineering analogy, the analogy of the large returns to be achieved from high technology in an industrial sense, as with the manufacture of steel. But over the great range of government activity technology in that sense is not the significant factor. Here the biological analogy may be a better one. This leads one to the biological solutions of hierarchy and autonomy, of communication and adaptiveness. This does not deny the crucial importance of centralising, as in the brain, a certain number of the most important functions—for example, of control ; but even that control goes hand in hand with a very high level of local autonomy over a great range of biological functions.

Deriving, I believe, from the over-simplified, mechanical view of what constitutes efficiency in the context of administration, are two subordinate ideas. The first of these is that to get on with the job one should engage in action and not talk. This is a fallacy to which administrators (but not politicians by the nature of their calling) are prone. Politicians know that a scheme cannot work unless the interests affected by it give it some degree of commitment. This involves, usually, a long process of explanation, persuasion and negotiation. To an increasing extent in modern times, successful administration involves a comprehensive programme of information, consultation, participation. This is, basically, to act on the value of trusting the people. To put this at its lowest, no scheme will work unless the people are prepared to accept it. The spectacular example here is that of incomes policies.

Another of these derived fallacies is that he who pays the piper calls the tune. This is used to justify a great deal of interference with autonomy and discretion within the public sector as the price for handing over public monies. As a matter of observation one can see that this is by no means a universal principle. Indeed, one can find areas where public money is handed over and no tune whatever is called. But in those places where the tune *is* called, sometimes one can see—notably in the field of local government—where not only is the piper told the tune to play but is also being told *how* to play it. This is not to say that there cannot be confrontation between a special or local interest and the general or national interest: that is where the hierarchical principle legitimately comes into play.

Many of these so called transfers of public money, which give opportunities for falling into the foregoing fallacy, arise from the failure to face the need for financial and fiscal reform. This in turn is an instance of the preference for the special over the general: it is easier, for example, to give *ad hoc* grants to local authorities than to think through what needs to be done about systems of local taxation. Those who pursue centralisation to the extent practised in this country get themselves encumbered with special issues so that the big general issues which only they can tackle—such as fiscal reform, to continue with this example—get neglected. This was the basic analysis of Irish public administration of the Public Services Organisation Review Group. If policy is to be separated from execution, if the special is not to impede the development of the general, there must, I believe, be a sophisticated programme for the decentralisation of the executive work of Irish government.

VII.   THE CASE FOR DECENTRALISATION

What case for decentralisation comes from the papers in this book? How adequate is that case in the light of what has been set out above?

The first point is the distinction between policy, which should in general be centralised, and execution, which need not be. Secondly, there is the argument that *all* the business of government should be seen as one, whether it is discharged through a government department, a state-sponsored body or a regional or local authority ; the kind of body used to discharge it should be related to the specific nature of the work done—e.g. the generation of electricity. Thirdly, some public business must of its nature be centralised (e.g foreign or defence policy, overall national planning, etc.) ; but the great mass of executive business does not fall into that category: in principle, this should be allocated amongst the various types of executive agencies according to its and their nature, irrespective of the existing historical allocations. In this re-allocation an extensive facet of the executive business of government, especially where it is thick on the ground, should be given to geographical or areal authorities.

Where it must remain with a central body, the field services of that body should match the organisation of the regional and local bodies, and adequate authority be devolved to the appropriate officials. Within both the field services and the regional and local services, work should be differentiated on hierarchical principles, ranging from community work at the community level, personal services at the district level, normal technological services at the county level, and planning and higher technological services at the regional level. At each of these levels there should be cross-over points to relate together cognate and inter-dependent services and to provide places where the general interest at that level can take precedence over the special, agency interests. This provides a method by which there can be public participation and representation at each level and which makes for efficiency in relating each kind of body to its appropriate task and in relating all these to one another. If autonomy appropriate to that task is given to each body at each level, then there can be a freeing of local creativity and initiative. For this, the standardising of administrative areas would be essential.

This would provide a decentralisation programme of devolution and deconcentration that would take some considerable time to implement in full. It is in the light of some such programme that proposals for local government reform or regional development or the re-structuring of departmental field services should be judged.

One's judgment of the adequacy or otherwise of this scheme depends of course on one's political values. Is one a universal centraliser (as most politicians and officials are in Ireland), or does one see a place for a significant degree of decentralisation ? How important is decentralisation to the development of our democracy ? It is part of my general argument that values of this kind are susceptible of intelligent scrutiny and analysis.

CONCLUSION

Since many of the papers in this book were written, a number of institutional advances have been made, and promise of others emerged. These changes enhance, if anything, the need to lay foundations for a scientific approach to the whole problem of institutional development. This involves engaging in analysis of the issues with a considerable degree of rigour. What is attempted here is no more than the early stages of such analysis and in only one aspect of our public institutions. Given the long time scale that applies to most of the important actions of government, an apparent deflection of energy from the task in hand to long term thought and analysis may be far from slowing up the final outcome ; it may quite substantially speed it, especially if it has the effect of raising the level of public understanding and discussion in advance of the making of official proposals. Analysis and discussion of this kind can be seen very effectively not to be irrelevant to the busy practitioner, but an essential back up to him. I would suggest that, to take a relevant example, the attempt to bypass this procedure in relation to local government reform vividly illustrates the force of this argument.

The paper in this book on machinery of government ends by suggesting that to overhaul a piece of machinery one needs a mechanic. But how useful is a mechanic without the *study* of mechanics ? The attempt to engage in a scientific study of institutional development is, I believe, important for its own sake, in the sense that knowledge is always valuable. It is important for the better advance of the study of public administration and government generally. It is important for the contribution it can make to national development as a whole and to the science and art of government in particular. But above all it is important to making our society more democratic.

INDEX